OUR NATIONAL FORESTS

OUR

National Forests

STORIES FROM AMERICA'S MOST IMPORTANT PUBLIC LANDS

GREG M. PETERS | *Foreword by*
MARY MITSOS, NATIONAL
FOREST FOUNDATION

Published in 2021 by Timber Press, Inc.
The Haseltine Building
133 S.W. Second Avenue, Suite 450
Portland, Oregon 97204-3527
timberpress.com

Printed in China
Text design by Kelly Galbreath
Text is set in Garamond Premier Pro, a typeface designed by Robert Slimbach in 2007
Jacket design by Pop Chart and Adrianna Sutton

ISBN 978-1-60469-963-0
A catalog record for this book is available from the Library of Congress.

To all the national forest fans out there; the employees of
the US Forest Service with whom I've worked over the years
and who taught me that the agency is made up of committed, caring
individuals working tirelessly for the benefit of the forests and the
American public; the communities that rely on these lands for
water and livelihoods; and the forests themselves. Also to Mom,
who (among so many other things) helped me become a better writer
all those years ago; to Dad, who took me camping in sun, rain,
and everything in between; and to my wife, Chrissy, whose
unwavering support gave me the confidence to embark on this
project and to see it to completion.

CONTENTS

NATIONAL FORESTS
and
NATIONAL GRASSLANDS
of the United States

FOREWORD

A COOL, CLEAR MOUNTAIN STREAM. A wide open prairie of waving tall grasses. A majestic range of western peaks covered in ponderosa pines. These are some hallmarks of America's cherished national forests.

But, if we look more closely and shift our lens from macro to micro, a very different world comes into view. It is the world of a small child cradling a butterfly. A family sitting on a riverbank watching the water flow. A solitary hiker quietly stepping along a mossy trail.

The pages that follow reveal both perspectives—the grand and the miniscule, the awe of world-class scenery and the amazement of personal discovery. At 193 million acres, our National Forest System is the centerpiece of America's public lands. It was originally conceived during the great clear-cutting of our country's forests in the late nineteenth and early twentieth centuries. In fact, this massive harvesting of our forests, many of them virgin lands, exposed the pressing need for a more sustainable path.

When the US Forest Service was established, it was charged with providing a renewable source of timber and clean water to a growing nation, both still integral parts of the agency's mission 115 years later. Over time, the system grew, as did Americans' understanding of why areas needed to be set aside for public good. Even the concept of public good expanded. By the mid-twentieth century, outdoor recreation was popular, and increasing mobility and middle-class means led millions of Americans to visit scenic places that previously were just images on postcards.

In recent decades, two major shifts have further demonstrated the relevance and importance of national forests. As a nation, we finally recognized that these public lands are not equally shared by all Americans, and the challenge of ensuring a diversity of Americans can engage in these places became ever more pressing. Through efforts to tell more inclusive histories, major outreach initiatives, and programs to link urban population centers with more remote forests things are starting to change. Though long overdue, we are telling the entire story about how National Forest System lands were originally the homelands of indigenous peoples.

The second shift is all around us—our changing climate. National forests are natural carbon sinks, increasingly seen as integral parts of natural climate solutions. The National Forest Foundation and many others are aggressively planting trees to help maintain the intactness and resiliency of our public lands; this is critical now, as our forests are stressed by unnaturally large fires and other disturbances, which compromise their ability to harbor healthy wildlife, provide clean air and water, and store vast amounts of carbon.

As "the people's lands," national forests are a vital part of a vital idea: that ordinary citizens, not the wealthy or well connected, own these places of beauty, of sustainability, of personal renewal. Our nation essentially created this concept of public lands. But it is a fragile idea. We must be willing to accept the mantle of stewardship—of real care—to ensure national forests endure.

The National Forest Foundation and many like-minded nonprofit organizations exist to foster meaningful personal connections to our forests. Our conservation projects, whether restoring a watershed or taking out young people to learn about the unique ecology of tallgrass prairie, make meaningful change on the ground. These projects also cultivate a deeper understanding and commitment among our fellow citizens so they, too, can become essential stewards of this amazing, uniquely American, legacy.

Whether it's the lowland swamps of coastal Carolina, the arid and rugged beauty of our Southwest, or Colorado's iconic snowy peaks, these incomparable places help define America's identity. They tell stories, reveal ancient patterns, and shape the communities in their shadows. They are places to admire, to explore, and, ultimately, to protect.

I hope this book takes you on a journey of discovery that opens up the richness and relevance of our national forests.

—Mary Mitsos, President, National Forest Foundation

PREFACE

OUR BLUE SUBARU IMPREZA RATTLED up the rutted dirt road, its headlamps piercing the night's darkness. My girlfriend, Chrissy, sat quietly in the passenger seat. I knew she was anxious. I was too.

We had no specific destination and drove ever deeper into the dark with the base understanding that the road led to a national forest. I didn't even know, in any meaningful way, what a national forest was, only that "they" reportedly allowed free camping and imposed few limits on where you could pitch a tent for the night. The day had been wearisome, and we longed to be out of the car and in our tent.

An hour and a half had passed since we had rolled through Billings, Montana, in the waning evening light. We couldn't afford a hotel room in the city and had planned on finding a spot to camp. The ragged gazetteer we employed for our road trip indicated that a national forest lay to the west of Billings, so we took the closest exit and motored into the growing darkness.

Eventually, we decided we were on the forest. I can't recall, nearly two decades later, which forest we thought we were on, or if we passed a sign that told us. I pulled over in a turnout that seemed flat enough to accommodate our small tent and we set up our camp.

I do recall waking up the next morning in front of a fence with a green cattle gate. Dried cow patties covered the ground. We hastily packed up and headed back down the road. As often happens, the drive back out of the woods, this time in the soft light of an autumn Montana morning, seemed far shorter than the drive in. Soon enough we pulled back onto Interstate 90 and continued our trip west to Whitefish, Montana.

Since that awkward camp, Chrissy and I have gotten married and moved to Missoula. With that wonderful, small city as our home base, we proceeded to spend as much of our time exploring the surrounding national forests as we could. And over the passing years, I've come to understand much more about the 193 million acres of forests, deserts, grasslands, and mountain ranges that comprise the National Forest System.

In 2010, I got a job with the National Forest Foundation, a nonprofit chartered by Congress in the early 1990s and dedicated to promoting the health and public enjoyment of these vast lands. I first managed their budding tree-planting program, soliciting donations from corporations, small businesses, and individuals, before becoming the communications director, a position I held until the final day of 2018.

That experience coupled with our immersion in the incredible national forests that surround Missoula have provided me with a much richer understanding of our national forests than that awkward camping spot outside Billings all those years ago.

It turns out that camping among cow pies wasn't actually my first experience on a national forest. In the early 2000s, I lived in an off-the-grid cabin outside of Girdwood, Alaska. The cabin was one of several that had been built on an old mining claim in the Chugach National Forest. While the land on which the cabin rested (precariously I might add) was privately owned, a few footsteps out the rickety door deposited me on the Chugach proper. It was a wonderful place to live if you were young and hale and undeterred by the cold, a lack of running water, or spotty electricity.

Chrissy paddling on Earthquake Lake in Montana's Custer-Gallatin National Forest.

However, looking farther back in my personal history, this rustic experience wasn't my introduction to national forests either. When I was in high school, my parents took our family to Utah to ski at the Alta Ski Resort in Little Cottonwood Canyon. The resort is on the Uinta-Wasatch-Cache National Forest, as is its neighbor, Snowbird (and several other world-class resorts). At the time, I had no idea that they were part of the National Forest System, a fact that did nothing to dampen my wide-eyed enthusiasm. I was completely blown away by the mountains in that canyon; they were so different from the rounded, weatherworn summits of Maine's Appalachian Mountains that rose a couple hours west of the coastal town where we lived. That it took years for me to fully realize the extent of my connection to national forests isn't surprising; many Americans might find themselves confused about exactly what our national forests are and what they mean.

INTRODUCTION

MY FIRST, THOUGH UNWITTING, EXPERIENCE with national forests, a family ski trip at Utah's Little Cottonwood Canyon, parallels the way many Americans become acquainted with these lands. More than 120 ski resorts on our forests host millions of skiers and snowboarders every year. And like sixteen-year-old me, many of them only know they're skiing at Vail or Alta or Jackson Hole or Attitash, without the faintest idea those resorts are on land they communally own with all Americans.

Skiing is, of course, expensive. I didn't realize as a teenager how fortunate I was to enjoy the beauty of the Wasatch Mountains on that family vacation. Nor did I realize how such activities are out of reach for so many.

Fortunately, America's national forests are open and accessible in myriad other ways to those who can't afford to spend a hundred dollars (or more) for a day of skiing. Recreation is probably the single most important avenue Americans have to enjoy these public spaces. Camping, hiking, rock climbing, fishing, hunting, wildlife watching, paddling, riding off-road-vehicles, and simply driving the vast network of national forests roads (more than 350,000 miles of them, several times the mileage of the interstate highway system) are just some of the less-costly ways that we come to know these places.

Most Americans are familiar, at least to some degree, with our country's magnificent national parks, either in concept or in practice. They have been described as "America's Best Idea" and to be sure, they are truly incredible. That a country would set aside its most beautiful landscapes for generations to come was a novel idea when it was proposed more than 100 years ago, and it remains inspiring today.

I adore our parks and cherish the time I spend exploring them. But our parks represent a relatively simple idea of preservation. These lands exist, as much as anything or any place can these days, somewhat outside the thrumming scrum of humanity. Of course, we've built roads through them along with lodges, campgrounds, marinas, dams, cell towers, and other infrastructure we deem necessary to further our enjoyment and appreciation of them. And, of course, human activities that occur outside park boundaries impact these landscapes too—air, water and light pollution don't stop at the entrance gate to Yellowstone or the Grand Canyon. Wildlife that wander out of a park's boundaries lose protective cover. And climate change is affecting everything, everywhere. But generally, the parks are monuments to preservation, managed for consistency of views, of experiences, of wildlife populations, of history, and of entire ecosystems. Some park rangers and supervisors will take issue with this simplified characterization. Surely, there are examples of parks that buck the preservation concept, but there is no debate that many parks are heavily regulated environments where simply stepping off of the paved path and onto the grass can result in a fine (or at the least, strong words of admonishment from a ranger). No trees are harvested in parks, no wildlife hunted (save fish or invasive species), no cattle or sheep graze their grasses, no miners trod their grounds in search of coal, oil, gas, or gold. And those humans who deign to explore them without securing the proper permits and paying the required fees violate laws and regulations at their peril.

Our national forests aren't like our national parks—even though many forests possess inspiring views, impressive populations of wildlife, and abundant recreational opportunities that rival them. If our national parks represent preservation, our national forests represent conservation. At least, that was the original conceit voiced by the Forest Service's first chief, Gifford Pinchot.

In the late 1800s, America was developing at a rapid pace. Many Americans, including John Muir and Gifford Pinchot, rallied for the preservation of the vast wildlands contained within the borders of the nation. What form that preservation would take was up for debate. The notion that any lands the United States controlled should be preserved, or even kept in the public estate, was bitterly argued. While it may be something of an oversimplification, Muir, who founded the Sierra Club, believed that these lands should be set aside and managed without human interference or manipulation. Pinchot believed that the sound management of these lands by humans for the benefit of humans was the correct way to ensure their lasting legacy. Historians have boiled these twin visions down to preservation (Muir's) and conservation (Pinchot's). In a broad generalization, Muir's vision is embodied by the national parks and Pinchot's by the national forests.

As Pinchot helped shape the concept of conservation in America, he drew from a British philosopher named Jeremy Bentham who espoused utilitarianism as a moral code. Bentham summed up his philosophy as "it is the greatest happiness of the greatest number that is the measure of right and wrong." In the early days of the Forest Service, local rangers were often the arbiters of what could and couldn't happen on national forests, tasked with balancing competing interests like grazing, mining, harvesting timber, providing water, preventing fires, and managing wildlife (the same is generally true today). Pinchot reworked Bentham's code as a way to help these early rangers make the difficult decisions they faced: "Where conflicting interests must be reconciled, the question shall always be answered from the stand-point of the greatest good of the greatest number in the long run."

Just how effectively Pinchot's utilitarian-conservation ethos has been practiced by the Forest Service in the century since he led it is a matter of much debate. Today, our national forests are managed for coequal uses: natural resource development (including timber, grazing, and oil, gas, and hard rock mining), recreation, water provision, and wildlife (including terrestrial and aquatic plants and animals). How the Forest Service balances these uses is informed by science, the American public, American politics, and the agency's long history of public lands management. But there is no debate that our national forests are far more open, accessible, and in many ways, democratic than our national parks.

Consider recreation and the aforementioned ski resorts that operate on national forests. Do these 120 or so businesses serve the greatest number in the long run? They sure provide millions of Americans with the opportunity to get outside during long winter months for fresh air, exercise, and time with family and friends. Many of them are pricey world-class resorts like Vail, Snowbird, or Jackson Hole, but count-less others are small, mom-and-pop operations where a day of skiing costs less than $50. National forests permit off-road-vehicle use in summer and winter, something that few parks do. There may be entry fees at certain locations, and many forests require parking stickers to utilize developed trailheads, but there are no entry gates at national forests like there are at national parks. Dogs are permitted just about anywhere, to the delight or dismay of forest users.

I recall a phone call with a social media influencer when I worked at the National Forest Foundation. She typically focused on national parks but was planning to include a national forest or two in her upcoming itinerary. Trouble was, she couldn't find where the designated backcountry campsites were when looking at national forest maps. It took me a moment to understand her conundrum. National parks (most of them anyway) specifically prescribe where you can camp each night of your stay, whether in the front country at a road-accessible campground, or in the back-country at a campsite that requires a permit and some amount of effort to access. National forests, generally at least, have no such prescriptions. You simply find a flat, safe spot to camp and set up your tent. She was amazed at such permissiveness.

This democracy and ease of use are accompanied by darker realities. All our national forests are taken lands (sometimes violently, sometimes through decep-tion or bureaucracy) and our modern names and boundaries erase thousands of years of Native American occupancy and stewardship. Many contemporary users abuse the privileges national forests extend—dumping trash, shooting trees and signs, overstaying camping limits, and worse. National forest history is rife with examples of poor land use management and abandonment of Pinchot's "greatest good" philosophy, itself arguably a relic of a different age. Controversy has dogged the Forest Service from its 1905 inception to today, and its legacy is viewed in drastically different lights by different Americans.

For many in the environmental community, the "Forest Circus" is a lapdog of industrial interests, intent on getting the cut out and willfully ignorant of the true values the land it manages should be providing. For others, the Forest Service basks in a halo of thoughtful management that embodies how technocratic bureaucracies delivered a multitude of goods and services to help build our nation. For some on the fringes of society, the Forest Service is like any other federal agency, bloated, overreaching, and run by a cabal of out-of-touch bureaucrats in Washington, DC, with no idea of how forests should be managed. Others, like myself, see a generally well-intentioned agency subject to a nearly impossible-to-achieve mandate of multiple-use that values timber, wildlife, clean water, recreation, grazing, oil and gas, and other uses as all equal and that is further subjected to the whims of each presidential administration and its short-term priorities.

Of course, these attitudes are just snippets of a wide spectrum. And the hard truth is that the majority of Americans probably don't feel one way or another about the Forest Service and by extension, the national forests. They have never experienced a national forest, and their general notion about America's public lands starts and stops with the national parks or local green space maintained by their city or state.

Regardless of how Americans feel about the Forest Service, or about how national forests should be managed, there is no debate about the incredible diversity of landscapes national forests contain. There is at least one national forest (or unit of the National Forest System like a grassland), and often many, in all but ten states in the country—only Massachusetts, Connecticut, Rhode Island, Delaware, New Jersey, Maryland, Iowa, and Hawaii lack a piece of the NFS. Even Puerto Rico has one, called El Yunque National Forest.

Some, like Alaska's 17-million-acre Tongass National Forest are almost too large to comprehend (for perspective, the Tongass could swallow 2.2-million-acre Yellowstone National Park seven times over and still have space). Others, like the 11,000-acre Tuskegee National Forest in Alabama, would fit onto the island of Manhattan with room to spare. The NFS stretches from the Atlantic, where North Carolina's Croatan National Forest is bordered by Bogue Sound, to the Pacific, where breakers crash on the beaches of California's Los Padres and Oregon's Siuslaw National Forests.

Geographic breadth is a decent metric of the system's size, but it falls short when compared to the biodiversity contained within these 193 million acres. El Yunque National Forest is the country's only tropical rainforest and home to more tree species (250) than exist on all other national forests combined. The verdant profundity of life found there is a stark contrast to the red-rock deserts of Coconino National Forest in Arizona—the rust-colored mesas that dominate this "forest" are as wholly different from a lush Caribbean island as sugar from salt. Yet even here, the variety of life is striking. In addition to its Mars-like red rocks, the Coconino also boasts the largest continuous tract of ponderosa pine trees in the world. Farther south, saguaro cacti raise their arms in defiance of the summer sun that relentlessly bakes Arizona's Coronado National Forest.

Meanwhile, in Montana, Wyoming, and Idaho, the national forests that overlay so much of the northern Rocky Mountains boast snow-capped peaks and dark green forests that seem to have no end when glimpsed from atop a summit. These

Oregon's Siuslaw National Forest touches the Pacific Ocean.

Puerto Rico's El Yunque National Forest is the country's only tropical rainforest.

In southern Arizona's Coronado National Forest, saguaro cacti reach for the sky.

Cathedral Rock on the Coconino National Forest in Arizona highlights that forest's red-rock splendors.

forests give rise to some of the largest and most iconic rivers in the country. The Columbia and Missouri begin their descents from Montana's conifer-clad national forests. The Snake River and the Green River both drain national forests in Wyoming as they flow to the Columbia and Colorado respectively. And the Salmon River, the famous River of No Return, starts its journey in the Idaho's Sawtooth National Forest. These forests—the Flathead, Bitterroot, Bridger-Teton, Shoshone, and Sawtooth—are truly the headwaters of our nation.

In Colorado, the swaying golden grasses of the Comanche National Grasslands are often overshadowed by the dozens of 14,000-foot peaks (including Maroon Bells, often cited as the most photographed mountains in the country) contained within the state's national forests. Twenty percent of California is covered by national forests, and they include species and landscapes as diverse as the ancient bristlecone pine forests on the Inyo National Forest (where single specimens have been growing for 5,000 years or more), the bone-dry, fire-prone chaparral of Angeles National Forest (more akin to vegetation found in Greece and Italy), and the redwood, spruce, and pine forests of Six Rivers National Forest, which tower above 1,500 miles of rivers and streams (providing at least 9 percent of the state's freshwater runoff).

The great forests of western Oregon and Washington comprise parts of the largest temperate rainforest on Earth, which stretches all the way up to the Chugach National Forest in Alaska. Mist-shrouded and covered in mosses, these forests are anchored by volcanoes—Mount Shasta, Mount Hood, Mount St. Helens, Mount Baker—that make other mountains look like foothills.

In Florida's three national forests, trail crews wield machetes to keep vegetation at bay, and hikers wade through both swampy bottomlands and across wide longleaf pine savannas in a matter of miles. Springs gush with clear water that slowly meanders across the flat landscape. Appalachian Trail hikers beginning their trek on Springer Mountain in Georgia's Chattahoochee-Oconee National Forest quickly appreciate why the trail is called "the green tunnel"—for its first 1,700 or so miles, it winds through a dozen national forests in the Appalachian Mountains with their thick canopy of hardwood and pine trees. When hikers reach New Hampshire, the penultimate state on a south-to-north hike, their well-worn boots put them atop wind-scoured summits more akin to the arctic or high alpine regions than to the verdant, biodiverse hotspots through which they've traveled so far—here the White Mountains rise in undulating waves of rock and lichen, belying their elevation just a few thousand feet above sea level.

My friends from Wisconsin, Michigan, Minnesota, and Missouri would cry foul if I failed to mention the vast national forests hosted by their home states. And they'd be right to do so. These dense woods boast towering pine and spruce, maple and birch, and dozens of other woody species, growing amid tens of thousands of lakes. Superior National Forest in Minnesota, home to the Boundary Waters, our country's most-visited Wilderness Area, is truly superior by any measure, not least its three-million-acre size, larger than most western national forests, and yes, larger than Yellowstone (forgive my double use of Yellowstone as a size comparison; it's a handy reference.

And still, there are more. The Wayne and Hoosier National Forests in Ohio and Indiana prove that those states offer far more than rolling farmlands and friendly Midwestern cities—especially in fall when the trees turn vibrant reds, oranges, and yellows. In southern Illinois, photographers flock to the haunting rock formations of the Garden of the Gods on the Shawnee National Forest. In Oklahoma and Arkansas, mountain bikers are building miles of trails through the Ouachita National Forest's captivating topography and pine-studded mountains. In Texas, the four forests in the eastern half of the state comprise some of the best public lands in

the notoriously privately owned Longhorn State, and residents flock to their meandering streams, refreshing lakes, and pine-scented forests. In spring, wild azaleas proliferate throughout Louisiana's Kisatchie National Forest; pine and hardwood forests rise from lush bottomlands in Alabama's Talladega National Forest, home to the Pinhoti National Recreation Trail; and Mississippi's six national forests cover an impressive 1.2 million acres of the state.

Each of these varied ecosystems supports a wide array of life. From the largest, California's sequoias and redwoods, to the oldest, the bristlecone pine, also found

in California, the diversity of trees on our national forests is astounding. The Pando Aspen Clone in Utah's Fishlake National Forest is the true winner of age and size superlatives. While each individual aspen in the grove may only live a couple hundred years, the root system from which they spring has been estimated at 80,000 years old, one of the oldest and largest living organisms on the planet.

The Forest Service estimates that our national forests host more than 10,000 species of plants and 3,000 species of wildlife. Listing them all would be mind numbing, but a few deserve special mention. In Alaska, ocean waters contained

in the boundaries of both the Chugach and Tongass National Forests support humpback and orca whales, sea lions, and salmon by the millions. So intertwined is the relationship between salmon and forests that cedar trees on the Tongass contain salmon DNA in their massive trunks.

Grizzly bears and wolves, two of the most feared and beloved predators in North America, depend on national forests. They're joined by other apex predators like coyotes, foxes, martens, wolverines, bobcats, cougars, and lynx. In the forests of Appalachia, the giant salamander *Cryptobranchus alleganiensis*, nicknamed hellbender, snot otter, or Allegheny alligator, lurks in the clear, fast-moving water. One

PREVIOUS Mount Hood National Forest's eponymous peak rises over Oregon.

CLOCKWISE FROM OPPOSITE Minnesota's Boundary Waters Canoe Area Wilderness in the Superior National Forest.

Garden of the Gods in Illinois's Shawnee National Forest proves there's a lot more to the Midwest than farms.

In Utah's Fishlake National Forest, the Pando Aspen Clone is considered one of the oldest and largest living organisms on Earth.

need not travel very deep into an eastern forest to find game animals like wild turkey, quail, grouse, and plenty of deer.

A 2012 report from the Forest Service noted that 429 species listed on the Endangered Species Act (32 percent of the 1,381 species that were on the list at the time) "were known to either use national forest/grassland habitats, or potentially be affected by Forest Service management activities." Additionally, the agency noted, "Some 251 other species are candidates for listing (i.e., meet listing criteria, but have not yet been formally proposed), and over fifty of those occur on national forest or grasslands." Of course, the vast majority of species, both floral and faunal,

that live on our national forests are far less charismatic than a grizzly bear, bald eagle, or moose, and they're not listed on the ESA. But that doesn't mean they're any less important.

Many species of wildlife, especially the megafauna we most value as a society (for better or worse), are often wide-ranging. They travel across landscapes as the seasons change, as they seek new home ranges and mates, and as humans push ever farther into the once-wild zones at the edges of our public lands. Our national forests serve a critical function in these travels as well.

Take the Greater Yellowstone Ecosystem. This vast swath of the Rocky Mountains is anchored by Yellowstone Park, but it's mostly comprised of five national forests that surround the park—Custer-Gallatin to the north, Bridger-Teton to the south, Shoshone to the east and Caribou-Targhee and Beaverhead-Deerlodge to the west. Bison, elk, grizzly bears, wolves, and countless other species move throughout this huge landscape with little regard for the human boundaries we've imposed. They follow ancient routes between winter feeding grounds and summer range; they

establish new packs in places where their ancestors were extirpated a century ago; they hunt and hide, breed and die, feast and fly never knowing or caring if they're in Yellowstone proper or in a national forest outside the park's boundaries.

While the Greater Yellowstone Ecosystem is, arguably, one of the best examples of how national forests help sustain national parks, it is by no means the only. North Cascades National Park, known as the American Alps, is likewise flanked by national forests, the Okanogan-Wenatchee to the east and the Mount Baker-Snoqualmie to the west. Olympic National Park is almost entirely surrounded by a national forest of the same name, and Mount Rainier is likewise encircled by the Mount Baker-Snoqualmie National Forest. Much of the north rim of the Grand Canyon is bordered by the Kaibab National Forest. The Cherokee National Forest and the Nantahala and Pisgah National Forests straddle Great Smoky Mountains National Park. Visitors to the Rocky Mountains National Park must first pass through the Arapaho and Roosevelt National Forests before they get to a park entrance gate. The list goes on—California's Kings Canyon and

ABOVE Alaska's Tongass and Chugach National Forests host incredible wildlife, including humpback whales and other marine life.

LEFT Grizzly bears fishing for salmon on Admiralty Island, part of the Tongass National Forest.

Sequoia National Parks, Oregon's Crater Lake, Montana's Glacier, Alaska's Glacier Bay, Wrangell-St. Elias, and Kenai Fjords, Minnesota's Voyageurs, and others are all bordered on one edge or another by a national forest.

Yet, as wild as some of these lands are, they are working lands. Timber is still cut and trucked to sawmills. Mines—hard rock, coal, oil, and gas—are still permitted. Transportation corridors, electrical and communications infrastructure, and dams can be found on forests from California to New Hampshire. Cattle and sheep graze on roughly ninety-six million acres of rangeland contained in the National Forest System—half the system's entire acreage. The resources these lands provide, and the incomes earned from their production, literally and figuratively put food on the table for millions of hard-working Americans.

If our national parks are considered inspiring, our national forests should, at the very least, be considered interesting. They are mirrors of our society. As we

Spread over Montana's Custer-Gallatin and Wyoming's Shoshone National Forest, the Absaroka-Beartooth Wilderness Area is a haven for wildlife and backcountry skiers.

battle over threatened species, natural resource extraction, recreational access, systemic racism, and the sad legacy of our historical treatment of indigenous cultures, our national forests reflect our desires and our decisions back onto us. This is what makes them so compelling and ultimately, American.

Laws, many written and passed more than fifty years ago, provide us with the opportunity to share our views on how our forests should be managed. While those same laws provide similar opportunities regarding national parks, those lands aren't managed for as many competing values as our forests. Our parks are static, or at least the management of parks is intended to maintain them in a specific way—our national forests are far more dynamic, and the arguments, lawsuits, and compromises that inform their management reflect that dynamism.

This book may be best described by what it's not, rather than what it is. Which is pretty close to the approach many board members and staff at the National Forest Foundation take when describing the forests to family members, neighbors, or colleagues: They're like national parks but different. They harbor wildlife, but they're not wildlife refuges. They're working lands, but they're not like private timberlands with their directives to maximize profit. They're not this, but they are kind of . . . sort of . . . like that.

This book is not exhaustive in its scope. There are simply too many stories to tell, histories to explore, tragedies and triumphs to highlight for any one book to cover them all. It's not a repudiation of the Forest Service or a record of its mistakes. Nor is it a glowing commendation of the agency that has overseen these lands for the better part of a century and a half. It's not a history of the Forest Service or of each national forest; there are historians far more qualified to write that type of book than I. In fact, many have, and I encourage you to read their work.

Mostly, this book is an exploration. The editors at Timber Press gave me a wide berth to choose stories, and I was free to follow where they led. I grounded this exploration in my own experiences and knowledge of our forests. I don't claim to be an expert, but I have spent the better part of my adult life immersed in these places, both literally (out in the woods, whether for fun or for hire) and professionally (mostly in front of a computer at the NFF, and as a conservation writer). Those experiences are of course, mine, and therefore limited. Certainly, there are topics I wish I could have covered or, at least, could have covered in more detail.

While I was writing this book, the Covid-19 pandemic raged across the globe. By the time you read this, I hope that it is only a bad memory, but as the death toll climbed over 500,000 Americans, our society was severely shaken. The pandemic laid bare the failings of our health care system and the wide fractures in how

The LeConte
Glacier dwarfs
a visitor in the
Stikine-LeConte
Wilderness on
Alaska's Tongass
National Forest.

Americans think about community and the ways we live our lives. It has also reinforced the immense need for natural spaces and public lands.

As Covid-19 rendered indoor spaces more and more dangerous, Americans turned to outdoor spaces, including our national forests, as a salve, both mental and physical. Across the country, campgrounds were full, recreational equipment like bicycles, kayaks, and even dehydrated backpacker meals sold out and people recognized how profoundly important the outdoors is to their lives.

Even as the virus spread across the country, so too did protests that challenged America's long history of systemic racism. How our nation will deal with this legacy remains an open question. For Black Americans, the outdoors has long been considered a dangerous place. And the economic inequality that has so plagued our country has meant that many Black, indigenous, and people of color (BIPOC) simply can't access public lands, even if they feel safe doing so. Sadly, even those national forests that flank urban areas, like the Angeles, are prohibitively difficult to reach for many Americans.

These twin events impacted the book. How could they not? A global pandemic rendered travel difficult at best or, at the height of the shutdown, downright impossible. The Black Lives Matter movement caused me to reckon with the topics I had chosen to cover and how my experiences as a white, straight, cis-gender male born into an upper middle class family, with all the privileges that affords, has shaped my view of the natural world and of America's public lands.

I hope this book encourages readers to learn more about our national forests. I hope it inspires more reading, more investigation, more engagement. At the least, I hope it inspires readers to visit these magnificent lands and draw their own conclusions about them. In the years I worked at the NFF, I was guided by a maxim that many in the environmental and conservation fields follow: If people know something, they may come to love it; and if they love it, they may work to protect it.

I believe our national forests need protection—though perhaps in different ways and from different threats than you might assume. They need it from extremism, as expressed in the dueling fringe views that these lands should be given over to state or local management and divorced from federal oversight (something that would expose them to the worst impulses of industry and waste) or that they should remain forever untouched by humans, unmanaged and left alone (we have manipulated them too much for too long for that to be a legitimate course of action). They need protection from apathy—too many Americans don't care about our public lands, don't engage in their management, and don't understand the incredible services and resources they provide, whether clean air, clean water, or carbon sequestration.

And they need protection from those parties who see public lands—and especially our national forests, with their permissive policies and lax oversight—as theirs to degrade, disrespect, and abuse.

I was once someone who knew little to nothing about national forests. Just twenty years ago, free camping anywhere was the sum total of my knowledge. I can't claim that I've followed Leave No Trace principles every time I've camped or hiked in a national forest. I've struggled to balance the righteous environmentalism that underlies many of my personal beliefs with the practical realities of managing a system as vast and altered as these lands. We live in the Anthropocene, a period in which our world is so manipulated by humans that it is defined by that manipulation.

If nothing else, I hope this book shares the complexities of our national forests—the conflicting mandates that govern their management, the varied histories that have shaped them, the diverse characters who have played or continue to play their part in the sweeping saga of these lands. I truly hope this book, like our national forests, is interesting.

NO FORESTS, NO WATER

---

*The Story of
Eastern National
Forests*

**O** **N THE WESTERN EDGE OF MICHIGAN'S** Upper Peninsula, adjacent to the Wisconsin state line, a forest of towering white pine and eastern hemlock, fragrant balsam fir, and sprawling sugar maple and paper birch trees rises tall and stately from a thick carpet of leaves and needles. Black bears, moose, and even timber wolves haunt the shores of more than thirty lakes that lie nestled in the thick woods. Bald eagles shriek from snags, loons sing their mournful melodies on crystal-clear waters, and otters scamper up and down rocky banks. It's as wild a landscape as one can find in the continental states.

This ancient forest is part of the Sylvania Wilderness Area, a roughly 20,000-acre parcel of land managed by the Ottawa National Forest, which itself covers just under 1 million acres of Michigan's Upper Peninsula. To the casual observer exploring the Ottawa's lakes, rivers, and forests, the trees of Sylvania might not

The Sylvania Wilderness Area on the Ottawa National Forest is one of a few examples of old-growth forest left in the Great Lakes region.

PREVIOUS The birthplace of modern forestry, Nantahala and Pisgah National Forests cover more than one million acres of western North Carolina.

look that different from any others within the Forest's boundaries. But other stands are largely second- or even third-growth forests and barely 100 years old. The trees in Sylvania are much, much older, and that makes them rare in this part of the world.

Michigan's vast forests once provided an almost incomprehensible amount of lumber to domestic and international markets. In 1869, Michigan alone produced 1.7 billion board feet of white pine, nearly 30 percent of the country's entire production that year (board feet is a measurement of volume and equals a piece of lumber 12 × 12 × 1 inches). Ten years later, that output doubled to more than 3 billion board feet and roughly 50 percent of the nation's production. But Michigan's forests were not inexhaustible—in 1904, the state only produced 1 billion board feet, and by 1931, it produced a scant 67,000 board feet of lumber, an amount that barely registered in the national total.

Logs from Michigan's once-vast forests stacked high and ready for hauling to the mill.

As private lumber interests ravaged Michigan's forests, they pocketed profits and externalized costs, both social and ecological. Lumbermen took the best trees and left those that were too small to produce seeds, or, if they did reproduce, didn't grow particularly well. Wildfires ripped through the cutover stands, sterilizing the soil and killing off any grasses and shrubs that remained after the sawyers had done their work. Lumber jobs disappeared along with the white pine stands. In some spots, homesteaders tried to farm amid the stumps, but farming methods used at the time further depleted the soil and farmers quickly abandoned their homesteads.

The forests of Michigan's neighbor, Wisconsin, fared no better. That state's booming timber industry first focused on softwood trees like pine, shipping them off to communities where mills and factories turned them into doors, windowsills, and furniture. Once the best trees were cut, lumbermen returned to harvest the smaller trees. Eventually, they turned to the state's hardwood, and those trees fell and were shipped to furniture makers, cabinet factories, and tanneries. After the forests were cleared and the fires came through, homesteaders attempted to turn the depleted lands into farms, but like their neighbors in Michigan, they, too, quit their doomed efforts.

In New Hampshire and Maine, timber was one of the first resources that settlers exploited. The British Navy prized the tall straight pines that grew throughout the region for ship masts and felled the best of them. Then settlers cleared the thick pine and hardwood forests for their farms. These uses obviously impacted the forests, but small-scale, family farms could only clear so many trees each year, and even the mighty British Navy's need for ship masts wasn't infinite. Things changed in the late 1800s as industrial timber companies arrived and with them intensive harvesting methods. In short order, once-forested hills were stripped of their sylvan cover all over New England. And just like in Michigan and Wisconsin, wildfire followed, including an 84,000-acre blaze that roared through New Hampshire's White Mountains.

Once the forests were cleared, farmers attempted, and largely failed, to turn cutover lands into productive farms.

Farther south, rail lines crept ever deeper into the mountains of Appalachia. Railroads needed lumber and they facilitated logging and mining—together the three industries ravenously consumed the timber of central and southern Appalachia. In 1908, the Secretary of State issued a report noting that 86 percent of southern Appalachian acreage was either cleared of trees, in some stage of regrowth after having been recently cleared, or covered in young second-growth forests. That same report also noted that 50 percent of timberlands in the region were owned by large companies, primarily timber and mining companies. It also mentioned that "practically all of it, whether cut or not" had been burned.

In the coastal plains of the southeast, longleaf pines were the prize. This remarkably useful tree grew in vast stands from Maryland to Florida, providing habitat for hundreds of species of wildlife. But demand for turpentine, resin, and lumber nearly eliminated the stately longleaf from the continent—just 3 percent of the tree's historical range is represented today in a few remaining stands that cling on in Florida, Alabama, and Mississippi.

Across the East and Midwest, the industrial depletion of forests followed similar patterns: first the best trees were cut, then any that remained. After the timber companies moved on to the next stand, fires baked the soil and killed the grasses and shrubs. Spring rains and snowmelt no longer percolated into the ground— instead water rushed downslope, inundating streams and creeks. Dirt, no longer held in place by forests, streamed from the denuded land, fouling rivers and killing aquatic life. Floods ravaged downstream communities and turned once-navigable rivers into impassable torrents. Disease soon followed and sickened the towns' most vulnerable.

It can be hard to visualize just how ravaged our eastern forests once were. Much of this landscape is forested today, and the forests feel old. But many of them have only stood for a hundred years or so. In my native state of Maine, it's not uncommon to see old rock walls cutting through a thick, shady forest, relics of farms long abandoned.

The rare, old-growth trees in the Sylvania Wilderness Area, were, ironically, preserved by a rich lumberman. In 1895, as Michigan and Wisconsin's forest industries were starting their long decline, Wisconsin timber baron A. D. Johnston purchased eighty acres of land just over the state border. Johnston wanted to cut the large pines that grew in this remote corner of Michigan, but after actually seeing the forest, he decided to preserve it. He brought his wealthy friends—other timber barons, auto industry executives, and iron magnates—to visit, and they bought neighboring properties, eventually forming the Sylvania Club. Lodges and cabins sprung up on the shores of the larger lakes in the area and the members hunted, fished, hiked, and entertained other affluent and connected friends, including Dwight Eisenhower, Lawrence Welk, and Bing Crosby. The very name of the club

Today, many eastern and Midwestern areas like the Green Mountain National Forest in Vermont are covered in thick forests.

comes from the Latin word for woods, *sylva*. One can't but wonder if the club's founders, many of them beneficiaries of rampant industrial logging, saw the irony in the name they chose for their northwoods Shangri-La.

In 1966, the Forest Service purchased Sylvania from the owners and added it to the Ottawa National Forest. Recognizing the value such an old-growth forest offered for recreation and research, they removed the cabins and lodges. According to the small nonprofit group Friends of Sylvania, the forest there is one of two remaining tracts of old growth in the entire Great Lakes region.

That the agency could purchase Sylvania at all, and that there was an Ottawa National Forest to which it could add this incredible parcel, was no small thing.

Loons are a common sight on the Sylvania Wilderness Area and throughout national forests around the country.

BIRTH OF THE NATIONAL FOREST SYSTEM

When we think of public lands today, we think of national parks, national forests, wildlife refuges, Bureau of Land Management lands, and state or county lands that have specified boundaries. You're either on public land or you're on private land (and likely trespassing). While the management and purpose of these public lands may be different, most of them (especially the ones under federal management) have one thing in common: they were carved out of what was once called the "public domain."

Following the Revolutionary War, the Louisiana Purchase, the horrific, bloody conquest of Native Americans, and other historical events, the United States found itself the "owner" of billions of acres of land—which it called the public domain. Much of this land was given to newly created states, sold off to speculators and industry, given to soldiers in lieu of pay, granted to homesteaders, and otherwise privatized. Abraham Lincoln, for example, gave the railroads huge swaths of the West in an effort to speed settlement. Over time, some of these lands became national forests, wildlife reserves, and national parks.

There are still public domain lands today, and most are managed by the BLM, though the Forest Service manages some as well. Should a modern-day prospector find gold, silver, copper, or other hard rock mineral deposits on such land, he or she could file a claim, work that claim for a period of time, and eventually come to own it.

Eventually, Congress provided frameworks for managing national parks, national forests, or wildlife refuges, but laws governing the use of private lands were scarce throughout much of US history. If owners wanted to clear-cut their land, there was nothing to prevent them from doing so. If a prospector wanted to reroute a stream to develop a mining claim, he simply rerouted the stream. Even today, only a few federal laws, like the Clean Water Act, the Endangered Species Act, and the very recent Waters of the United States law, restrict what private landowners can do with their land. As long as those practices don't violate local ordinances, jeopardize an endangered species, or foul a stream covered under the Clean Water Act or the Waters law, landowners can essentially do whatever they want with their property.

The authority of the federal government to create forest reserves (precursors to national forests) from the public domain was first codified in the General Revision Act of 1891. The bill, signed by President Benjamin Harrison, included the following one-sentence amendment: "The President of the United States may, from time to time, set apart and reserve, in any state or territory having public land bearing forests, in any part of the public lands, wholly or in part covered with timber or undergrowth, whether of commercial value or not, as public reservations."

Harrison acted quickly after signing the act, designating more than 1.2 million acres of land around Yellowstone National Park as the Yellowstone Park Timberland Reserve (now part of the Shoshone and Bridger-Teton National Forests) in September of 1891. By the end of his term, he'd set aside more than 13 million acres of forest reserves in the West. But the act didn't include any administrative or management framework for the reserves, and illegal timber harvests, illegal mining, rampant poaching, and other abuses continued.

It wasn't until 1897 when Congress passed the Forest Service Organic Administration Act that a framework for administering and managing the federal forest reserves materialized. The primary goals of the Organic Act were to prevent precisely what was happening to private timberlands in the East and Midwest—the wholesale depletion of forests by mining and timber companies, the destruction of forests by wildfire, and, perhaps most importantly in the relatively arid West, the degradation of water that flowed from the high-elevation, forested watersheds to the communities and farmers that needed it downstream. The act's language is plain: "No national forest shall be established, except to improve and protect the forest within the boundaries, or for the purpose of securing favorable conditions of water flows, and to furnish a continuous supply of timber for the use and necessities of citizens of the United States."

Here, for the first time, we see the connection between water and forests and, more specifically, between federally managed forest land and downstream water supplies. Gifford Pinchot reinforced the idea when he penned *A Primer of Forestry* in 1905, explaining, "A forest, large or small, may render its service in many ways. It may reach its highest usefulness by standing as a safeguard against floods, winds, snow slides, moving sands, or especially against the dearth of water in the streams."

Historian Char Miller, in an article about Pinchot published by the Yale School of the Environment (formerly the Yale Forest School, which Pinchot founded in 1900), notes that "in the West there was an articulation from the bottom up and from the top down that landscapes like the mountain ranges of the West were essentially valuable more for water than for timber. Timber was great, but water was absolutely essential, and in the arid parts of the West this was even more important."

In 1905, the Forest Service was born, with Pinchot as its first chief. But the concept of federally managed forests was not universally embraced by many of the era's politicians, especially those from western states where the reserves were located. They felt that the best use of these public domain lands would be realized by private interests. Logging and mining would create jobs and prosperity, homesteaders would build farms and towns, and the United States would stretch from the Atlantic to the Pacific. They viewed the lands as practically inexhaustible and argued that the federal government had no role to play in managing them. So what if one forest was stripped of its trees? Another lay just over the horizon.

Even today, fringe elements in the West reject the federal government's right to manage (or as they say own) land at all. Cliven Bundy, a rancher in Nevada who refuses to recognize that the federal government can charge him (as it does every rancher who uses public lands) for grazing his cattle on BLM land, is the best-known leader of these radical groups. He owes the government more than $1 million in unpaid grazing fees and led an armed standoff with BLM officials in 2014 when they attempted to remove his cattle from public land. Unfortunately, the government prosecutors botched the case against Bundy, and he has yet to be held accountable for his actions. If anything, he and his acolytes have been emboldened. His son, Ammon Bundy, organized an armed takeover of the Malheur National Wildlife Refuge in Burns, Oregon, in 2016, protesting the arrest of Oregon ranchers who intentionally set fire to BLM lands (and who, it should be noted, declined his "help").

Of course, these voices effectively lost the battle—today we have, and cherish, a vast array of lands managed by the federal government—but they tried their best to limit the government's ability to set aside land from the public domain. In 1907, just two years after the Forest Service was established, Oregon senator Charles

Fulton added an amendment to the annual agricultural appropriations bill that prohibited the president from establishing new forest reserves in Oregon, Washington, Idaho, Montana, Colorado, and Wyoming. The amendment also revoked the president's authority to unilaterally create forest reserves anywhere, instead resting that power solely with Congress, and it changed the name of these tracts of land from forest reserves to national forests (a change that Pinchot supported as it helped clarify that the forests were to be actively managed and used as opposed to just reserved). President Roosevelt was effectively forced to sign the bill, but in a bit of political gamesmanship, he and Pinchot worked furiously in the days leading up to the bill's signing to establish sixteen million acres of forest reserves in the very states the Fulton Amendment declared off limits.

By 1910, the National Forest System had grown to more than 162 million acres, 115 million of which were established by Roosevelt. But national forests were still largely a western phenomenon. Roosevelt did designate national forests in the East, carving out of the public domain Florida's Ocala National Forest in 1908 and Minnesota's Superior National Forest in 1909, and what would become the Chippewa National Forest in 1902 from lands originally ceded to the Ojibwe people—but even with these additions, the vast majority of the federal forest acreage was located in the West. Eventually, of course, the East and Midwest would boast dozens of national forests. Today, they cover significant parts of the Appalachian Mountains

Florida's Ocala National Forest was one of the first forests established east of the Mississippi River.

from New Hampshire's wind-scoured White Mountains to the dark hollows of Georgia's Chattahoochee-Oconee National Forest, and they include tracts farther west, from Michigan's lake-studded forests to the dry pinelands of eastern Texas. Their inclusion in the National Forest System hinged on the role they played in regulating water, an argument successfully leveraged by a politician from Massachusetts named John Weeks.

THE WEEKS ACT

Weeks was born in New Hampshire but moved to Massachusetts, where he founded a successful Boston-based financial firm in 1888. Like many wealthy businessmen, Weeks moved into politics and was elected to Congress in 1905 as a Republican. He had grown up near the White Mountains in New Hampshire and owned a summer home there. During his vacations, he witnessed the damage that unrestrained logging had caused in New Hampshire and was inspired to seek solutions. His chance came in 1907 when he was appointed to the House Committee on Agriculture. His primary focus on the committee was to craft a bill that could gain support from his fellow conservatives and establish eastern forests.

The concept of establishing national forests in the East wasn't new, but it hadn't gained much support in Congress. Throughout the second half of the nineteenth century, a growing environmental movement in the United States had decried the wanton waste and destruction of natural resources that defined the times. The creation of western forest reserves was, in part, an effort to prevent the destruction so evident in the East and Midwest from despoiling the West.

Advocates of federal management pointed to Michigan's ravaged forests, New Hampshire's denuded mountains, and the fouled rivers of Appalachia as cautionary tales of what might befall western landscapes without federal management. With the Organic Act, the early environmental movement won a decisive victory—many of the West's vast forests would be managed (for better or worse) by the federal government in order to prevent clear-cutting and destructive fires, and to provide water for downstream communities. But the East's forests were private and subject to whatever uses their owners determined.

That didn't mean eastern forests were simply abandoned to the worst impulses of early American industry. Groups like the Appalachian National Park Association and the Society for the Protection of New Hampshire Forests had been lobbying Congress to create federally managed lands in the East since the late 1890s. But they faced an uphill battle. Western politicians who supported conservation efforts feared losing funding to the new (as yet unestablished) eastern forests. Others felt that national forests should have never been established to begin with. Yet others felt that states should manage lands as they saw fit and federal management was unnecessary (another view still held in corners of the West today). According to the Forest History Society, more than forty bills to create eastern national forests were introduced between 1901 and 1911. None passed.

One of the biggest barriers was the simple fact that the US government had no constitutional authority to purchase private lands and add them to the federal estate. The West's forests were carved out of the public domain, but public domain lands in the East and Midwest were scant. Despite this, the movement made incremental progress throughout the first decade of the twentieth century. In 1901, the Appalachian National Park Association, which was founded in 1899 in Asheville, North Carolina, convinced the North Carolina state government to allow the federal government to acquire lands for the establishment of forest reserves should it want to. South Carolina, Alabama, Georgia, Tennessee and Virginia soon followed suit.

John Weeks was the architect of the act that paved the way for the federal government to purchase lands in the eastern United States for inclusion in the National Forest System.

The cause of eastern forests was also taken up by groups like women's gardening clubs and the American Forestry Association, which elevated the issue to a national audience through its monthly magazine. Eventually manufacturing associations that relied on lumber joined the cause, believing federal management of eastern forests would stabilize the volatile timber market.

Nature contributed to the cause in her own destructive way when an early spring storm sent floodwaters ripping down the Monongahela River in West Virginia in March 1907. The surging waters inundated Pittsburg and wrought more than $100 million in damages. The flooding was blamed squarely on deforestation.

The following year, Weeks introduced the first version of his bill, which made little headway in Congress. In July, he amended it, adding language that stipulated the purchased lands would be managed as forest reserves for the purpose of protecting navigable waterways. It was a critical change.

If the Organic Act of 1897 enshrined water provision as a key component of western forest reserves, the Weeks Act of 1911 elevated it to the primary purpose for the creation of eastern forests. Weeks's logic was clever if a bit convoluted, and it centered on the role water played in interstate commerce. The Constitution didn't give the federal government permission to purchase private lands, but the Commerce Clause gave it authority to regulate interstate trade. Trade at the time was facilitated by rivers, still major transportation corridors in the early twentieth century. In short, the argument was this: river travel facilitated interstate commerce; river travel was threatened by flooding; flooding was caused by deforestation; defor-

estation was caused by private industry operating without oversight on private lands; thus, protecting the forested watersheds of navigable rivers through federal management would prevent (or reduce) flooding, and that would ensure interstate commerce could continue unabated.

Weeks, the former banker, had found the legal footing that would allow the federal government to purchase eastern lands for forest reserves. It was a massive victory for the American conservation movement and its legacy is felt by every person who hikes the White Mountain's Presidential Range, summits North Carolina's Mount Mitchell, or paddles the tannin-stained lakes of the Sylvania Wilderness in Michigan. Even more importantly, the Weeks Act is why tens of millions of urban residents in the East and Midwest can turn on their tap and get clean, fresh water at minimal cost.

The Weeks Act detailed how the government would evaluate and purchase private lands. A National Forest Reservation Commission was established and held its first meeting just days after President William Howard Taft signed the Weeks Act. The commission appointed purchase agents who would identify potential land, called a purchase unit, and submit it to the commission. Once the Geological Survey ensured the unit would, in fact, protect a navigable waterway, and the commission approved it, the government offered a fair-market price to willing sellers.

Other provisions in the act improved the cooperation between the Forest Service and states, largely focused on fire prevention. It also provided funding to states

with forest protection programs, so they could better manage those lands. And it launched a program of restoration and rehabilitation that transformed the cutover, degraded lands of the East into the verdant, sprawling forests that exist today.

The first national forest established under the Weeks Act was the Pisgah National Forest in North Carolina. It has a fascinating history that charted the course for how most of the eastern national forests were eventually restored to ecological health.

In the 1880s, Gilded-Age capitalist George Vanderbilt began purchasing vast swaths of cutover forests in North Carolina to add to his opulent Biltmore Estate. The lands were in rough shape, and in 1892, Vanderbilt hired a young Gifford Pinchot to develop and implement the first real forest plan in the United States.

After he graduated from Yale in 1889, Pinchot determined that he would become a professional forester, despite the fact that such a profession didn't really exist in the United States at the time. Lacking both lands to manage and real-world training in forest management, Pinchot travelled to Europe to study forestry in France, Germany, and Switzerland. When he returned to the United States in 1890, he was hired by Phelps, Dodge and Company to analyze the company's timber holdings in Pennsylvania. Shortly thereafter, Pinchot was invited to join Bernhard Fernow, the head of the USDA's Division of Forestry (a precursor to the Forest Service), on a mission to review forest lands in the Southeast. Fernow, a German immigrant trained in European forestry practices, was another leading figure in the establishment of the Forest Service.

Deforestation caused a flood in 1907 that inundated Pittsburg.

Shortly after these two assignments, Pinchot was approached by Vanderbilt to apply his newly learned forestry knowledge to the ravaged forests that surrounded the Biltmore.

When Pinchot arrived at Vanderbilt's estate, he possessed both the training and experience to develop a restoration and management plan for the vast acreage. An article in the *North Carolina Historical Review* quotes Pinchot as describing the lands he was charged with managing as "deplorable in the extreme." At the time of Pinchot's 1892 arrival, Vanderbilt's estate ran for six miles along the French Broad River and covered a total of 7,000 acres, much of it purchased from landowners who owned small parcels they had exhausted through intensive forestry and agriculture practices common at the time.

Pinchot desperately wanted to prove that managed forests could provide both profitable and sustainable timber in perpetuity. The prevailing view was of America's forests as inexhaustible. Once one stand was cut, lumbermen simply moved on to exploit the next tract. Managing forests wasn't something that happened in the

George Vanderbilt's Biltmore Estate remains one of the most opulent residences ever built in the United States; it's also considered the birthplace of scientific forest management.

United States. In fact, one of Pinchot's main jobs in his early days at the Biltmore was to develop a display for Chicago's 1893 World's Columbian Exposition. The display was intended to demonstrate that European-style forest management had a place in the United States and that forest management was vital to maintaining a supply of timber into the future.

Pinchot's efforts at the Exposition and beyond were successful. His eventual reward: a position as the first chief of the United States Forest Service, a federal agency wholly dedicated to the very practices he'd first experimented with at the Biltmore.

His successor there, a German named Carl Schenck, continued to practice forest management on Vanderbilt's growing holdings, and with the wealthy businessman's support, founded the first formal school of forestry in the United States—the Biltmore Forest School—on the estate. Today, the historic school and its 6,500-acre campus is preserved as the Cradle of Forestry in America and offers public tours and interpretation that detail the country's history of forest management.

When George Vanderbilt died unexpectedly in 1914, his widow, Edith, sold 87,000 acres of the land he had acquired in western North Carolina to a very willing buyer—the US government. That land is now the heart of the Pisgah National Forest. Modern-day mountain bikers zooming across its vast network of trails can be forgiven if they assume the verdant forests that now cover its steep, rolling mountains have always been there.

While Pinchot no longer ran the Forest Service when the Weeks Act was passed, his efforts at Biltmore helped lay the foundation for how the agency would both rehabilitate these cutover lands and manage them into the future. Many of the Forest Service's early leaders received training at the Biltmore Forest School, and the very concept of managing forests in a sustained manner for multiple purposes is still the core of the Forest Service's mission. Certainly, these practices were not above reproach then or now (some argue that forest management techniques honed in northern European forests didn't translate to the diverse forests of the eastern United States, and the Forest Service has, at times, sacrificed its water-related mission to timber, mining, and other industrial interests). Regardless, the restoration and relative sustainability of America's eastern forests is an undoubtable success story.

While the Pisgah National Forest may have been the first eastern national forest purchased under the Weeks Act, it was by no means the last. Between 1911 and 1945, roughly twenty-four million acres of national forests were established in the East and Midwest, including some of the most iconic national forests in the country today, like West Virginia's Monongahela, Vermont's Green Mountain, New

Hampshire's White Mountain, Georgia's Chattahoochee-Oconee, Michigan's Chippewa, Ohio's Wayne, Indiana's Hoosier, Tennessee's Cherokee, Kentucky's Daniel Boone, and Virginia's George Washington and Jefferson National Forests.

All told, twenty-three different states, from Maine to Florida and from Minnesota to Texas, host national forests that were established from lands directly purchased through the Weeks Act. Today, nearly 60 percent of Americans—198 million people—live within a day's drive of an eastern national forest. For these Americans, eastern national forests provide some of the best, if not the only, recreational opportunities around. But their true value is still rooted in the very reason they were first established: clean water.

Adjacent to Pisgah and the largest of North Carolina's national forests, Nantahala National Forest spreads out below Wayah Bald Tower lookout.

FROM TREES TO TAPS

In 2013, then Forest Service Chief Tom Tidwell gave an address at a meeting organized by the American Water Resources Association. In his remarks, Tidwell provides a glimpse of how the Forest Service views its modern role in water management.

The national forests and grasslands, the lands my agency manages, are the single most important source of water in the country. These lands have over 400,000 miles of streams, over three-and-a-half million acres of lakes and wetlands, over half the nation's hydroelectric power supplies, and almost a fifth of the nation's surface water supply. These lands furnish drinking water to about sixty million Americans living in 3,400 communities, including great cities like Atlanta, Georgia; Denver, Colorado; and Portland, Oregon.

In a sense, the Forest Service is the nation's largest water company. For more than a hundred years, a critical part of our mission has been sustaining the health of our nation's forests to protect the quantity and quality of our nation's water supply.

Nearly 20 percent of Americans rely on surface water (from a lake, river, or stream, as opposed to an underground aquifer) from the national forests when they turn on a tap, likely without the vaguest idea of where that water originates. But, as Tidwell's comments also highlight, water is used for more than just drinking. Those 3.5 million acres of lakes and wetlands and the 400,000 miles of rivers and streams provide not only clean surface water for communities, but also some of the best recreational opportunities in the country.

The agency estimates that 75 percent of recreational activities, activities that generate billions of dollars in revenue for local communities, outdoor retailers, hospitality services, and more, occur within a half-mile of a waterbody. Waterbodies on national forests host nearly forty-six million annual visits from anglers alone, generating $2 billion in revenue, supporting 51,000 jobs, and providing $246 million in federal taxes. Canoeing, kayaking, and pleasure boating pump millions, if not hundreds of millions, of additional dollars into local economies.

Of the 12,700 miles of Wild and Scenic Rivers that course through the United States, the Forest Service manages more than 5,000 miles. This protective status is afforded to the most pristine and undeveloped rivers in the country through the Wild and Scenic Rivers Act, which was signed by Lyndon Johnson in 1968. No dams may be built on Wild and Scenic Rivers, and riverside development is limited as well. That the Forest Service manages 40 percent of these

Areas of the Pisgah National Forest were once completely cutover.

Fishing on the Wayne National Forest in Ohio is just one water-based recreational activity that helps drive local economies.

incredible waterways is no accident. Between the western forests that were established, in part, to protect water supplies, and the eastern forests, which were established expressly to protect freshwater resources, many of our nation's finest rivers lie on national forests. These include classic western rivers like the mighty forks of the Flathead River in Montana, the emerald-hued Rogue River in Oregon, and the headwaters of the Snake River in Wyoming, alongside eastern gems like the Allegheny in Pennsylvania, the Ontonagon in Michigan, and the Eleven Point River in Missouri—all of which lie on national forests and are managed by the Forest Service.

Yet clean drinking water and recreation only account for two of the many resources fresh water provides. The production of food, whether fruits and vegetables, grains and cereals, or meat and poultry, especially in the western United States, is almost completely reliant on fresh water flowing from forested watersheds. Industry too, from the manufacturing of semiconductors to the clothes we wear, depends on

water in nearly every aspect of its production. But even adding these consumptive uses to water's already labored list of services fails to capture its true value.

Wildlife are as dependent on clean, fresh water as humans are. While we can turn a tap and enjoy potable water for pennies a gallon, fish, crustaceans, amphibians, insects, and a wide array of aquatic plants literally live in water. Ducks, geese, raptors, herons, and myriad other winged creatures rely on water for food and habitat. Elk, deer, bears, cougars, and hundreds of other creatures whose lot, like ours, is to live firmly planted on dry ground, slake their thirst from the bubbling springs that rise cool and clear from underground streams and from the creeks and rivers that carry snowmelt and rainwater.

Despite the great progress made in reforesting the cutover forests of the East and Midwest, despite the fact that one-in-five Americans relies on drinking water that flows from the lakes, rivers, and streams under the Forest Service's management,

BELOW Moose are one of the many species that, like humans, rely on clean water from national forests.

LEFT The French Broad River runs through North Carolina's Nantahala National Forest.

despite the fact that water-based recreation on national forests adds billions to the country's GDP, and despite the fact that protecting water is the keystone in the Forest Service's foundation, water quality and quantity are still threatened today.

IT TAKES A VILLAGE

One of the Weeks Act's legacies is close cooperation between Forest Service staff and state and urban land managers. The agency maintains offices in metropolises like New York City and Chicago where staff and researchers work with local managers to study and improve urban forests. (In July of 2019, Forest Service scientists discovered a new species of jewel beetle in a cemetery in Brooklyn.) It also operates several research stations, which conduct all kinds of research into all kinds of forest issues. Their research is shared with state land management agencies, other scientists and academics, and the public. The agency manages other facilities as well. For example, at the Forest Products Lab in Madison, Wisconsin, agency staff have helped develop cutting-edge technologies that take wood and turn it into a fantastic array of products including clothes, computer chips, and composites that can be used in cement bridges and other industrial applications.

Unsurprisingly, a good portion of the Forest Service's research efforts are in water, and specifically, the condition of the nation's forested watersheds. The 20 percent of the US population who get their water directly from our national forests are joined by many, many more who get their water from forested lands in the United States that aren't managed by the Forest Service. In fact, according to the agency, the numbers swell from the roughly 60 million people in 3,400 communities who get their water from a national forest to about 180 million people in 68,000 communities who get their water from forested lands—whether managed by a different federal agency, a state, or a private landowner.

And so, as directed by the spirit, if not the precise letter, of the Weeks Act, the Forest Service works across boundaries to evaluate and inform the management of this most critical of resources. In 2011, the agency unveiled its Forests to Faucets 2.0 data set and associated research. Forests to Faucets utilizes GIS technology to, in the agency's words, "determine the relative importance of small watersheds to surface drinking water. Imbedded in the data is the vital role forests play in protecting source water: the extent to which these forests are threatened by development, insects and disease, and wildland fire."

While the project may hold little interest to the average American who (like most of us) takes the luxury of on-demand potable water for granted, it is truly valuable to local municipalities that rely on the water that comes from forests. The municipal water managers who serve the 180 million Americans that rely on surface water from forested watersheds cannot afford the luxury of obliviousness. Threats to forests abound: wildfire, insects and disease, industrial development, residential development, ever-increasing demands for a finite resource, and looming over them all, climate change. Any one of these can severely impact a forest's capacity to provide water. Yet funding for forested watershed management, whether federal, state, or private, is scarce. The taps turn on and we drink, blissfully unaware of the role that healthy forests play in our quenching.

But there is hope. Cities are starting to invest in forest management. That is, their residents are starting to fund investments in the forested watersheds that provide them with drinking water, showers, flowers, and green lawns. Payment for Watershed Services, or PWS, programs, are bubbling up in cities as diverse as New York and Santa Fe. Some, like the ones in Flagstaff, Arizona, and Denver, Colorado, fund reforestation and restoration efforts following a wildfire that impacted the watershed. Others, like one in New York City, pay for trees, shrubs, and riparian plants to be planted along streams and rivers that are part of the city's watershed. Yet others, like one in Santa Fe, New Mexico, help the Forest Service thin overstocked forests so they don't burn as badly when a wildfire inevitably ignites.

Many of the watersheds that receive PWS funding are informed by Forests to Faucets 2.0, and the Forest Service is both a benefactor and a proponent of PWS. It has to be. In 2018, the Forest Service budget for "vegetation and watershed management" represented only 3 percent of the total budget. To be fair, the agency taps into other budget line items for managing the health of our forests, all of which are watersheds on which some living creatures depend, so the actual expenditures that improve or protect watersheds are likely higher. But the fact that the program dedicated to managing watersheds receives such a small percentage of the yearly budget stands in contrast to its immense value and historical emphasis.

I've never been to the Sylvania Wilderness, or for that matter, to the Ottawa National Forest. In fact, despite growing up only a couple hours from the White Mountain National Forest in New Hampshire, I've spent remarkably little time in the national forests established by the Weeks Act. It's a hole in my national forest resume and one I look forward to filling. But I don't need to visit these tracts to know their importance and to understand the value they provide our nation.

I have backpacked into the Bob Marshall Wilderness, which lies on the Flathead National Forest just north of my home in Missoula, Montana, outfitted with a small inflatable packraft, a fly rod, a week's worth of supplies, and a plan to float for four blissful days on the South Fork Flathead River. I'm no angler, but even I caught a glistening cutthroat trout on my first awkward casts in that gin-clear water. I've dipped my Nalgene into a rivulet of water cascading from the earth on Idaho's Clearwater National Forest and drank the raw, pristine liquid unworried about disease. I've camped alongside bright blue alpine lakes in the Rattlesnake Wilderness immediately north of Missoula, which until 1985 provided the city's drinking water and today serve as a backup supply should the aquifer from which we now draw our water ever run dry or become despoiled.

I've also watched runoff, brown and thick with sediment, shimmer down a rough dirt Forest Service road and into a creek. I've toured the charred hillsides of the Angeles National Forest, just east of the star-pocked streets of Los Angeles,

The Cherohala Skyway stretches between the Cherokee and Nantahala National Forests, just one of the scenic byways on America's national forests.

after a wildfire ravaged its precious watersheds. I've raised money to plant trees there and in a dozen other watersheds that, like the Angeles, provide nearby communities with their water. I've shared stories of how Forest Service staff and nonprofits are partnering to reintroduce beavers into the watersheds where they belong—after centuries of indiscriminate trapping removed them and their pollution- and runoff-trapping dams—so that they might help heal these broken hydrological systems at no cost to humans.

I've studied the data from Forests to Faucets 2.0, and I've helped broker charitable contributions from corporations like Coca-Cola, Disney, and Molson Coors that have restored degraded watersheds and planted trees that will filter runoff and snowmelt as they grow. I've worked to reduce the vast and undermaintained network of more than 350,000 miles of roads that fragment our national forests and send sediment and pollution into the small creeks and rivers they parallel.

Through all of these experiences, I've learned that the real value of forests lies not in the timber they produce or the beauty they provide. In my travels and my work, I've come to know what Gifford Pinchot and George Perkins Marsh, the grandfather of American conservation, knew—that forests and water are inextricably linked. This knowledge is as tragically unappreciated in today's world as it was throughout history. The cedars of Lebanon made that now-dry country the verdant jewel of the Mediterranean, until they were cut for ships, temples, and railroads. As they felled tree after tree, the ancient Greeks transformed much of their landscape from a rich, fertile forest into the arid chaparral ecosystem it is today. Our nation's heritage of national forests was founded in part to avoid such a fate and in part to remedy the very ills that industrial deforestation caused.

On the landing page for the Forests to Faucets program, the Forest Service authors conclude with a short sentence that, though written in the stilted, half-bureaucratic, half-scientific prose that so much of the agency relies on when describing its work, is worth emphasizing here: "In perhaps its most important role, this work can serve as an education tool to illustrate the link between forests and the provision of surface drinking water—a key watershed-based ecosystem service."

Take just a moment to consider what these authors are saying. This massive set of data, culled and refined over more than a decade and created to inform water and forest managers of the very real threats the water supplies they manage face, may find its greatest value in teaching us, the public at large, one simple fact: that forests equal water.

2

SEEDS OF REFORESTATION

The Art and Science of Growing Trees

ON EARTH DAY 2018, the nonprofit National Forest Foundation launched a campaign to plant fifty million trees on America's national forests in five years. The campaign marked a huge increase in the organization's tree-planting efforts. As it happened, I was the NFF's communications director at the time and had started my career at the organization managing its tree-planting program.

In the ten years prior to launching the campaign, the NFF had helped the Forest Service plant eleven million trees. Ramping up in such a big way was both exhilarating and a bit terrifying. But the need to replant our forests was obvious. The press release announcing the campaign noted that the Forest Service estimated that more than one million acres of our national forests needed some kind of reforestation.

Given that the national forests stretch across 193 million acres, this backlog may not seem particularly worrisome to the casual observer—1 million acres is about half a percent of the total amount of national forests in the country. However, nearly half that 193 million acreage is considered rangeland not forest. Further, many of the areas most in need of reforestation serve as watersheds to downstream communities, provide critical habitat for endangered species, or have been so ravaged by severe wildfire that there is little chance they'll recover without human intervention.

Regardless of the need and irrespective of the NFF's ambitions, the campaign generated one major question: How could the Forest Service source nearly ten million native tree seedlings a year, all matched for the elevation, aspect, climate, and forest type of each specific planting location where there was a need?

The science of forest management is called silviculture, which the Forest Service defines as "the art and science of controlling the establishment, growth, composition, health, and quality of forests and woodlands to meet the diverse needs and values of landowners and society such as wildlife habitat, timber, water resources, restoration, and recreation on a sustainable basis." Growth, then, is a key component of the mission, and reforestation, the art and science of growing and planting seedlings, has been part of the Forest Service's culture since before it was even a federal agency. In its history of reforestation, the Forest Service states that "the Organic

Administration Act of 1897 explicitly provided for the establishment of national forests to improve and protect forests to secure favorable conditions of water flows and to furnish a continuous supply of timber. The act provides for reforestation work in support of the these aims."

Generally, fire is the largest driver of reforestation needs; the Organic Act of 1897 mentions fire repeatedly, going so far as to spell out punishments for those who might purposefully or accidentally ignite a fire on one of the new forest reserves. And so, the Forest Service and its precursors wasted no time in building the infrastructure, both physical and institutional, to replant forests following fires. In 1902, just five years after the Organic Act was passed and three years before the Forest Service was offi-cially founded, the Charles E. Bessey Nursery was established in Halsey, Nebraska.

Fire is the largest driver of refor-estation needs on our national forests.

Bessey Nursery is the oldest Forest Service nursery in the country and where the agency's tree-planting program first took root.

Nebraska may seem an odd spot to grow trees. It's smack in the middle of the notoriously treeless Great Plains. Why the Forest Service chose Nebraska for its tree-seedling program hints at both the agency's early ambitions and its self-assumed technical prowess. It's also an interesting story.

The nursery's namesake, Charles E. Bessey (1845–1915) holds a special place in the history of American botany and horticulture. Bessey was born in a log cabin near Milton, Ohio. After the Civil War (for which, at age 16, he was too young to enlist), Bessey worked as a timber surveyor in Michigan. In 1869, he graduated with a botany degree from Michigan Agricultural College, and in 1870, he landed a teaching gig at Iowa Agricultural College (today Iowa State University). His tenure in Iowa lasted until 1884 when he was offered the deanship of botany at University of Nebraska in Lincoln, which would remain his home for the next two decades.

Bessey was beloved by his students, and he was active in national and regional botany and horticultural organizations, including serving as the state botanist and as the head of the Nebraska State Horticultural Society's Forestry Committee. He is credited with advancing the science of botany, especially botany education, by moving past simple plant classification and into the laboratory-based microscopic study of plants, plant disease, and other such scientific query. He also pushed the science of horticulture—the propagating and growing of plants—into new frontiers as well.

He advocated for and helped write the Hatch Act, an 1887 law that established a partnership between the federal government and land-grant universities to institute experimental agricultural stations funded by the government and managed by the universities. Shortly after the Hatch Act passed, Bessey was appointed to a two-year term as the first director of the Nebraska Agricultural Experiment Station.

The idea of planting trees in Nebraska wasn't Bessey's alone, though he is credited with bringing the idea to the Federal Division of Forestry (the precursor of the Forest Service) in 1891. According to John F. Freeman's excellent history *High Plains Horticulture*, Bessey persuaded Bernhard E. Fernow, chief of the Division of Forestry at the Department of Agriculture to "provide the seedlings and funding for an experimental conifer test plot in the Sandhills." Fernow agreed, provided that Bessey could find suitable land and labor for the experiment at no cost to the government. Fortunately, one of Bessey's colleagues, an entomology teacher named Lawrence Bruner, owned land with his brother, and they offered it to Bessey for the experiment.

The experiment didn't take long to establish—by summer, nearly 20,000 ponderosa pine, jack pine, Scotch pine, and Austrian pine had been planted along with shelter trees of boxelder, hackberry, and black cherry. In keeping with the experimental nature of the effort, Fernow directed Bessey and the Bruners to plant some of the seedlings on cultivated land and some on land that hadn't been plowed under. The trees on the cultivated land died fairly quickly—that fall only 5 percent of those seedlings were alive—but the trees on the land that hadn't been plowed fared better, showing a 50 percent survival rate.

Charles Edwin Bessey helped establish the nursery named after him and expanded the science of horticulture.

The late nineteenth and early twentieth centuries were heady times for scientific study. Advances in technology and a growing network of land-grant universities brought science to the general public and helped transition agriculture and horticulture from a trial-and-error discipline to one governed by science. Bessey played a leading role in this during his tenure in both Iowa and Nebraska. He brought the first microscopes to the University of Nebraska-Lincoln and enlisted his students in helping him catalogue all the plant species that grew in the state.

On his plant-collecting rambles throughout the state, Bessey noticed that Nebraska sat at a confluence of eastern and western plant species. In the far northwestern corner of the state, the Pine Ridge area was blanketed by ponderosa pines, and local farmers told Bessey about the decaying

stumps they found on their farms. Bessey became convinced that Nebraska, and especially the Sandhills region, once supported forests and could support them once again—the sandy soil there was similar to that in Michigan where Bessey worked as a timber surveyor and he reasoned that the water table was high enough to support trees. The seedling survival success at the Bruners provided Bessey with proof that Nebraska could once again be forested.

While the experiment at the Bruners proved that seedlings could grow in Nebraska, the funding was exhausted almost immediately, and they had to essentially abandon the project. But Bessey wasn't deterred. Over the next several years, he continued to press the case that federal lands in Nebraska could, and should, be devoted to growing trees. While there's no doubt Bessey appreciated forests for their beauty, his primary motivation was utilitarian—settlers and cattlemen needed fence posts, timber for homes, and wood for fuel. Growing trees in Nebraska could provide these much-needed resources, while providing erosion

Early planting efforts on the Dismal River Forest Reserve, precursor to the Nebraska National Forest.

control, habitat for wildlife, and watershed protection. His arguments, rooted in the real needs of the time in which he lived, were as much practical and economic as they were dedicated to furthering scientific inquiry.

Bessey leveraged his leadership positions in Nebraska's horticultural arena to advocate for reforestation of the Sandhills. Eventually, his arguments were echoed by other Nebraskans and made their way to the federal government. In 1900, the Division of Forestry decided it would send a delegation to western Nebraska to judge for itself the suitability of Nebraska, and especially the Sandhills, for growing trees.

After surveying the western Nebraska landscape, including the now ten-year-old plantation on the Bruner's land, the feds concluded Bessey was right: trees could, and should, be grown in Nebraska. One of the members of the survey party was Forestry Division chief Gifford Pinchot. Conveniently for Bessey, Pinchot was a trusted advisor to Theodore Roosevelt who became president in 1901.

With Pinchot's support and Bessey's lobbying, Roosevelt acted in April 1902, designating 85,000 acres of land around the Dismal River and another 123,000 acres near the Niobrara River as forest reserves (in 1908, the reserves were collectively renamed the Nebraska National Forest). Calling them forest reserves was aspirational—they weren't forested at the time they were set aside—but Roosevelt, Pinchot, Bessey and others were confident that someday, a revenue-producing forest would rise from the plains. The reserves would be managed by the federal government, but the actual planting and any forestry or horticultural experiments would be conducted by students and professors of the university.

One of the first tasks was creating a nursery to grow seedlings for this novel afforestation experiment. Within months of Roosevelt's designations, the first seedbeds were established at the Niobrara Reserve and planted with ponderosa pine seeds collected in the Pine Ridge area of northwestern Nebraska and the Black Hills of South Dakota. Successful propagation wasn't immediate, but over time, the nursery honed its horticultural techniques and produced seedlings for other forests in addition to the Nebraska National Forest. Also, over time, a real-deal forest sprouted from the thin, sandy soil once dominated by swaying grass. Today, it covers roughly 20,000 acres of the otherwise treeless Great Plains. Thus began the nation's first federally managed tree nursery and the western hemisphere's largest hand-planted forest.

Today, the Bessey Nursery is still operational. The state-of-the-art facility produces roughly 1.5 million bare-root conifer and hardwood seedlings every year, though it can produce as many as 4.5 million seedlings a year.

McCloud Nursery on the Shasta National Forest was one of the early Forest Service nurseries; here staff weed seedlings in the shadow of Mount Shasta.

THE SEED ORCHARD

To successfully grow a tree on a national forest, managers need a healthy seedling. Seedlings, somewhat obviously, come from seeds, which come from trees. So, while the seedling may be the end product that facilities like the Bessey Nursery produce, it's only one small part of the tree-planting process.

The Bessey is one of six federally managed nurseries in the country. These facilities are supported by seed extractories (some of which are co-located with the nursery like at Bessey and at the Coeur d'Alene Nursery in Idaho) where the precious seeds are extracted from the cones, hulls, and other seed-dispersal apparatus that trees have developed to propagate naturally. And some of them, like Bessey and Coeur d'Alene, also function as seed banks, where various seeds are kept in well-organized bins in huge walk-in coolers. If a forest needs seedlings of a particular species from a particular location, elevation, or zone, like Engelmann spruce for planting on the White River National Forest in Colorado, the nursery can pull those seeds from the seed bank and sow them for planting. But before any of that can happen, nursery staff need seeds, and to get seeds they need cones.

In the West, most of the reforestation efforts involve cone-producing conifer trees (deciduous trees also produce seeds, but don't produce cones—think of an acorn or winged maple tree seeds). Decades ago, cones were collected in the wild. Forest

Service staff trudged through the woods, eyes aloft in search of the tallest, straightest, best-looking specimens. When they found a winner, they climbed high into the canopy and hand-collected cones. This doesn't really happen anymore. Since the 1960s, the Forest Service has transitioned from collecting cones in situ to growing and managing cone orchards where genetically superior trees are grown in an organized way solely to produce cones and seeds for nurseries.

The Plains Tree Orchard, formally known as the Plains Tree Improvement Area, is only an hour from my home in Missoula, and, as it turned out, I'd driven past it dozens of times, never really knowing it was there. From the highway that runs along its southern border, the orchard doesn't look like much, but once you turn down the dirt driveway and make your way to the small collection of outbuildings and offices, the breadth of the operation becomes readily apparent.

Spread across roughly 120 acres that the Forest Service purchased in 1991 specifically for growing cones, the orchard is a study in efficiency and would make Charles Bessey proud. It provides cones for a wide swath of Montana and Idaho, beginning near Great Falls, Montana, and stretching west across the Idaho Panhandle and south to the Salmon River.

From the road, the Plains Tree Improvement Area doesn't look like much.

This broad area is split into two zones, a northern blue zone that is generally colder and wetter, and a southern red zone that is hotter and drier; the two zones overlap in the middle a bit as well (I don't know if they call it the purple zone, but they should). Home gardeners might understand this system, as it's similar to the hardiness zones listed on plant tags. The same species grow across the entire region, but trees adapt to their local growing conditions and produce seeds (in cones of course) that are also adapted to the local conditions. Planting seedlings from trees that are adapted to colder, wetter environments in dry, hot sites isn't a good way to successfully replant a forest. The same is true of trees that grow at 7,000 feet in elevation vs. trees that grow 4,000 feet above sea level. So in addition to tracking which zone the cone stock comes from, the staff also track what elevation it is best suited for.

When I visited the Plains Tree Orchard in 2017, it boasted two full-time staff—Valerie Walker, the Lolo National Forest Genetic Resources Forester who runs the operation, and Elliott Meyer, the genetic resource and silviculture assistant. A few locals help out with mowing and watering as needed.

The orchard grew out of an effort to selectively breed white pine trees resistant to white pine blister rust, a fungal infection that decimated wild white pine trees roughly sixty years ago. White pine blister rust is transmitted to the trees from shrubs like gooseberry and currants. It eventually causes the trees to die. There are several types of white pine found throughout North America, including the western white pine, a beautiful and valuable tree that once grew throughout western Montana and northern Idaho (it's Idaho's state tree). Ensuring its future was a priority for the Forest Service.

When Forest Service employees were still heading out into the woods to collect cones, their mandate was to find the healthiest trees, confident that any descendants would share the parents' genes and that they too would grow straight and tall, resist disease, and fight off insects. When the white pine blister rust appeared, staff noticed that some white pines were able to fight off the disease even as their neighbors succumbed. They collected cones from these trees and brought them back to district and supervisor offices where they extracted seeds and grew out seedlings in test plots. While the agency may not have known the precise genetic code that allowed these trees to beat the blister rust, foresters hypothesized that the progeny from these blister-resistant trees would also be blister resistant.

The experiments proved successful, and descendants of these blister-resistant white pines now grow throughout the northern Rockies. After this initial success, the concept of selectively propagating high-quality specimens was expanded to other native trees and to other desired characteristics, like cold hardiness and drought tolerance. Over the years, these trials, carefully monitored and studiously tracked, helped silviculturists pinpoint exactly which trees performed the best. Those best-of-the-best trees were planted in organized plots in cone orchards, where they grow seeds that are preprogrammed with all the genetic codes needed to produce healthy, valuable, and disease-resistant trees.

At Plains Tree Orchard, roughly 8,000 trees are grown in twenty-five square plots, spaced far enough apart to prevent cross-pollination and inbreeding. Nearly three miles of six inch irrigation pipe snake between the plots. While these

Each tree in the Plains Tree Improvement Area is marked with a tag that details important information.

trees represent decades of careful, selective breeding, they don't look like they're the best of the best. Many are topped and spread out in strange, Dr. Seuss–like shapes, pruning that makes it easier to harvest cones, irrigate the trees, and keep grass between and beneath the plots mowed. Each plot contains trees from a particular zone and elevation—blue zone, high-elevation larch trees are over there, red zone, low-elevation ponderosa pine trees in that plot, and so on. Each tree is marked with a metal tag that provides critical info like species, zone and elevation, and where it is in the plot. Cones are harvested and sent to seed extractories, where the seeds are extracted, labeled, and stored in seed banks. When an order for trees comes in, nursery staff pull seeds from storage and plant them as either containerized or bare-root seedlings, depending on the specific order.

Other silvicultural techniques are on display at the orchard as well. The western white pine isn't the only tree susceptible to white pine blister rust. High in the sub-alpine zones of the Rocky Mountains, including Montana and Idaho, whitebark pines grow gnarled and twisted. These tough trees provide pine nuts, a critical food for the Clark's nutcracker bird and for grizzly bears, and are a bellwether for the health of these high-elevation environments. But they too have been seriously impacted by the blister rust.

On the opposite side of the orchard from the white pines, behind a curtain of late-season weeds, small whitebark pine trees grow in neat rows a few feet apart. On the top of each roughly eighteen-inch high tree is a small cluster of reddish, gray cones. For those unfamiliar with whitebark pines, the small size of these trees may not register as out of the ordinary. But as I found out, these diminutive saplings are proof of horticultural sleight-of-hand.

Because the blister rust impact on whitebark pine trees is a relatively new phenomenon, the agency still collects wild blister-resistant whitebark pinecones when staff find them scattered on the wind-swept ridges of the Rocky Mountains. The seeds from these cones are carefully cultivated for a couple years in controlled environments and subjected to blister rust when they're big enough. Those that do, in fact, have genetic resistance to the rust are grown out for another year or two. They are then grafted onto the rootstock of much older whitebark pine trees. And that's where the magic happens. Once grafted, the young seedlings are fooled into thinking they're much older, and they start to produce cones—something wild whitebark pine trees don't do until they're roughly eighty years old.

BEATING THE BLIGHT

Valerie and Elliot are quick to point out that they aren't genetically altering or modifying trees, just selectively breeding them. But there are efforts within and outside of the Forest Service to genetically engineer trees, specifically the American chestnut. For nearly forty million years, the American chestnut tree grew throughout the eastern United States. Like the western white pine, it was valuable to humans and wildlife. The American Chestnut Foundation describes it this way:

More than a century ago, nearly four billion American chestnut trees were growing in the eastern United States. They were among the largest, tallest, and fastest-growing trees. The wood was rot-resistant, straight-grained, and suitable for furniture, fencing, and building. The nuts fed billions of wildlife, people and their livestock. It was almost a perfect tree, that is, until a blight fungus killed it more than a century ago. The chestnut blight has been called the greatest ecological disaster to strike the world's forests in all of history. The American chestnut tree survived all adversaries for forty million years, then disappeared within forty.

Like the white pine blister rust, the chestnut blight is an introduced pathogen. It effectively kills mature above-ground parts of the chestnut tree but does not affect the root system, allowing the plant to send up doomed sprouts. Because of this, scientists don't consider the American chestnut extinct, labeling it instead "functionally extinct."

Unlike some white pine trees, which have genetic resistance to the white pine blister rust (and which served as the impetus for the cone collecting program the Forest Service manages), American chestnuts show very limited genetic resistance to the chestnut blight. However, another species, the Chinese chestnut, is blight resistant, and it offers hope to those working to restore its once-abundant American cousin to its former range. The American Chestnut Foundation (ACF), which is leading these efforts with help from and in cooperation with the Forest Service, has embarked on a two-pronged approach to creating blight-resistant American chestnut trees.

The first prong follows traditional breeding methods that silviculturists have been utilizing for centuries, namely crossbreeding American chestnuts with Chinese chestnuts that show resistance to the blight. The result is essentially a half-Chinese, half-American hybrid. ACF staff then breed this hybrid with an American chestnut several more times until the resulting seedling is $\frac{1}{16}$ Chinese and $\frac{15}{16}$ American. These trees contain most of the wild genetics of American chestnut and the blight-resistance of the Chinese chestnuts. This approach is effective, but it's time consuming and expensive.

The second prong involves something called transgenics. Transgenic organisms are also called genetically modified organisms, which proponents claim will save humanity and opponents claim will cause humanity's ruin. However one feels about genetically modified organisms in the food supply, the science behind them is fascinating and, in the case of the American chestnut tree, presents a compelling opportunity for saving a species whose demise was caused by humans messing with the environment to begin with. If saving the white pine through selective breeding is like playing checkers, saving the chestnut through genetic engineering is like playing chess—against a computer.

Researchers at the ACF have discovered a gene from the wheat plant that effectively neutralizes the fungus that causes blight, thus preventing it from damaging the chestnut tree. They're able to insert that gene into the American chestnut (which the scientists argue is safe since we've been growing and eating wheat for millennia) and voilà—the transgenic American chestnut trees are no longer susceptible to blight.

Of course, the ACF isn't simply releasing its transgenic trees into the wild. The research shows promise, but there is a lot more work and study required before these trees are used in any large-scale restoration efforts. The Environmental Protection Agency, the US Department of Agriculture, and the Food and Drug Administration all have regulatory frameworks for transgenic plants, which the ACF must clear before they can begin planting their genetically modified trees in earnest.

If the American Chestnut Foundation's transgenic work portends the future of horticulture (especially for the revival of iconic species imperiled by foreign disease or pests), and Charles Bessey and his fellow Nebraskans' turn-of-the-century efforts mark the start of large-scale, science-based tree propagation efforts, the Plains Tree Improvement Area lies somewhere in between, straddling the past and the future. My visit happened to be in fall when cones of the stately ponderosa pine were ready for harvesting.

I watched as a temporary worker scaled a tall, three-legged orchard ladder to harvest the cones. These hand-sized treasures contained genetic material honed by decades of precise, controlled and highly selective breeding—once plucked from the branch, the worker stuffed them into a humble burlap sack tied with a small paper tag bearing the species, elevation, zone, and other relevant information written in shaky cursive. Eventually, the sacks would go into a truck to make the trek down Interstate 90 to the Coeur d'Alene Forest Nursery and seed extractory where the cones would be dried out, separated from their seeds, and ground into mulch.

Following their journey, I meet Aram Eramian, the Coeur d'Alene Nursery supervisor, who walks me out of the nursery office and into the 220-acre campus. Around us lie greenhouses, sheds, warehouses, and an assortment of tractors, four-wheelers, and other contraptions. Of course, there are also large, rectangular plots of green where small trees grow in neat rows. It's immediately clear that this operation is also a blend of the past and future, of cutting-edge technology and tried-and-true horticultural methods, and of elegant, purpose-built machinery and boot-strapped engineering.

We wander over to a sprawling warehouse where cones, like the ponderosa pine-cones harvested at Plains, are dried out. Large, rectangular wooden trays, roughly ten feet long by five feet wide and eight inches tall rise from a red base to a height of twelve or more feet. Another red tray caps the structure. Blue ducting connects the base to a heater and blower which pumps warm air—Aram says it's between 105 and 110 degrees—through the base and up into the trays. Both the trays and the bases show their age—the Forest Service–green paint on the trays is chipped and faded and the red base is covered with a thick layer of dust. But it's all perfectly functional. The cones are laid in the kiln trays, stacked on top of each other and subjected to warm air for several days. In time, the cones dry out and open up, releasing their seeds.

The shed at the Plains Tree Improvement Area contains dozens of sacks of cones, marked and ready for shipping to seed extractories.

Once dried, the cones are pulled from the trays and put through a large tumbler where they are rolled and bounced until the seeds fall out. From there, the seeds are taken to the extractory, a white cinder block building filled with Rube Goldberg-esque contraptions. Though the tumbling process separates the seeds from the cones, it doesn't result in a bare seed ready for storage. Conifer trees like the ones grown at the Coeur d'Alene Nursery produce single-winged seeds. In nature, the cones dry out on the tree, high up in the air. Once opened, the single-winged seeds fall out and are carried by the wind (or by animals and birds) to the forest floor. If conditions are favorable, they'll overwinter and sprout the following season.

The Coeur d'Alene Nursery in Idaho is a modern nursery and seed extractory.

In the extractory, the seeds are first subjected to the scalper, which removes any bits of cone or other large debris that made it through the tumbling process. Then they're run through the de-winger, which removes the wings. From there, they undergo two more separation processes that further strip the seed of its protective coatings. Finally, Aram and his staff are left with live seed—a tiny speck of genetic coding that if planted, miraculously grows into a hundred-foot tall, oxygen-giving, water-cleaning, habitat-providing tree. But the nursery staff don't simply plant these seeds, rather they soak them in water for at least forty-eight hours (depending on the species) then store them in carefully labeled containers that are put into one of four giant walk-in coolers where six-degree Fahrenheit temperature mimics the deep freeze of a northern Rocky Mountain winter.

The whole operation is both quaint and modern. Analogue tracking—paper tags noting the source of the cones or seeds, the date of collection, the collector, and more—follow the cones and seeds through each step of the process. The machinery itself is adapted from grain processing equipment designed to separate wheat and other cereal grains. With a few homegrown modifications, it works perfectly for separating cones from seeds. High-tech irrigation equipment, well-maintained greenhouses, and precise growing methods leverage the most up-to-date horticulture techniques and add an aura of digital modernity to the operation. Whether old school, new school, or a hybrid, it's remarkably efficient. In 2016, Aram's team of twenty-five people processed 6,000 bushels of cones and grew nearly five million seedlings.

The seeds aren't planted until an order comes into the nursery. Reforestation often follows a wildfire, disease outbreak, or blow down (when trees are blown over in a particularly strong storm), though not always. Sometimes managers want to improve species diversity in a particular stand or need to plant a particular species to improve wildlife habitat or to help restore a stream or river, and, of course, replanting is required after a timber harvest.

Regardless of the reason, the local silviculturist determines the needed species, the quantities required, the elevation where they are planting, and what zone they are in. The final step is determining whether they want bare-root or containerized seedlings. Bare-root seedlings are grown for two years in large outdoor beds before being lifted from the soil and processed for shipping to the forest that ordered them. Containerized seedlings are grown in Styrofoam blocks with dozens of small holes in them or in small plastic tubes. The holes or tubes are filled with potting soil and the seedlings are grown for one year before being shipped to the forest that ordered them. Each option has its advantages and disadvantages and local silviculturists match their preference with the site conditions and other factors.

CLOCKWISE FROM LEFT Cones are placed in stacked cone trays, which dry them out making it easier to extract seeds.

This large freezer stores years (and millions of dollars) worth of seeds in the nursery's seed bank.

Aram Eramian holds the fruits of his team's labor: seeds.

Federal law requires that the Forest Service nurseries keep a ten-year supply of seed stock on hand, which for the Coeur d'Alene Nursery, equates to seeds worth about $2.5 million in the deep freeze. Federal law also prohibits Forest Service nurseries from competing with private nurseries, so they can't sell their seedlings to the general public—though the Coeur d'Alene Nursery does provide seedlings to the Idaho Department of Conservation and the Bureau of Land Management.

Interestingly, Aram tells me that the nursery gets no funding from Congress or the Forest Service's annual budget. Instead, it's a business, though an atypical one to be sure, and the money the agencies pay for seedlings pays for the cost of operation. If there's a bit extra at the end of the year, Aram invests in new tractors, tools, greenhouses, or irrigation equipment.

The Coeur d'Alene Nursery is one of six nurseries the Forest Service still operates (five of them have seed extractories on site, and the agency operates two other extractories as well). The Plains Tree Improvement Area is one of five such orchards in Idaho and Montana alone. Together, these facilities, and those like them across the country, produce and process a huge number of cones and grow tens of millions of seedlings each year.

Of course, the final piece of the reforestation puzzle is actually planting a seedling in the ground. This process also bridges the past and present. Prepared seedlings are kept in refrigerated trucks after they leave the nursery until the day they go into the ground. Workers, many of them from South America on work visas or college students on a summer conservation work crew, lug large sacks brimming

BELOW Bare-root seedlings in a nursery bed, ready for lifting after two years of growth

LEFT Containerized seedlings in one of Coeur d'Alene's high-tech greenhouses

with seedlings across the forest, searching for microsites where the trees will have the best chance of survival. These specific locations may be tucked behind a boulder, on a slight shift in the slope aspect, or snugged up against a fallen tree—all spots where a bit more shade or moisture might make the difference between life or death. A specialized tool creates a hole and a worker carefully places the seedling in the void. Once they've filled the hole with soil so that no air can dry out the tender roots, they take a few steps and dig another hole.

Professional planters can complete the entire process in ten seconds.

Forest Service staff monitor the planting and check back on the trees in one, three, and five years. Sometimes competing vegetation needs to be removed, other times, the seedlings suffer unforeseen drought or other natural events that impact survival rates. Elk and deer can damage seedlings too, and in some locations the Forest Service installs protection to keep hungry ungulates at bay.

An early planting project by a CCC crew on the Lolo National Forest in Montana.

When the National Forest Foundation announced its campaign to plant fifty million trees in 2017, the organization had helped the Forest Service plant eleven million trees over roughly ten years. In 2019 alone, it planted five million trees. Each one of those seedlings was the descendant of a genetically superior tree, precisely matched to the zone and elevation where it could grow into a hundred-foot adult. Each one was grown specifically for its planting project by a crew of horticultural professionals in a modern, self-sustaining nursery, and each was carefully planted by a professional tree planter mindful of the slightest variations in topography and location that would give the seedling its best chance at survival.

Charles Bessey would be proud.

3

FROM THE DUSTBOWL TO MIDEWIN

Restoring America's Grasslands

"E'RE GRASS FARMERS," Wade Spang, supervisor of the Midewin National Tallgrass Prairie, tells me proudly. "Other national forests grow trees, but we grow grass." Spang and I are in a sprawling outbuilding near Midewin's modern visitor center. Giant green John Deere tractors line one end of the hanger-like building. Spang is dressed in his Forest Service greens, the drab olive green and brown uniform that Forest Service staff wear in their official duties. He walks with a slight limp as we move through the cavernous building and out into the harsh August sunlight.

PREVIOUS
Midewin National
Tallgrass Prairie
on a misty summer
morning.

I'm on official duty as well, though my uniform is less formal than Spang's. The previous evening, I had hosted a small, but lively, fundraising and trivia event at an organic farm-to-table restaurant in Chicago, which is an hour or so north of Midewin. I had been to the prairie once before, on a whirlwind tour. Work duties kept that visit short, just a half a day. This time, I was eager to explore the surrounding landscape, though I had little conception of how a tallgrass prairie should look, either its modern incarnation as represented by Midewin or what it might have been one-hundred and fifty years earlier when Illinois was considered "the West." Fortunately, someone else did.

On a stagecoach ride from Chicago to Peoria in July 1840, Eliza Steele awoke to find herself surrounded by tallgrass prairie, one of three prairie ecosystems found on America's vast Great Plains. Her description of the scene is evocative, and the Forest Service sometimes references it when describing their end goals for Midewin.

I started with surprise and delight. I was in the midst of a prairie! A world or grass and flowers stretched around me, rising and falling in gentle undulations, as if an enchanter had struck the ocean swell, and it was at rest forever. Acres of wild flowers of every hue glowed around me . . . What a magnificent sight! Those glorious ranks of flowers! . . . How shall I convey to you an idea of a prairie? I despair, for never yet hath pen brought the scene before my mind. Imagine yourself in the center of an immense circle of velvet herbage, the sky for its boundary upon every side; the whole clothed with a radiant efflorescence of every brilliant hue. We rode thus through a perfect wilderness of sweets, sending forth perfume, and animated with myriads of glittering birds and butterflies. . . . You will scarcely credit the profusion of flowers . . . We passed whole acres of blossoms all bearing one hue, as purple, perhaps, or masses of yellow or rose; and then again a carpet of every color intermixed, or narrow bands, as if a rainbow had fallen upon the verdant slopes. When the sun flooded this mosaic floor with light, and the summer breeze stirred among their leaves, the iridescent glow was beautiful and wondrous beyond any thing I had ever conceived.

Mrs. Steele (as her book attributes authorship) had embarked from New York City on a 4,000-mile journey through the vast American frontier. Her adventure included steamships, trains, and stagecoaches. A talented, if somewhat discursive writer, she recorded her travels through a series of letters to "E" that were collected and published in 1841 as *A Summer Journey in the West*, a year after her trip. Little is known about Mrs. Steele, aside from what can be gleaned by careful reading of her travelogue, but she must have been an independent and adventurous (and well-funded) woman to have taken such a trip.

In the 1840s, tallgrass prairie extended from eastern Illinois north and west to Minnesota and south along the western boundaries of present-day Iowa, Missouri, and Arkansas, finally terminating in eastern Oklahoma. Mixed grass prairie picked up where the tallgrass left off, extending farther west through the Dakotas, Nebraska, Kansas, and Texas, before climate and soil proved too dry. Finally, in the far western range of the Great Plains, the foothills of the Rockies climb through short grass prairie, the third type of prairie found in the United States.

Of course, these transitions don't follow clear lines on a map, but rather mark subtle changes in climate and soil. Tallgrass prairies grow where rain is more abundant and where the soil is deeper; receiving between thirty and thirty-five inches of precipitation annually. As the climate gets drier farther west, tallgrass prairies give way to mixed grass, which in turn give way to short grass in the arid plains. Or at least, it used to be that way. Today, most of the Great Plains, and especially where the tallgrass prairies once swayed in a rainbow of flowers, are some of the most productive farm and agricultural lands in the world.

Climate and soil weren't the only reasons the prairies existed as they did. Dozens of Native American tribes lived across the entire Great Plains and they regularly used fire to manipulate the landscape (as they did across all of North America). Those fires, plus ones caused by lightning, cleared trees and recycled nutrients back into the soil. Immense herds of bison, elk, and pronghorn roamed the plains, providing food and other resources to the people who lived there. European incursion into the area had significantly altered the makeup of tribal cultures and politics in the Midwest by the time Eliza Steele traveled through Illinois (itself a state for only twenty-two years when she arrived), but it had only just started to disrupt the ecology of the region—an ecology that had been in place for at least ten thousand years. At the time, Illinois was still very much the western frontier. The Black Hawk War, a short, bloody battle between white militia groups and a group of Indians comprised of Sauks, Meskwakis, and Kickapoos and led by Black Hawk, had ended in 1832, just eight years prior. Chicago was incorporated as a village in 1833, just one year after Black Hawk was defeated, and it became a city in 1837, when its population climbed to 4,000 people.

While the Black Hawk War marked the end of Native American resistance in the Midwest, it presaged the beginning of how the Great Plains would be transformed from prairie to farm. Just three years prior to Eliza Steele's epic summer road trip, a blacksmith in Grand Detour, Illinois, had invented a new steel plow designed specifically to break up the thick, clay soils around his home. In 1838, he sold his new plow to a neighbor and then another and another as word of mouth

Wildflowers at Midewin hint at the splendor Eliza Steele witnessed in 1840, before the tallgrass prairie was plowed under.

spread. By the time Mrs. Steele rhapsodized about the prairie, John Deere had begun mass-producing his new plow, and in 1841, he was producing between 75 and 100 plows a year. Fourteen years later, in 1855, Deere's factory had sold more than 10,000 of the "plow that broke the Plains."

As it turned out, the same climate and soil that fostered an incredible diversity of wildflowers and six-foot-high grasses was equally fertile for crops. With Deere's plow and a couple horses, hardworking homesteaders quickly brought the tallgrass prairie to heel, plowing up the rich soil and planting corn and other crops in place of wildflowers and grasses. By the turn of the century, all but a few remnants of America's tallgrass prairie were gone. Estimates of remaining tallgrass prairie range from 1 percent to 4 percent of its former 170-million-acre extent.

BEYOND BOMBS

Though Illinois is nicknamed the Prairie State, not much prairie actually remains. Today, only 2,500 acres of virgin tallgrass prairie still exist in Illinois, just 0.01 percent of its former 20-million-acre range. It is an imperiled landscape.

The largest, still extant tracts of native tallgrass prairie overlay the rugged Flint Hills in Kansas and parts of Oklahoma. Here, rocky hills of flint, limestone, and shale are covered with a thin layer of soil. The soil cap is deep enough to support tallgrass prairie plants, but too shallow to accommodate a plow, thus sparing it the fate of most prairies. Today, cattle grazing is the primary land use throughout the Flint Hills, and ranchers use prescribed fire in spring to regenerate the prairie grasses just like Native Americans and lightning did in previous millennia. While much of the landscape is privately owned, a few reserves, like the Nature Conservancy–managed Joseph H. Williams Tallgrass Prairie Preserve in Oklahoma and the National Park Service–managed Tallgrass Prairie National Preserve in Kansas, provide a glimpse of how so much of the Great Plains once looked.

Modern travelers following Eliza Steele's stagecoach route from Chicago to Peoria, would most likely take Interstate 55 southwest out of the city, rolling smoothly on a ribbon of pavement at speeds that would have seemed impossible to her. The route zips through the city's vast suburbs before passing through industrial zones where factories belch acrid smoke into the thick Midwestern air. As travelers leave the city and its enterprises behind, I-55 merges with Historic Route 66 and rolls along the Des Plaines River, past bedroom communities, and into the rural agriculture fields that comprise most of the Midwest.

In an hour or so, depending on traffic and weather, the route passes Joliet, Illinois, a midsized city of roughly 150,000 people. In addition to being the birthplace of Dairy Queen, Joliet boasts attractions such as the Old Joliet Prison, made famous in *The Blues Brothers* film, as well as the Chicagoland Speedway, the Historic Route 66 Welcome Center, and the Rialto Square Theatre. But most often it's associated with the Joliet Army Ammunition Plant, also called the Joliet Arsenal, a sprawling bomb-making facility that employed over 10,000 workers during World War II.

When war began in 1939, the United States lacked manufacturing capacity necessary to build bombs and other related military supplies. Because the specialized equipment required to make the materials of war prohibited the reengineering of existing factories, the government began purchasing land and building munitions and ordnance manufacturing facilities. And so this quiet corner of Illinois was transformed from small farms run by descendants of the pioneers who broke the thick prairie sod with John Deere plows just a few generations before into a 40,000-acre weapons manufacturing center.

Two separate facilities were built. First was the Elwood Ordnance Plant, which built bombs, mines, artillery shells, and other munitions. It was followed by the Kankakee Ordnance Works, which manufactured the explosives, primarily TNT, that went into the bombs its sister facility built. In 1945, the two plants were officially combined to form the Joliet Arsenal. At its zenith, the Joliet Arsenal's roughly 10,500 workers manufactured more than one billion pounds of TNT and loaded more than 926 million ordnances. TNT manufacturing ceased in 1976 following the end of the Vietnam War, and by 1977 both plants were permanently shuttered.

Were Eliza Steele able to time travel, she might recognize the "sea of grasses and flowers" in the prairie preserves of Kansas and Oklahoma. But the Joliet Arsenal of 1977 could show her little natural splendor.

Manufacturing TNT, bombs, and other weapons of war was (and still is) a dirty process. As the Department of Defense worked to shutter the Arsenal in the late 1970s, it identified fifty-three "areas of concern" where toxins threatened the landscape. In 1987, the Environmental Protection Agency placed specific areas of the Arsenal grounds on the National Priorities List. The NPL is a list of toxic sites the federal government has identified as "of national priority among the known releases or threatened releases of hazardous substances, pollutants, or contaminants throughout the United States and its territories." Sites placed on the NPL are also called superfund sites and require formal, organized, and generally very expensive remediation efforts.

Historic aerial photo of the Joliet Arsenal long before it became Midewin.

Remediation at the Joliet Arsenal began in earnest following the site's listing on the NPL. Over the next two decades, the EPA, the Illinois Environmental Protection Agency, the DoD, and eventually the Forest Service worked together to remove the worst of the pollutants. According to a 2008 report from the EPA's Federal Facilities Restoration and Reuse Office, "As part of the cleanup, 280,000 tons of explosive-contaminated soil was treated at a bioremediation facility constructed on-site. . . . Approximately 120,000 tons of non-explosive-contaminated soil and 487,000 tons of ash were excavated and disposed appropriately off-site. Additionally, more than 8,100 munitions and explosive-related items were removed and disposed."

In 1993, the DoD determined that the roughly 23,500 acres it owned south of Joliet (basically the Arsenal) was "excess federal land" and no longer needed by the military. To help formulate a plan for this incredible asset, the State of Illinois created the Joliet Arsenal Citizen's Planning Commission, a citizen's group made up of local business leaders, conservationists, and state and federal officials. With the help and support of Congressman George Sangmeister, the group's work led to the passage of the Illinois Land Conservation Act of 1995, which established a process for transferring 15,000 acres of the land to the Forest Service, roughly 3,000 acres to the State of Illinois for development of a large business park, 455 acres to Will County for a landfill, and 982 acres to the Department of Veterans Affairs for the Abraham Lincoln National Cemetery.

By 1996, clean up was well underway. The work of the Joliet Arsenal Citizen's Planning Commission had been codified in the Illinois Land Conservation Act, and the 15,000 acres of the former Joliet Arsenal transferred to the Forest Service from the DoD had officially become Midewin National Tallgrass Prairie.

The name Midewin came from the Planning Commission, and it hints at the optimism of those early prairie boosters. It also helps connect the present to the past by recognizing that the land was once stewarded by others. As the Forest Service explains:

> Midewin (pronounced mi-DAY-win) is the name of the Grand Medicine Society of the Anishinaabeg, which includes the Potawatomi (Bodéwad-mik) people who were historic residents of this part of Illinois. As a society of healers and leaders, the Midewin keep the greater Anishinaabe society in

balance. These indigenous values are reflected in the current use of the name and represent healing the natural world and providing balance to our urban, technology-filled lives. . . .

The US Forest Service recognizes the significance of this Potawatomi name and is committed to its respectful use. We are conscientious in explaining its meaning and acknowledging its importance. We believe that the restoration of the prairie is in keeping with the purpose of the Potawatomi Midewin society, and our intention is to honor that purpose.

To be honest, Midewin doesn't look much like its cousins in Kansas and Oklahoma—at least not yet. While much of the toxic legacy left by the army has been cleaned up, other infrastructure remains. The Joliet Arsenal was considered the most advanced munitions manufacturing center in the world during its heyday and as such required substantial infrastructure to operate.

According to the Forest Service, the DoD modified 45 percent of the land area on the Arsenal's sprawling campus. When it was transferred to the Forest Service,

The Tallgrass Prairie National Reserve in Kansas is managed by the National Park Service and offers a glimpse of what Midewin may look like someday.

Midewin was crisscrossed by nearly 200 miles of roads and 160 miles of narrow-gauge railroad. More than 1,400 buildings, most of them abandoned, haunted the grounds. To store TNT, the army built 392 igloos, concrete bunkers that rise from the flat landscape like small ocean swells covered with sod roofs. Natural wetlands were drained, streams were straightened and channelized, and the whole area was wrapped in thirty-seven miles of eight-foot-high chain link fencing garnished with three-strand barbed wire.

Despite the abundant infrastructure and toxic legacy, much of the Arsenal's land was leased to local farmers and ranchers during the decades the army wasn't building bombs.

All told, less than 3 percent of the 15,000 acres the Forest Service received in 1996 consisted of native prairie vegetation. Additional transfers from the DoD added to its size—Midewin is now about 19,000 acres—but not to its percentage of native prairie. Growing that statistic is now up to a new army, one made up of biologists, ecologists, conservationists, and volunteers.

On the day I visited Midewin, I spent the morning touring some of the prairie with Paul Botts and Emily Leu. Paul is the president and executive director of the Wetlands Initiative, a Chicago-based NGO (non-governmental organization) dedicated to restoring wetlands in the Midwest. Emily, a regional manager for the four REI stores scattered around Chicago, joined us because the outdoor retailer helps fund the Midewin Youth Corps, a six-week internship program that brings high school students from the North Lawndale College Prep school in Chicago's Southside to Midewin. She'd never been to Midewin and in addition to exploring the prairie, we spent some of the morning alongside the youth crew.

First launched in 2012, the Midewin Youth Corps is one part of the broad restoration effort that has been evolving at Midewin since 1996. For six weeks each summer, these teenagers brave the humidity, bugs, dirt, rain, wind, and simmering sun as they work alongside Forest Service staff and other volunteers to raise a native tallgrass prairie. On the day we visited, they were planting prairie milkweed on an

Seed collection, largely done by volunteers, is a critical component to Midewin's restoration.

OPPOSITE
Midewin has hundreds of bunkers like these, once used for storing TNT and other munitions, legacies of its industrial past

upswell in the plains. Prairie milkweed is a subspecies of the common milkweed plant, and the planting project was aimed at improving habitat for the imperiled monarch butterfly, which relies on milkweed to reproduce.

Some of the students sat or kneeled in the dirt, digging small holes with a trowel. Others lugged buckets of water from a truck parked a hundred yards away. A group of young women in dirt-stained jeans and dark green Youth Crew t-shirts pulled the tender milkweed seedlings from black plastic pots and gently placed them in the holes. They talked freely among themselves and with the volunteers they knew from a summer's worth of work but were shy and reticent with us interlopers.

Citizen volunteers have played an important role at Midewin since the concept of turning an abandoned WWII-era industrial munitions complex into a tallgrass prairie was first proposed. On its face, it seemed outlandish, but like the spindly roots of the prairie milkweed, it slowly grew into a reality.

One of the main challenges in healing Midewin is sourcing enough native plant seeds to grow thousands of acres of wild, native prairie. Sadly, too few examples of native tallgrass prairie exist today for Midewin to utilize them as seed sources—those remnant prairies that do exist are too small and too ecologically fragile to provide seeds for a project as large as Midewin. (Though Midewin staff do work with other prairie reserves to source seeds for some especially difficult-to-find species.)

For a bit of perspective, Midewin is about 19,000 acres. Each acre of native tall-grass prairie hosts hundreds of species and thousands of individual plants. Imagine trying to plant a garden like that on 14,400 football fields (end zones included), and the massive undertaking of restoring a full complement of prairie plants begins to come into focus. With all the plants conveniently available, it would be daunting; without a viable source of native seeds, it's basically impossible.

So Midewin staff and an intensely dedicated cadre of volunteers have created seed gardens, where native tallgrass prairie plants are grown for the express purpose of harvesting their seeds. Tallgrass prairies have been compared to tropical rainforests in terms of biodiversity, and the restoration goals at Midewin call for producing more than 350 different species that fill the prairie's diverse ecological niches: tallgrass vegetation, wetlands, savannas, and oak woodlands. When Wade Spang told me that Midewin staff are grass farmers he wasn't joking, but he was being modest—they are also wildflower farmers.

A DUST BOWL LEGACY

Of the 175 different units in the NFS (a unit is Forest Service speak for a specific national forest or grassland) 20 of them are national grasslands. Midewin is its own, unique unit: a national tallgrass prairie.

National grasslands lie in predominantly western landscapes. Most of the four million acres that make up our national grasslands are in the Great Plains. This is due to both geographical and historical causes—geographical because the Great Plains are, somewhat obviously, comprised mostly of grassland and prairie ecosystems; historical because of the Dust Bowl.

Just twenty-two years after Eliza Steele's western adventure, Congress passed the Homestead Act of 1862. Over the next three decades, six million people moved into the Great Plains, pushing farther and farther west, past the fertile tallgrass prairie, through the less-fertile-but-still-farmable mixed grass prairie, and into the semi-arid short grass prairie at the far western edge of the Plains. At first, much of this marginal land was used for grazing (though poor grazing practices caused their own issues and the harsh winters proved tough on cattle and sheep), but a period of wet summers and mild winters encouraged the ever-increasing settlers to plow up the thin topsoil and plant crops. During these years with abundant rain and mild winters, crops

flourished. But when drought hit, the crops dried up, and the desiccated soil blew away in the incessant prairie winds.

A Midewin view similar to what Eliza Steele might have experienced

The first major drought came in 1930 and lasted into 1931. A few years later, in 1934, drought returned—in 1936 another arrived, and between 1939 and 1940, yet another. The causes and the history of the Dust Bowl are well chronicled, and its legacy still touches us today.

Franklin D. Roosevelt responded quickly, establishing the Soil Erosion Service in 1933. In 1935, it became the Soil Conservation Service (now the Natural Resources Conservation Service) and, like the Forest Service, it was housed in the Department of Agriculture. Its mission was to work with farmers to stabilize soil and reduce erosion. Other New Deal programs like the Soil Conservation and Domestic Allotment Act, the Federal Surplus Relief Corporation, the Civilian Conservation Corps, and a massive effort, called the Great Plains Shelterbelt, to plant 200 million trees from Canada to Texas, helped both stabilize the soil and reduce human and animal suffering caused by the catastrophe.

One important policy measure called the Bankhead-Jones Farm Tenant Act of 1937 served two purposes. First it authorized a credit program for tenant farmers

so they could borrow money to purchase their own land to farm. While this aspect of the program was not considered a huge success, it did specifically help African American farmers gain ownership of farmlands in a meaningful way. Second, it authorized the Federal Government to purchase submarginal lands (those deemed unsuitable for agriculture). The newly minted Soil Conservation Service (SCS) managed the program, buying up the degraded lands and implementing conservation measures to reduce erosion and reestablish vegetative cover.

Author and historian R. Douglas Hurt describes the objectives of this land buy-back program as a multi-step process. "First, the federal government planned to purchase the most severely wind-eroded or 'nuisance lands' known as 'blow hazards.' Then, federal officials planned to halt wind erosion, turn the land-use projects into demonstration areas where famers could observe the best soil conservation techniques, and eventually, return the land to grazing under government management."

Over the next half-decade, the SCS experimented with a number of techniques to halt soil erosion and restore vegetative cover on these projects. In a foreshadowing of the modern-day seed-sourcing challenges facing Midewin, the

The "plow that broke the Plains" buried in blowing soil in Cimarron County, Oklahoma.

OPPOSITE Farms like this were a common sight in 1938 as the Dust Bowl, caused by extended drought and intensive plowing, ravaged the Great Plains.

SCS struggled to source seeds, resorting to Russian thistle and other weeds in a last-ditch effort to keep soil from blowing away. Fortunately, it was eventually able to source enough native seed to restore blow hazards to a more natural mix of prairie plants. By the early 1940s, "normal" precipitation returned to the southern and western Great Plains, and with it, vegetation. Once the rains and grasses returned, the SCS started leasing some of the project lands to ranching cooperatives and even individual ranchers. But because these ranchers leased the land and didn't own it, the SCS was able to keep a close eye on their grazing practices, helping ensure the range didn't become degraded again. In January 1954, the SCS transferred the now-restored lands to the Forest Service.

Our national grasslands were born from the twin ravages of the Dust Bowl and the Great Depression. The designation wouldn't be created until 1960, but the seeds of these unconventional "forests" were sown in the 1930s.

Today there are twenty national grasslands, not including Midewin. They span more than four million acres across twelve states. Thirteen of them are in the Great Plains, and together they host more than one million visitors a year. In 2012, the

Forest Service celebrated the seventy-fifth anniversary of the national grasslands (using the 1937 Bankhead-Jones Farm Tenant Act as the official start). In a press release about the anniversary, then Forest Service Chief Tom Tidwell noted, "Our national grasslands remain beautiful examples of successful restoration programs. These lands are once again rich habitats brimming with native wildlife, grasses, and wildflowers. They are also economic engines, generating jobs and bolstering rural American communities."

Economic benefits are indeed a positive legacy of these one-time blow hazards. The Forest Service estimates that cumulatively, our national grasslands "provide tremendous benefits, including pollination of native and agricultural plants, estimated at $6 billion annually. Livestock grazing and energy ventures including oil, gas, coal, and wind also contribute to the economic benefits provided by these lands. They help prevent drought and floods, maintain biodiversity, generate and

preserve soils, contribute to climate stability, and protect watersheds, streams and river channels."

Our national grasslands provide a focal point for understanding the Forest Service's role in range management, but their creation did not mark the agency's foray into this field. Grazing has long been one of the primary uses of public lands, especially in the West, and the Forest Service has been formally managing grazing since the early 1900s. Nearly half the 193 million acres it manages today is rangeland. Of course, the national grasslands are included in this accounting, but the Forest Service's rangeland portfolio includes ecosystems as varied as Florida's lush grass and pine savannas, Wyoming's arid sagebrush-steppes, and high-elevation meadows in the Rocky Mountains. During the late 1800s, cattle and sheep roamed freely across huge swaths of unclaimed public lands, which, as so often happens with public commons, soon became severely degraded due to overstocking and overgrazing.

ABOVE West Pawnee Butte on the Pawnee National Grasslands in eastern Colorado.

LEFT The Dakota Prairie Grasslands cover large swaths of North and South Dakota.

Recognizing the dangers of this laissez-faire management scheme, Congress charged the nascent Forest Service with developing a grazing program, and by 1907, the agency had implemented new regulations requiring permits, limiting herd sizes, establishing grazing seasons, and requiring grazing fees. Other land management agencies, like the Bureau of Land Management, followed the Forest Service's lead when they began to manage grazing on public land. Grazing is so codified in the cultural and land-use legacy of western public lands that it is allowed in formally designated Wilderness Areas, where riding a mountain bike or even using a chainsaw or other machine to fight wildfire is prohibited.

WHO DOESN'T LOVE A BISON?

One grazer that has been absent from the Great Plains for more than a century is the American bison. It's estimated that in the early 1800s, between thirty and sixty million bison roamed the vast interior of North America. This huge swath of land is sometimes called the Great Bison Belt, and it extended from the Gulf of Mexico (and even into the northern reaches of present-day Mexico) to Alaska. Generally arid, it was dominated by grasses (today much of it is still grassland, but huge portions have been converted to farms). Bison played a central role in this ecosystem, grazing the grasses, fertilizing the soil with their scat, and tilling it with their hooves. They also played a central role in the culture of the people who lived throughout the Great Bison Belt before Europeans arrived. In addition to providing food and resources for clothes, homes, and other necessary items, bison were the foundation of many cultural and religious traditions.

The first challenges the bison faced were European cattle and horses. Introduced diseases and competition for forage, along with unregulated hunting, eliminated the eastern herds by the dawn of the nineteenth century—by 1802, bison were extirpated from Ohio. But this was just the start. Beginning in 1830, before John Deere had even conceived of his plains-breaking plow, the decimation of the bison began in earnest.

According to a grim timeline compiled by the US Fish and Wildlife Service, the scattered herds of bison west of the Rocky Mountains disappeared in the 1840s. In the 1860s railroads finally crossed the Great Plains, splitting the Plains bison into northern and southern herds. The southern herds disappeared in a decade; by 1874 an estimated three to four million bison in the southern plains states were dead. Nine years after that, in 1883, the northern herds were gone and only 325 wild bison, 0.001083 percent of the low-end estimates of the pre-Columbian extent of North America's bison, remained. One of the greatest faunal populations on Earth had been all but eliminated in a few decades.

Motivation for the slaughter can be attributed to many things, not least of which was the federal government's desire to deprive Plains Indians of their food and cultural foundation and force them onto reservations. Greed, ignorance, bloodlust, wanton destruction, racism, and privilege all played their devastating roles as well.

In 1910, roughly thirty years after the slaughter ended, the American Bison Society estimated that there were 2,108 bison in North America—1,076 in Canada and 1,032 in the United States. Of the 1,032 in the United States, only 151 were in public herds, with the remainder held by zoos or private individuals.

Today, an estimated 500,000 bison are scattered across the United States. The Yellowstone herd, which consisted of just 25 in 1883, numbers roughly 5,000 animals. The Department of the Interior manages seventeen herds (including the Yellowstone herd) on public lands, with a total of about 10,000 bison. The remainder are managed by other public land management agencies, Native American tribes, conservation organizations like The Nature Conservancy, and private ranchers

This historic print from 1871 depicts bison hunting along the Kansas-Pacific Railroad.

(Ted Turner "owns" about 51,000 bison spread across fifteen ranches). In 2016, President Barack Obama designated the bison as the country's national mammal. For some, the bison represent a conservation success story, for others, their decimation is one of the most egregious chapters in US history.

One place bison fans can see these 2,000-pound herbivores is at Midewin. In October of 2015, the National Forest Foundation, in partnership with The Nature Conservancy and Midewin, brought twenty-seven bison (three bulls and twenty-four cows) to a 1,200-acre pasture at Midewin that had been built expressly for the herd. The goal of the project is to monitor if and how the bison change the vegetation community in the area where they roam. Grasslands evolved with grazers, not just bison, but also elk, deer, and pronghorn. Though they didn't evolve in North America, cattle are grazers too, and a variety of studies have shown that they graze differently than bison. While recent research has cast doubt on whether there's a big difference in the grazing styles, Midewin is now a living laboratory where range managers can study the effects of grazing bison compared to grazing cattle.

Regardless of how well the Midewin landscape responds to the bison, the bison have responded well to Midewin. As of 2020, the herd has grown to more than seventy-five animals. In addition to playing a role in Midewin's ecological restoration, the bison are also a potent lure to visitors.

There's a long-standing maxim in conservation circles: people support what they love, and they love what they know. In other words, if people know about Midewin—if they come and visit, explore and appreciate this landscape—they'll be more likely to volunteer, donate, or engage in policy and planning. Flipped, the maxim is equally true: if nobody knows about Midewin, nobody will care about Midewin. The bison experiment was actually part of the original vision for the land when the Citizen's Planning Commission first crafted its plan in the 90s. The bison serve as a hook for visitors from the third-largest city in America, and if just a tiny fraction of Chicago's more than 2.6 million residents do visit, there's a good chance that some of them will become enamored.

It seems to be working. Visitation at Midewin has steadily climbed since the bison introduction. According to the Forest Service's National Visitor Use Monitoring

ABOVE Bison rest in their specially built pasture at Midewin.

LEFT A massive pile of bison skulls hints at the scale of the slaughter.

105

program, about 17,000 people visited Midewin in 2008. By 2018, that number had ballooned to 71,000, a 317 percent increase (though still just a fraction of the visitation that other forests receive). The agency estimates annual visitor spending adds roughly $2 million to the local economy.

To be fair, bison aren't the only reason people are visiting. Midewin staff have also done a great job designing and implementing events that draw visitors—they have a great Facebook feed, and better online information about visiting than many other national forests—but bison are a big draw for sure. Virtual visits are even more popular; in 2016, the NFF, EarthCam, and the Forest Service teamed up to install a web camera at Midewin that overlooks the bison pasture. In its first four years, EarthCam's live stream of the Bison Cam logged more than 2.1 million views.

As we wrap up our visit to Midewin, Supervisor Spang takes us to another outbuilding where volunteers and staff are sorting seeds for future planting projects. The room is lined with a variety of contraptions designed to separate seeds from the plant that produced them. A huge walk-in cooler hums in the background, storing seeds ready to be prepped for planting. Spang explains some of the machinery and how the various seeds are processed. It's a fascinating example of homespun

Canada goldenrod and smooth blue aster dance in the breeze at the River Road seedbed in Midewin.

engineering—most of the machines were originally built to process grains and have been repurposed for grasses and flowers.

We walk back outside into the shimmering sun. It's nearly midday and the air is turning oppressively hot. The Midewin Youth Corps have finished their lunch and have headed back out to the fields. It's time to head back to the city, and as I crank the air conditioning and steer my rental car back toward Chicago, I think about what Midewin represents, both to its fans and to the Forest Service. There's no doubt its staff are proud of this small, unique unit of the National Forest System. Despite funding challenges (individual forest budgets are largely based on a complex matrix of land size, staff size, visitation rates, and how much revenue they produce; Midewin ranks low in all categories) and the massive restoration task they face, staff are devoted to healing the land and realizing Midewin's future.

The history of America's prairies is riddled with mistakes. In a few generations, bison all but disappeared, diverse native ecosystems were re-engineered into monocultures, and topsoil was plowed up, dried out, and blown away. The Forest Service often notes that Midewin is a work-in-progress and a grand experiment—perhaps to mitigate visitor expectations but also because both things are true.

That it's a work-in-progress is evident everywhere you look—hundreds of bunkers and dozens of old buildings still haunt the prairie, non-native plants still dominate the landscape despite years of progress, and visitor infrastructure is still somewhat minimal.

The experimental aspect is both obvious and more subtle. It's an experiment in restoring native tallgrass prairie on a formerly toxic industrial site. It's an experiment in leveraging volunteers and creating multi-faceted partnerships between public and private entities. Perhaps most importantly, it's an experiment in healing. The bison are, arguably, the most charismatic manifestation of this healing and they represent a small attempt to undo one of our nation's most tragic mistakes. But the healing is evidenced in every volunteer hour logged, every native seed gently hand planted, and in every blooming wildflower that evokes Eliza Steele's long-ago wonder.

They grow a lot of grass at Midewin, and they grow a lot of flowers too. But the main crops at Midewin aren't plants at all—though they're just as beautiful and just as paradoxically fragile and robust as the prairie milkweed or the orange coneflower. As it turns out, Midewin staff and volunteers are growing hope, redemption, and optimism. Hard work, dedication, and commitment are the fertilizers of choice for these crops. Fortunately for us all, they're easier to source than native tallgrass prairie seeds.

THE ORIGINAL PEOPLE'S LAND

*Native Voices
and the Struggle
to be Heard*

UST SOUTH OF STUNNING Glacier National Park, on Montana's dramatic Rocky Mountain Front, lies a landscape known as the Badger-Two Medicine. For the most part, the Badger-Two Medicine is as beautiful and wild as it was when it was brought under federal management more than 100 years ago as part of the Lewis and Clark National Forest. This is where the northern plains meet the Rocky Mountains, and the towering reefs and fins of gray rock that rise from the aspen- and conifer-covered foothills are truly spectacular.

PREVIOUS
The Badger-Two Medicine area is on the Helena-Lewis and Clark National Forest on the front range of northern Montana's Rocky Mountains.

It is also a sacred landscape to the Blackfeet Nation whose reservation lies just to the east. For thousands of years, far, far longer than the Forest Service or the United States of America have existed, the Blackfeet have revered this intense landscape. The Badger-Two Medicine is where the Blackfeet people came from. It's their traditional homeland, but it's more than that. It's their church but also more than that, too. It's both the source and the repository of their very identity.

Today, the West is comprised of private lands and public lands like national forests, national parks, and wildlife refuges, which are managed by distinct federal agencies for specific purposes (states, counties, and towns also manage public land throughout the West, but the majority of western public lands are federally managed). In the 1870s and 1880s, the West hadn't yet been divvied up in the way we understand it today. It was generally either public domain (land that was owned by the federal government on behalf of all American citizens, but not allocated for a specific use), land controlled by Native Americans that hadn't been ceded to the US government, or land held in trust by the government for Native Americans. Many politicians, especially western ones, wanted the public domain land to be given over to private industry, states, and individual Americans. Others, particularly those in the growing conservation movement, felt that private interests would focus exclusively on short-term profits and render the land barren and wasted. They wanted the federal government to control and manage at least some of the public domain in perpetuity, ensuring the natural resources these lands offered also endured. At the time, however, the federal government's ability to set aside land was limited at best.

Congress created Yellowstone National Park in 1872 by drafting and adopting legislation expressly for that purpose. It was the first national park in the country and is generally considered the first in the world. When it was established, there were no federal land management agencies, so oversight of the park fell to the army, which struggled mightily to prevent rampant and illegal poaching, timber harvests, and mining during the park's early days.

The Forest Reserve Act of 1891 was, in part, an attempt to prevent the abuses Yellowstone endured from afflicting other public domain lands in the West. The act gave a US president authority to remove timber reserves from the public domain and place them under the management of the federal government. Once there, they could be protected (theoretically at least) from unregulated timber harvests, homesteading, and other human-caused abuses. President Benjamin Harrison, who signed the Forest Reserve Act, wasted little time in executing his new authority. Just twenty-seven days after signing the law, he set aside more than 1.2 million acres of land around Yellowstone as the Yellowstone Park Timberland Reserve. Over the course of his administration, he established more than thirteen million acres of forest reserves.

His successor, Grover Cleveland, built on this legacy, adding twenty-five million acres of forest reserves to the federal estate, including the Lewis and Clark Forest Reserve, which was part of a twenty-one-million-acre suite of reserves established in late February of 1897, just two weeks before his final term ended. The Badger-Two Medicine, along with millions of acres of other lands Native Americans had ceded to the US government, was included in this last-minute designation.

Although the Forest Reserve Act allowed the president to unilaterally establish forest reserves from the public domain and place them under federal stewardship, it wasn't until 1897, when President William McKinley signed the Organic Act, that Congress figured out how it wanted those lands to be managed. McKinley, a conservative Republican, established just seven million acres of forest reserves during his administration, but his successor, Theodore Roosevelt was far more active than any president before or since, adding over 200 million acres of land to the federal estate during his eight years in office. Roosevelt also pushed for and enacted the Transfer Act of 1905, which created the Forest Service, renamed the forest reserves as national forests, and transferred management responsibility for them from the Department of the Interior to the Department of Agriculture, where the Forest Service was freshly located.

Legal authority wasn't the only barrier preventing the federal government from establishing forest reserves, national parks, or other protected lands. The inconvenient fact that the United States was inhabited by diverse societies of indigenous people was another.

Historians have struggled to estimate how populated the Americas were prior to colonization. Little empirical data exists, and we are generally left to rely on the (often biased) accounts of colonizers and government officials. In short, estimates range from about 10 million to 50 million, with some scholars claiming near 100 million. Population estimates for what became the United States follow similarly varied estimates, but it's safe to assume there were between 5 and 10 million (or more) people in the United States prior to European "settlement."

What is less debatable is the widespread impact disease had on Native American populations. Smallpox, influenza, bubonic plague, measles, and a host of other diseases spread through native populations in advance of physical occupation by white colonists. A recent article in the online journal *The Conversation*, written by scholars from University College London argues that this "great dying" marks the start of the Anthropocene, a geological epoch defined by human manipulation of the Earth (as opposed to prior geological periods, like the Holocene or the Pleistocene, defined by climatic or evolutionary forces).

These authors claim that 100 years after Columbus "discovered" the Americas, nearly 90 percent of the indigenous populations of South and Central America were dead—a number they estimate at fifty-six million people. "Most were killed by diseases brought across the Atlantic by Europeans, which had never been seen before in the Americas." In North America, "the population decline was slower but no less dramatic due to slower colonization by Europeans. US Census data suggests the Native American population may have been as low as 250,000 people by 1900 from a pre-Columbus level of five million."

While scholars may argue over numbers and percentages, diseases, wars, and cultural upheaval so reduced the populations of America's indigenous peoples that their ultimate conquest was far easier than it might have been. This decimation perpetuated widespread historical revisionism that fueled racism and persists today—the myth that the United States, and especially the American West, has been, since time immemorial, a wild landscape, populated by small bands of roving, uncivilized, stone-age hunter gatherers.

In truth, most Native American cultures, in North, Central, and South America were agrarian. As disease reduced their populations, farming became prohibitively difficult, and many turned to hunting and gathering. This shift from farming to hunting had significant impacts; not least of which was a change in the atmosphere. The same article from *The Conversation* notes: "In their absence, previously managed landscapes returned to their natural states, with new trees absorbing carbon from the atmosphere. So large was this carbon uptake that there is a drop in atmospheric carbon dioxide recorded in Antarctic ice cores, centered around the year 1610."

This context is vital to understanding how the United States created the system of public lands we have today. While many of us may not have learned it in school, North America before European settlement was home to millions of people who thrived in complex societies, heavily shaped the natural environment, practiced advanced agriculture, and created intricate religions. Disease unequivocally played an early and devastating role in the subjugation of North America's indigenous peoples, but war and vicious public policy cemented it.

PROMISES MADE AND BROKEN

One thing we probably all learned in school was that the first permanent British colony in the United States, Jamestown, was established in Virginia in 1607. Jamestown nearly collapsed, and without the help of the local Paspahegh tribe it would have. Despite this initial and critical help, the two parties eventually went to war, and the Jamestown settlers effectively wiped out the Paspaheghs in half a decade.

This pattern of early settlement, critical indigenous help, and fractured relationships descending into open hostility was repeated throughout the first 150 years of North America's colonization. The French and Indian War, a series of wars between the British and French that raged from 1754 to 1763, embroiled native tribes from present day Virginia to Nova Scotia and from Ohio to the Atlantic coast. Colonists exploited existing alliances and historic animosity, bribed, cajoled, and otherwise conscripted more than a dozen tribes who all suffered tragic consequences during this bloody period. By the time of the Revolutionary War, the British had come to "own" much of what is now the eastern United States.

If Jamestown typified the early history of European and Native American relations, the Treaty of Fort Pitt presaged the relationship the US government would foster with Native Americans during the late eighteenth and nineteenth centuries. Signed in 1778, it is the first written treaty between the US government and any Native American tribe. In it, the Lenape, or Delaware people, agreed to let Revolutionary troops pass through their territory for the purposes of waging war against the British in exchange for clothing, food, and munitions. More importantly, it also recognized the Delaware as a sovereign nation, granted them full rights to their territorial land, and even provided an opportunity (conditional on

Congressional approval) for other tribes to join the Delaware and form an independent state with Congressional representation. Here is the precise text:

> Whereas the enemies of the United States have endeavored, by every artifice in their power, to possess the Indians in general with an opinion, that it is the design of the States aforesaid, to extirpate the Indians and take possession of their country to obviate such false suggestion, the United States do engage to guarantee to the aforesaid nation of Delawares, and their heirs, all their territorial rights in the fullest and most ample manner, as it hath been bounded by former treaties, as long as they, the said Delaware nation, shall abide by, and hold fast the chain of friendship now entered into. And it is further agreed on between the contracting parties should it for the future be found conducive for the mutual interest of both parties to invite any other tribes who have been friends to the interest of the United States, to join the present confederation, and to form a state whereof the Delaware nation shall be the head, and have a representation in Congress; provided, nothing contained in this article to be considered as conclusive until it meets with the approbation of Congress. And it is also the intent and meaning of this article, that no protection or countenance shall be afforded to any who are at present our enemies, by which they might escape the punishment they deserve.

Congress never provided such approbation. For that reason or others lost to history, the treaty fell apart within a year, and the Delawares joined the British to fight against the Americans. Today, the tribe still exists—in Oklahoma and Kansas, a thousand miles from the territorial homeland promised to them in perpetuity by the treaty.

When they colonized the Americas, European nations generally followed the Doctrine of Discovery. It was, at its core, both a way to divvy up non-European lands (Africa, Australia, and the Americas) and a justification of Euro-Christian superiority. When "new" lands were "discovered," they were claimed by the government that sponsored the discoverers—Columbus, for example, despite being Portuguese, claimed Hispaniola for Spain because Spain sponsored his expedition across the Atlantic. Jamestown, by contrast, was sponsored by the British and therefore, the British claimed the lands around Jamestown as theirs. Any indigenous peoples living on those lands were seen as inferior, uncivilized non-Christians, and their fate was left to the colonial power claiming their lands.

When the United States overthrew the British, it continued to follow the Doctrine of Discovery. Over time, the Doctrine of Discovery was tweaked and expanded into the uniquely American concept of Manifest Destiny—essentially a belief that the United States, both culturally and politically, was preordained by God (the Christian one) to stretch from the Atlantic to the Pacific.

In 1803, just fifteen years after New Hampshire became the final state to ratify the new US Constitution, President Thomas Jefferson pushed through the Louisiana Purchase. This deal, which included lands west of the Mississippi River and east of the Rocky Mountains, effectively doubled the size of the United States. However, France, which sold the land to the United States, only controlled a small portion of the vast region. In practice, the United States purchased the right to take lands west of the Mississippi (legally or otherwise) from the indigenous people who lived there without interference from other European powers. Over the next decades, the US government sponsored expeditions, like that of Lewis and Clark, and built forts as it attempted to gain control of the newly acquired land. It also continued to broker (and then break) treaties with Native American tribes.

Even though the United States "owned" the lands east of the Mississippi, settlement in the region moved slowly in the first decades of the nineteenth century. The British colonists who settled the northeast had mostly killed or subjugated the Native Americans who once lived there, but large populations still lived in the Southeast. The Indian Removal Act of 1830 allowed the government to forcibly relocate more than 60,000 Native Americans from the Southeast, pushing them west of the Mississippi to "Indian Territory" in present day Oklahoma. These relocations became known as the Trail of Tears. Tens of thousands of people died during the forced marches and yet more perished from disease and starvation once they arrived.

Settlement of the West was also hampered, in part, by slavery. Southern states resisted government programs that sought to bring settlers west of the Appalachians because they wanted those lands to be open to slavery. Northern politicians insisted that any new states (or territories that might become states) should be slave free. As a result, few government programs emerged until the Civil War started in 1861. When the war broke out, southern politicians lost their roles in the federal government along with their ability to influence legislation, and President Lincoln was able to pass the Homestead Act of 1862. This law offered 160 acres of "federal" land to citizens willing to live on, improve, and then own their 160-acre plot. Lincoln also gave the railroads large swaths of the West so that they could build rail lines across the continent and facilitate settlement.

These twin actions, the Homestead Act and the railroad land grants, effectively opened the West to US citizens. They also exacerbated what had become known as the Indian Problem. In the Southeast, the Indian Problem was solved through forced relocations, but as white settlers moved west, new conflicts emerged. Some Native Americans refused to sign treaties and move onto reservations, and they waged war on both settlers and the US Army, which was dispatched to quell the hostilities.

TRICK OR TREATY

Throughout its early history, the United States generally regarded Native American tribes as sovereign nations—even if they were nations comprised of people it considered inferior. Historically, these relationships were formalized through treaties, not unlike the Treaty of Fort Pitt, where an Indian Tribe gave the US government certain things (like the right for troops to travel through Indian territory) and the US government gave the tribe certain things (food, clothing, guns). Over time, the thing the tribes gave was land. In return, the government placed them on reservations and promised protection, food, schools, and healthcare, while assuming ownership of the surrounding lands the tribes had ceded. In some treaties, tribes maintained their rights to hunt and fish on lands outside reservation boundaries and that hadn't (yet) been given to white settlers, industry, or other private interests. These are known as reserved treaty rights or reserved rights.

Tribes often signed treaties after war, under duress, and with terms and concepts they couldn't fully understand—and the government often broke those treaties eventually. The Treaty of Fort Laramie, signed in 1868, was a particularly egregious and notorious example in which the Black Hills of South Dakota, a vast sweep of mountains and forests in the northern Great Plains, were promised in perpetuity to the Dakota, Lakota, Nakota (known collectively as the Great Sioux Nation) and Arapaho peoples. A 2018 article in the *Smithsonian Magazine* sums up the result: "The treaty established the Great Sioux Reservation . . . [and] designated the Black Hills as 'unceded Indian Territory' for the exclusive use of native peoples. But when gold was found in the Black Hills, the United States reneged on the agreement, redrawing the boundaries of the treaty, and confining the Sioux people—traditionally nomadic hunters—to a farming lifestyle on the reservation. It was a blatant abrogation that has been at the center of legal debate ever since."

According to the Bureau of Indian Affairs (BIA), the agency in the Department of the Interior that manages the federal government's relationship with tribes, "from 1778 to 1871, the United States' relations with individual American Indian nations indigenous to what is now the United States were defined and conducted largely through the treaty-making process. These 'contracts among nations' recognized and established unique sets of rights, benefits, and conditions for the treaty-making tribes who agreed to cede of millions of acres of their homelands to the United States and accept its protection . . . Indian treaties are considered to be 'the supreme law of the land.'"

During that time, the United States ratified 368 different treaties and negotiated at least 45 more that were never ratified. After 1871, "relations with Indian groups have been formalized and/or codified by Congressional acts, Executive Orders, and Executive Agreements." Today, according to the BIA, there are currently 574 "federally recognized American Indian and Alaska Native tribes and villages" in the United States.

Because the US government's policies and US citizens' attitudes concerning Native Americans were grounded in a paternalistic and binary Christian versus non-Christian view, western expansion was ironically seen as a way to save Indians from themselves. White Americans saw Indians as inferior and in need of salvation. Government officials felt the same and brokered treaties that worked to end their traditional ways of life. Nomadic hunter-gatherers and communal farmers had no place in individualistic American society. But family owned farms did. Placing Native Americans on reservations under the custody of the US government construed two benefits: Indians would learn how to be Americans and Americans would be able to safely settle lands formerly occupied and stewarded by Indians.

Through treaties, the government came to hold aboriginal land in trust. That is, the lands that Native Americans had lived on and managed for millennia were placed under the care of the US government. Indians were forced onto reservations where they were promised food, clothes, schools, and healthcare, though in general, those promises were barely kept, if kept at all. As more whites moved west and demand for land intensified, the government moved toward a policy of assimilating Indians into American society.

Assimilation was, in part, a response to the deplorable conditions seen in many reservations. Despite treaty-obligated promises of security—food, housing, schools, medical facilities, and help in developing the natural resources that might exist on a given reservation—conditions were dire for many tribes. In order to harvest timber,

The Black Hills are sacred to several Great Plains tribes and were once promised to them in perpetuity.

for example, or lease grazing lands to white settlers, tribes had to work through the Department of the Interior's Office of Indian Affairs (OIA, precursor to the BIA), and specifically Indian Agents within it, a cumbersome and slow process. Poverty was rampant (and still is on many reservations, a legacy of these failed policies).

The overarching goal of assimilation was to turn Native Americans into American citizens (because the federal government regarded Native American tribes as sovereign, but dependent, nations, Native Americans as a general rule weren't citizens of the United States until 1924 when President Calvin Coolidge signed the Indian Citizenship Act). In practice that meant that Indians had to abandon their polytheistic, land-based religions, forsake their languages, and reject their communal practices to embrace Christianity, European models of farming, and American capitalistic society. Even those whites sympathetic to the plight of Native Americans in the nineteenth century recognized that their societies, beliefs, and land tenure could not survive the onslaught of settlement, concluding that the sooner they were brought into mainstream American society, the better off they would be.

The government pursued assimilation in various ways. The Dawes Severalty Act, also called the General Allotment Act, signed by President Cleveland in 1887, is one of the most notorious and proved to be the most damaging. During the treaty-making period, the entirety of a Native American nation's lands would be divided up. Some was absorbed by the federal estate (often becoming national forests or national parks) and some (usually the least valuable part of their former territory) became that nation's communally owned reservation. Prior to Dawes, these reservations were held in trust by the US government. As such, the feds, through the OIA, managed the reservation lands for the benefit of all the members of the tribe that lived there. This communal ownership and federal trust responsibility were a problem for those in government who felt they allowed traditional Native American cultures to persist (even if in an extremely limited and reduced manner) and thus forestalled the inevitable absorption of Indians into American society.

The Dawes Act authorized the president to divvy up the communally owned reservation lands and allot them to individual members of the tribe if the tribe so desired. In short, it imposed the American notion of private land on people who regarded land as sacred and unownable.

If Indians were given their own land, the thinking went, they would be one step closer to becoming American citizens, both literally and figuratively. In fact, citizenship was specifically written into the law. Indians who received an allotment and who "adopted the habits of civilized life" could petition to become American citizens. The

Dawes Act whittled away at tribal sovereignty and self-governance as well (if Indians were American citizens, they weren't members of a sovereign nation and therefore didn't need their own government).

Though allotment did help Native Americans own land, such ownership was complicated. Heads-of-household (generally adult males) received ownership of 160 acres of land. Children got 80 acres. When an Indian landowner died, that ownership was divided equally among the heirs. In practice, this meant that in a couple generations, allotted land was so divided among owners that it was too small to farm effectively, any revenue generated from it was too little to be helpful to any family, and selling the land required such complicated legal administration as to be nearly impossible.

Conveying private ownership to Indians wasn't the only effect of the Dawes Act; it also contained a provision that allowed non-Indians to come to own formerly Indian land. When the government surveyed a given reservation and divided it into 160-acre plots, there was often more land than there were tribal members to allot it to. This "surplus" land was sold to whites, land speculators, or purchased by the government and absorbed into the federal estate. Over time, the Dawes Act was amended to further benefit whites and harm Indians, effectively removing nearly all barriers to whites acquiring Indian land.

The primary function of the Dawes Act was to reduce Native American holdings in a monumental and unalterable way. Scholars have estimated that Indians lost roughly eighty-six million acres of land (roughly the state of Montana) between 1887 and the mid-1930s, when the administration of Franklin D. Roosevelt finally forged new policies that tried to reverse some of the worst effects of the Dawes Act. And it's important to remember that Dawes only impacted reservation land—Indian nations had already lost hundreds of millions of acres through treaties negotiated in prior decades.

One example from Minnesota highlights just how the Dawes Act further reduced Native American land holdings. In 1855, the Ojibwe Tribe ceded nearly all of northern Minnesota to the federal government except for a few small reservations. By the mid-1880s, the lumber industry had ravaged Minnesota and the last large stands of white pines that still stood were on the small reservations where the Ojibwe lived.

In 1889, two years after the Dawes Act was passed, Minnesota Representative Knute Nelson drafted a law he called "An act for the relief and civilization of the Chippewa Indians in the State of Minnesota." (Chippewa is another name for the Ojibwe Tribe.) Its intent was to use the legal authority granted by the Dawes Act to divide up and allot lands in the reservation and once completed, permit the sale of timber from those allotments. Some Ojibwe wanted to sell the valuable timber from their allotments along with the surplus lands that were "created" following division. Indians were supposed to get work cutting logs as well as money from their sale. But corruption ran rampant, and a growing conservation community pushed for reform, including protecting some of the reservation lands by adding them to the federal estate as a park or forest reserve.

In 1902, Congress passed the Morris Act, which laid out a new framework for the lands in question—all of which were, at the time, part of the Ojibwe's Leech Lake Indian Reservation. In short, the Morris Act provided opportunities for logging, while also establishing a 225,000-acre forest reserve (covering nearly nine-tenths of the reservation) to be managed by the Bureau of Forestry which was housed in the Department of Agriculture (USDA). At the time, the bureau, headed by Gifford Pinchot, was primarily focused on research. The new Minnesota forest reserve was the first opportunity the bureau had to actually manage, not just study, a forested landscape. Never mind that the legislation had reduced the reservation's size by nearly 90 percent.

Three years later, the Transfer Act of 1905 shifted the management of all the forest reserves in the country from the Department of the Interior to the USDA and established a new agency to manage them—the Forest Service, which was led by Pinchot.

Theodore Catton explores this saga and many others in his excellent book *American Indians and National Forests*. He does a far more thorough job of detailing this complicated history than I can, and I recommend readers interested in learning more about this topic make the time to read it. However, even this brief synopsis sheds light on the conflicting motivations of Pinchot and Roosevelt (who signed the Morris Act).

The Ojibwe reservations in northern Minnesota weren't the only lands that held valuable natural resources—specifically timber. Many reservations across the West contained vast and valuable timberlands. They were held in trust and managed by the OIA for the benefit of the tribes, at least until Congress or a president moved forward with allotment. Both Pinchot and Roosevelt feared that as these lands were allotted and the surplus lands sold off, private interests would render them denuded, degraded, and despoiled. Between the options of watching those lands get sold to the timber industry or somehow bringing them into the federal estate where they could be managed more sustainably, they chose the latter when the opportunity presented.

MANAGING TRUST

The Office of Indian Affairs had its own forestry department, even though in its early days most staff lacked forestry training. During the allotment period, its mission was confounded by two distinct but equally potent policies. Essentially the entire OIA was one of planned obsolescence. If allotment worked as planned, there would be no reservations to manage, no tribal forests to oversee, no tribes to look after. Indian land would be privately owned by Indians or whites. Tribal nations would cease to exist and therefore, no federal agency would be needed to oversee them. But allotment proceeded slowly on a tribe-by-tribe basis, and so those tribal lands that were still managed in trust were required to be managed by the OIA for the long-term prosperity of the tribe. On the one hand, the OIA was supposed to close up shop; on the other hand, it was tasked with managing lands until the government

This cutover private timberland outside Leadville, Colorado (eventually absorbed into the Pike and San Isabel National Forests) was never part of a reservation, but it's a good example of what Pinchot and Roosevelt feared might happen to privatized tribal forest lands.

completed the messy work of allotment, which might take decades or longer. Those dual purposes were at odds and reconciling them was nearly impossible.

During the first few decades of the twentieth century, tribal forests that were still part of reservations held in trust were caught in a battle between the USDA's Forest Service and the Department of the Interior's OIA. The Forest Service felt that they were best positioned to care for the tribal forests—after all, long-term management of forests was their mission. For the conservation-minded staff in the agency, this was especially true for those forests that might become surplus lands. Once identified, those forests could potentially be incorporated into the federal estate and managed for long-term sustainability. Alternatively, those surplus forests could be sold off to private interests, cut over, and resold to settlers, speculators, or other interests.

In the end, the price tag for purchasing the entirety of what might become surplus tribal forest lands proved too high for the federal government to afford. In the late 1920s, a joint memo from the Forest Service and OIA's forestry branch estimated the price of all the unallotted tribal forest lands, not including the timber on them, at $100 million.

The election of Franklin D. Roosevelt in 1932 and the crushing weight of the Great Depression provided opportunities for change. Roosevelt installed Harold Ickes as his Secretary of the Interior, and Ickes, in turn, placed a progressive named John Collier in charge of the OIA. Collier was a leading critic of assimilation policies and believed that Native American cultures and traditions could be brought into American society, essentially reversing assimilation's intent. Collier hired a young Forest Service employee named Bob Marshall to lead the OIA's forestry department.

During Marshall's five-year tenure, the OIA worked to reduce the worst impacts of the allotment years. Marshall, known for his role in promoting the concept of wilderness, used his position as the head of the OIA's forestry program to this end, conceiving a 1937 order that designated 4.8 million acres of thirteen Indian reservations as "roadless" or "wild." Mechanized transport was prohibited, as was road building and other development. Of course, neither Marshall nor any other bureaucrats asked the tribes involved before they issued the order. Marshall, feeling that Indians deserved some land where they could practice their traditional ways of life away from whites, imposed his own land management ethos in a well-intentioned but nevertheless paternalistic effort.

In 1933, the Roosevelt administration created the Civilian Conservation Corps. This work-relief program was open to unemployed, single men 18–25 years of age. Young men across the country signed up for the program and went to work planting forests, building roads, erecting buildings, restoring rangeland,

and completing other public works projects from coast to coast. Much of the recreational infrastructure on our national forests today was built by the CCC. In fact, nearly half the CCC camps were located on national forests and three-quarters of all their projects were overseen by the Department of Agriculture. Recognizing the opportunities the CCC presented for Indian country from an employment and a restoration perspective, Harold Ickes spearheaded a separate Indian-only CCC program within the OIA.

Totem poles still stand amid the ruins of a community house in Kasaan, Alaska.

An Alaskan CCC crew works to restore totem poles as part of a partnership between the Forest Service and Alaska native tribes.

One of its most successful projects involved Native American totem poles in Alaska, which showed that the Forest Service and tribes could work together to restore cultural artifacts while also restoring traditional practices. Under the Forest Service's supervision, tribal members with carving skills were put to work restoring hundreds of totem poles that their ancestors had created. Young apprentices learned from the carvers, and the project both preserved cultural heritage and advanced it at the same time.

In 1934, Congress passed the Indian Reorganization Act (IRA). It was the centerpiece of Roosevelt's new policies toward Indians and it repealed the Dawes

Act. The IRA stopped allotment and prescribed long-term management directives for tribal forests and rangeland in line with Forest Service directives of sustained yield and watershed protection. The law also sought to reassert tribal sovereignty and self-governance, though in practice, this remained grounded in a paternalistic view of tribal culture. While Indians could create their own governments, the OIA directed how those governments were formed and implemented.

By the time Roosevelt's New Deal was in full force, Native Americans had lost an incredible amount of land. All public lands designated at the end of the nineteenth and start of the twentieth century were carved from land once owned entirely by tribes. Allotment further reduced Indian land holdings by dividing up and selling off reservation lands, themselves just a fraction of the aboriginal lands Indians once controlled. In some instances, surplus lands were brought under federal management as national forests.

While Native Americans remained marginalized in American society throughout the first half of the twentieth century, the Roosevelt administration improved conditions on reservations and in the political arena. The threat of allotment and further reductions in land was effectively eliminated. The CCC provided employment and also resources to improve lands still owned by tribes.

NEGOTIATIONS CONTINUE

Despite progress, tribal lands in the mid-twentieth century were still managed by whites, and paternalistic views of Native Americans would persist for decades.

Certainly, Indians used the public lands, especially the national forests, that neighbored their reservations for hunting, fishing, and other traditional practices like berry and mushroom picking. But as Theodore Catton points out, there is anecdotal and empirical evidence that the uniformed forest and park rangers patrolling the forests and the parks reminded tribes of their military suppressors, even if, in the mid-twentieth century, those memories were cultural rather than lived for many Indians. Additionally, the Forest Service's obsession with wildfire prevention ran counter to the indigenous people's use of small, intentional fires to encourage berry growth, forage for deer and horses, and, as it turns out, maintain long-term forest health. Such practices were illegal, and Indians were prosecuted for starting forest fires. And, of course, there were more and more whites moving west, using the forests for grazing, hunting, and as the century progressed, recreation.

The decentralized management structure of the Forest Service has long meant that local rangers and forest supervisors have tremendous decision-making authority. Recall that Gifford Pinchot's oft-repeated quote, which came to define both conservation and the Forest Service's very mission, was initially an instruction he penned to help guide local rangers. While it is often referred to in its short-hand version, "the greatest good of the greatest number in the long run," Pinchot's complete instruction read: "When conflicting interests must be reconciled, the question shall always be answered from the standpoint of the greatest good of the greatest number for the long run." As one might imagine, reconciling the conflicting interests of Native Americans and an ever-increasing number of whites was something forests ranger did often, with mixed outcomes.

In Washington State, the supervisor of the Columbia National Forest (present-day Gifford Pinchot National Forest), J. R. Bruckart, granted members of the Yakama Nation exclusive access to a small huckleberry patch, after migrants fleeing the Great Depression arrived and, through desperation and intensive harvesting, effectively commercialized the forest's other berry patches. The 1932 accord became known as the Handshake Agreement, and although the Forest Service posted boundary signs and other basic educational messages, it did little actual enforcement of the boundary. For the most part, it didn't need to; white locals voluntarily followed the rules and the agreement was written into the forest plan in 1990, an enduring example of cooperation between the Forest Service, white forest users, and the Yakama Nation. Ironically, the berry patch is now threatened by another force, the exclusion of fire, which has allowed the dense northwest forest to crowd it out.

While the Yakama Nation forged a durable agreement with the Forest Service and the public at large, other tribes fared less well in similar negotiations during the first two-thirds of the twentieth century. In Alaska, despite the objective success of the totem pole program, the Forest Service strongly resisted Haida and Tlingit claims that they held aboriginal title to valuable timberlands on the Tongass National Forest. In the end, Congress passed the Tongass Timber Act of 1947, which set the stage for industrial timber harvesting on the Tongass, an issue that still haunts this sprawling forest.

In the 1950s, the US government yet again changed its policies toward Native Americans as it pursued "termination." In short, termination sought to end the trust relationship between the federal government and the tribes by settling, once and for all, tribal land claims, dispensing of tribal property and obviating the need for the newly christened (since 1947) Bureau of Indian Affairs.

Indians did not universally embrace the concept, in fact, most opposed it. However, the Klamath tribe in Oregon did want to terminate its relationship with the federal government, and in so doing, sell its valuable tribal forests for a one-time payment to all members of the tribe. After significant legal and political maneuvering, the federal government became the main buyer. This was largely a result of harvesting restrictions imposed on timber sales, which aimed to prevent short-order clear-cutting, which could damage watersheds important for downstream users like farms and white communities, and to avoid depressing timber prices through the huge influx a quick sale and harvest would create. In July 1961, President John F. Kennedy established the Winema National Forest, comprised largely of lands the Klamath sold to the government that year.

As the political winds shifted in the late 1950s and 1960s, termination lost its supporters and was scuttled as a federal policy. Once again, the government committed itself to caring for Native Americans and their lands, for better or worse.

In 1980, roughly forty-five years after FDR officially ended allotment and reinstated tribal sovereignty, President-elect Ronald Reagan appointed James G. Watt as his Secretary of the Interior. The DOI has a broad set of often-conflicting

A Native American huckleberry camp on the Kootenai National Forest in Montana, circa 1938 mandates. Yes, it oversees the National Park Service, but it's also responsible for oil and gas leasing that occurs on land and waters within the United States, including the national forests. And, of course, it also oversees the Bureau of Indian Affairs, which despite schizophrenic federal policy, still manages the federal government's relationship with Indians along with tribal lands still held in trust. In short, the DOI is responsible for safeguarding America's most beloved natural places and for developing the nation's most controversial energy sources.

Watt is generally regarded as one of, if not the most, anti-environmental Secretaries of the Interior in recent time (history has yet to fully judge the environmental record of the Trump Administration, though I suspect even Watt will appear quaintly benign when compared to Ryan Zinke or David Bernhardt). He was controversial at the time and only lasted two years before he was forced to resign following disparaging remarks he made about affirmative action during a speech to the Chamber of Commerce.

During his short tenure, Watt permitted forty-seven oil and gas leases on the Badger-Two Medicine area. His authority over the sub-surface mineral and gas resources was well established under federal law. However, his under-the-radar approach was questionable at best, and many local conservationists and the Blackfeet have argued it was illegal as well. Most importantly, they argued that a thorough, legally defensible, environmental review was never completed, a requirement under the 1970 National Environmental Policy Act. Second, the Blackfeet Nation, whose reservation borders the Badger-Two Medicine and for whom the Badger-Two Medicine is the religious and cultural foundation upon which their tribal identity rests, were never consulted regarding the lease. The Blackfeet hold reserved treaty rights to the Badger-Two Medicine and the federal government is obligated to consult them regarding management of the area. That consultation never happened, an omission that paralleled so many of the decisions the federal government has made over the centuries in regard to tribal land.

For the next four decades, the Blackfeet and local conservationists worked to rid the Badger-Two Medicine of the leases. A series of lawsuits and countersuits played out over several presidential administrations. In time, some of the lessees voluntarily relinquished their leases in response to public pressure. In 2006, Congress prohibited any new leases in the Badger-Two Medicine, and in 2016–17, more than three decades after they had been issued, the Obama Administration's Secretary of the Interior, Sally Jewell, cancelled the remaining oil and gas leases on the Badger-Two Medicine.

Two oil companies, Moncrief Oil and Solenex LLC, sued the government, claiming the cancellation was illegal and the leases should endure. In 2018, a US District Court judge reinstated the leases, but a few months later, Moncrief Oil voluntarily gave up its lease, noting, "Even though Moncrief Oil believes that this valuable oil and gas lease could have been developed while protecting and even benefiting the wilderness, the sensitivity to this special area outweighs development, and therefore has agreed to relinquishment of the lease to the federal government after the prior proper ruling by the court." Solenex LLC remained committed to drilling until, in June of 2020, the US Circuit Court in Washington, DC, ruled that the cancellation was legal.

While that may seem the end of the saga (Solenex may appeal), and it is certainly an outcome worth celebrating, the Blackfeet continue their fight to protect, and to help manage, the Badger-Two Medicine. This time, they're working in close coordination with the Forest Service and with the legislative support of Montana's Democratic Senator, Jon Tester.

Just days after the Circuit Court affirmed the lease cancellations, Tester introduced the Badger-Two Medicine Protection Act, which would designate the 127,000 acres as a cultural heritage area. This novel land designation would maintain some existing uses such as livestock grazing and non-mechanized recreation, while prohibiting future commercial timber harvest, new road construction, motorized vehicles or mountain bikes, and any new structures such as water facilities, pipelines, or buildings.

Perhaps most importantly, it also, "requires the Forest Service to consider new management proposals put forward by the Tribe [and] to consult with the Tribe on management." Such consultation is something the Forest Service and the federal government at large (as evidenced by the leases' very issuance in the first place) have had a poor history of doing. But it's something the agency has redoubled its efforts on in the last three decades.

In 1988, over one hundred years after the US signed its last treaty with a Native American tribe, the Forest Service established the first Tribal Government Program Manager position in its Washington, DC headquarters. That single position expanded to become the Office of Tribal Relations, which aims to "facilitate consistency and effectiveness in Forest Service program delivery to tribes and to institutionalize long-term consultative and collaborative relationships with tribal governments through new policy and direction."

The office is further supported by regional and local staff who assist in executing its mission, which includes providing oversight of Forest Service programs and policy that may affect tribes, preparing and implementing new and existing policy and direction, clarifying the agency's responsibilities regarding tribal trust and reserved rights, developing and supporting education and training for employees of the Forest Service and other agencies that help them work more effectively with tribal governments and other partners, and exploring innovative ways to interact with tribes, tribal members, and others to enhance the agency's service to Native American communities.

Some may dismiss this effort as too little, too late. Six national-level staff is certainly a small group of folks in an organization that has more than 30,000 employees, but in the twenty-odd years the program has been in existence, it has helped better include Native American voices in the conversation about how national forests are managed.

For the Blackfeet, such cooperation is welcome, if decades late. The fate of the Badger-Two Medicine is now, as so many other matters concerning Native Americans in our nation's history have been, in the hands of Congress. If, and

A decades-long battle over oil development on the Badger-Two Medicine is finally nearing its end; with Congressional approval, this area will be forever protected from natural resource development and managed in cooperation with the Blackfeet Nation.

only if, Congress passes the Badger-Two Medicine Protection Act will this sacred landscape, a place that 80 percent of Montanans want protected from industry, actually get the legal protections it deserves.

In the long days of the Montana summer that passed after a panel of judges on the DC Circuit upheld the government's cancellation of the drilling leases, several Blackfeet leaders penned an opinion letter in the *Flathead Beacon*, a community newspaper based out of Kalispell, Montana, the largest town near the Badger-Two Medicine. I can think of no better way to close this chapter than to quote their eloquent words:

Recently, a panel of judges in Washington, DC, ruled that the last industrial lease in the Badger-Two Medicine must be canceled. And while the Blackfeet Nation is grateful for the court's ruling, we recognize that this company is not likely to give up. They will be back. . . .

And we recognize that, despite the outcome, there were no Blackfeet judges on the court's panel. There were no Indigenous attorneys in the room, no Blackfeet jurors. The fate of our traditional territory was, yet again, in the hands of people far away.

It is past time for that to change; it is time to make room for the voices of people who for too long have been silenced. It is time to permanently protect our sacred lands, in alignment with Blackfeet's vision and tribal interests. That is why we have worked with so many of our friends and neighbors to draft a proposal that will protect the Badger-Two Medicine once and for all.

The Blackfeet have been granted a profound connection to the Badger-Two Medicine since time immemorial. It is our last cultural refuge, home to many of our cultural origin stories, a stronghold for our ceremonies and traditions. It is where we practiced our culture in safety after the federal government outlawed Blackfeet ceremony. It is where we still seek healing and solace, guidance, and renewal. . . .

If our experience teaches us anything, it is that soon, someone will bring another fight to our doorstep. Someone always has another plan that will erode our cultural heritage. Our Blackfeet Traditional Knowledge System is intact—thanks in large part to the Badger-Two Medicine—but it is in fragile condition. It cannot withstand additional pressure. It cannot withstand another fight.

Today, we share an opportunity to protect the best of Blackfeet tradition and Montana heritage. The Badger-Two Medicine is, above all else, a place of healing, and our world needs it as much as it needs us.

CROWD CONTROL

*Just Because Bears
Do It, Doesn't Mean
Humans Should*

THE SKI SLIDES A FEW INCHES ACROSS the softening snow. I pause and take a deep, labored breath before shuffling the other ski forward. I pause again and take two breaths and then a third before I resume my comically slow plod up the mountain. It's as fast as I can manage, though my legs feel strong and my enthusiasm for the day's adventure remains high. Slide, pause, breathe; slide, pause, breathe.

We started our day in inky predawn light, but now the May sun stands high in the sky. Intensely bright, the sunlight reflects off the white snow and works its way around my dark sunglasses, assaulting the edges of my eyeballs. I squint reflexively but it doesn't help much. I'm thirsty, and I just want to stop and drink all the water I'm carrying. I think I'm hungry too, but it's hard to tell.

Above me, Dave Downing, a friend and former colleague, cuts the track I'm following up the snowy slope. As he nears the edge of the snowfield, he reverses direction and zigzags a new track across the white expanse. Slowly, almost imperceptibly, we gain on gravity and climb higher into the Colorado sky. Across the snowfield, Marcus Selig, another friend and former colleague, kicks his boot into the snow, his skis slung across his shoulder. He's abandoned the route Dave and I are on, opting instead to bootpack up the slope. His going is as slow as ours—kick a toehold into the snow, pause a moment, kick another one, pause a moment, kick again.

We are on the Pike-San Isabel National Forest, in the Sawatch Range, slowly making our way up the Angel of Shavano. Shaped like a regal cherub with wings spread wide, the angel appears on the eastern face of Mount Shavano each year as winter snowpack melts into spring snowfields.

Spring is a special time for skiers, and especially for backcountry skiers who eschew developed resorts in favor of wild slopes and crowd-free mountains. Avalanche risk is generally low, sunshine is generally abundant, and frozen, bulletproof snow magically softens into what skiers call corn each afternoon, allowing for easy skiing and mellow turns. But it's the summit elevation that truly drew us to this peak and lures us slowly, ploddingly forward.

Mount Shavano is a fourteener. Its summit sits 14,231 feet above sea-level, making it one of over fifty peaks in Colorado that reach more than 14,000 feet of elevation. For hikers, skiers, and outdoor-minded-folks, Colorado's fourteeners are a magnetic draw that lure hundreds of thousands of recreationists each year. Forty-eight of Colorado's fourteeners lie on the state's vast national forests, including Mount Shavano, which is on the Pike-San Isabel National Forest.

The most famous and heavily visited fourteener in Colorado is Pikes Peak, located west of Colorado Springs on the Pike-San Isabel National Forest where it reaches 14,115 feet. The Ute band of Tabeguache, whose descendants still live in the region, call the peak Tavakiev which means "sun mountain" and their traditions include it as their creation site. The Arapaho, who arrived later, call it Heey-otoyoo, which means "long mountain." The first Anglo-American to document the peak was Zebulon Pike in 1806, and though it already had several names and he never reached the summit, his name eventually prevailed as moniker, formally adopted by the federal government in 1890.

Today, a road and a railroad both access the summit, facilitating visits for the more than 600,000 people who come every summer. Visitor centers (including a new, 38,000-square-foot Summit Complex completed in 2021) sell "tourist-trap standards and special high-elevation donuts that collapse when brought to lower elevations. A plaque on the summit commemorates Katharine Lee Bates's inspiration for "America the Beautiful"—penned after a visit in 1893.

One might think it'd be easy to define a fourteener—after all, measuring a mountain's elevation is an empirical exercise. The official list of Colorado's fourteeners includes fifty-three peaks; however, a handful of peaks, named on USGS maps and reaching above 14,000 feet, aren't on the list. They don't make the cut due to the fact that they don't rise at least 300 feet from the saddle that connects them to another, more prominent, peak. So, the true definition of a Colorado fourteener is a peak that rises above 14,000 feet in elevation *and* has at least 300 feet

Dave Downing (front) and Marcus Selig (back) all geared up and ready to bag a fourteener.

of relief from a saddle that connects it to another fourteener. The tallest fourteener, and the tallest mountain in Colorado, is Mount Elbert, at 14,433 feet. The shortest fourteener, Sunshine Peak, is a scant twelve inches above the threshold, topping out at 14,001 feet.

Cars and cog railways aside, getting to the top of a fourteener isn't easy. Even the "easy" fourteeners require hikers to work for their summit views. Grays Peak, generally considered the easiest fourteener, necessitates a 7.5-mile round trip that includes a 3,000-foot climb from the summer trailhead, at roughly 11,280 feet, to the summit, at 14,270 feet. Quandary Peak, another "easy" fourteener, imposes a 3,450-foot climb over 3.25 miles to gain its summit. For hardened outdoor athletes

accustomed to Colorado's lofty altitudes, it's a pretty straightforward day hike. For visitors from the coast (or even from mountain towns that sit at lower elevations), it's an entirely different matter.

There are a lot of reasons climbing a fourteener is high on the outdoor-adventure bucket lists maintained by Colorado's residents and visitors alike. Public access is perhaps the simplest explanation. Forty-eight of the peaks rest on one or more of Colorado's thirteen national forests or grasslands, making them accessible by anyone with a car. No permits are required to scale them; there's no gate or high-priced entrance fee; climbers don't need to fill out cumbersome paperwork or sit through a mandatory ranger talk to start their hike. They just show up, park

ABOVE A cog railway brings visitors to the top of Pikes Peak on the Pike-San Isabel National Forest.

LEFT Marcus bootpacking up the steep slope.

their car, and head out. Many of the fourteeners are in the Front Range, an easy morning drive from Denver, Colorado Springs, or Fort Collins, putting them in close proximity to millions of people living in some of the fastest growing communities in the West.

But there are dozens of spectacular hikes on public lands spread all across the Front Range (and throughout Colorado for that matter), so access alone can't account for the fourteeners' popularity. Summits exude a magnetism that pulls people upward, and the higher the summit, the stronger the pull. Fourteeners are literally the highest points in Colorado. Figuratively, they're the peak of adventure for the more than 300,000 people who attempt to climb them each year.

Once largely the province of highly experienced mountaineers, these peaks are accessible in a new way today. In the last couple decades, information about climbing and skiing fourteeners has proliferated. Gerry Roach, who *Outside Magazine* called Mr. 14er in a 2010 interview and profile, published his classic book

Hikers on Quandary Peak get to share the high alpine habitat with mountain goats.

Colorado's Fourteeners: From Hikes to Climbs in 1992. The first edition contained black-and-white photographs, black-and-white-topographic maps and 197 different route descriptions. The third edition, published in 2011, contains 256 routes, color photos and maps, GPS coordinates, and dozens of alternate routes for climbers and hikers disinterested in the standards.

And Roach's book is just one resource among many. Legendary ski mountaineer and the first person to ski all of Colorado's fourteeners, Lou Dawson, published two guidebooks detailing winter routes and ski descents on Colorado's fourteeners in 1994, just two years after Roach's book first came out. Dawson divided the state in half for his two-volume set, and though the books are now out of print, they're considered classics by fans of Colorado's high peaks. Then Chris Davenport raised the bar. In one year, from 22 January 2006 to 19 January 2007, Davenport traversed 200,000 vertical feet in his quest to ski all of Colorado's highest peaks. A coffee-table book jammed with inspiring photos documents his effort.

Aspen local Christy Mahon became the first woman to ski all of Colorado's fourteeners in 2010. It took her six years, five years longer than Davenport, but seven fewer than Dawson. Unlike Davenport, who is a professional skier and mountaineer, Mahon had a full-time job at an art gallery and devoted her weekends and holidays to the project.

All these people are top-notch athletes, trained in ski-mountaineering and climbing, and they all have a deep resume of high-elevation mountain travel. Local newspapers, ski magazines, and online adventure outlets write glowingly about their exploits, but often gloss over the years of training, tutelage, and hard-won experience required to successfully navigate the mountains. That makes sense—Americans are drawn to stories of achievement. We see ourselves in the triumphant photo at the top of a peak, but we don't always grasp the years of training and preparation it takes to get there.

At about 12,800 feet, my head starts to hurt. I can't seem to get enough water, but I try to ration the two liters I brought, sipping gingerly between breaths. I decide to take a longer break and drop my pack onto the snow. Dave is a hundred feet above me, working his way up the slope. Marcus is still across the snowfield, doggedly if slowly, kicking his boots into the softening snow as he climbs ever higher. Though we've worked our way up nearly 3,000 feet of elevation, we still have 1,400 feet to climb. I'm not sure I can make it.

My quest to ski just one fourteener is proving far more challenging than I'd anticipated. I'm a lifelong skier, experienced in mountain travel and trained in avalanche awareness. I even spent a few days in Salida acclimating to the higher elevation. I knew it wouldn't be easy, but I'm surprised at how much I'm struggling. I can't catch my breath for more than a moment and only when I'm still. As soon as I start to climb again, I'm gasping for air.

Of course, most people don't try to ski a fourteener; they try to climb one in the height of summer when most (or all) of the snow has melted and the weather is much friendlier. While that reduces the risk of being caught in an avalanche or taking a serious fall while skiing back down, it doesn't eliminate risk entirely. Big mountains have big consequences—something that's easy to overlook when sitting at a desk, reading trip reports, or watching online videos.

The internet has radically reshaped recreation just like it has reshaped so many other aspects of our culture. While Roach's guidebook may have been the first comprehensive take on hiking fourteeners, it is no longer even a primary source. In 2000, Colorado local Bill Middlebrook launched 14ers.com, "the premier resource for climbing the high peaks in Colorado." National sites like Summit-Post.org include detailed information about climbing routes on Colorado's fourteeners. Even the *Denver Post* website hosts information about climbing them. Add to this the ubiquity of GoPro cameras, the omnipresence of Instagram, and an ever-growing cadre of bloggers, vloggers, and adventurers recording and posting their experiences online, and it becomes clear how and why fourteeners have become a defining centerpiece of recreation in Colorado.

Also driving the fourteeners' rise in popularity is the simple fact that Colorado's population (especially in Denver and other Front Range communities) has exploded in recent years. According to the *Denver Post*, the Denver Metro Area, which includes Boulder, has grown by 15 percent since 2010. El Paso County, where Colorado Springs is located, grew by 14.7 percent from 2010 to 2018. Births account for some of the growth, but thousands, if not tens of thousands, of the new residents are outdoor-minded people itching to tick off their first fourteener.

Outdoor recreation is a double-edged sword. In recent years, it's been seen as a cure for all sorts of maladies—physical, emotional, and cultural. Much of the current nature-as-cure philosophy has stemmed from Richard Louv's book *Last Child in the Woods*, which made the New York Times Bestseller List in 2008 and earned the author an Audubon Medal "for sounding the alarm about the health and societal costs of children's isolation from the natural world—and for sparking a growing movement to remedy the problem."

Children aren't the only ones suffering symptoms of the "nature deficit disorder" Louv's book made famous. Many Americans have turned to nature for improving their general well-being and to help a variety of conditions. Doctors prescribe nature walks, pointing to peer-reviewed studies that catalog the benefits of time outdoors (in addition to the previously known benefits of exercise). Veterans struggling with PTSD set off on outdoor expeditions to find peace. Forest bathing, a less active, more immersive form of nature therapy first practiced by the Japanese, has found its way to the United States and has become increasingly popular in just the last few years. Advocates point to improved happiness, reduced stress, and other physiological benefits that accrue from a mindful approach to being outdoors.

But outdoor recreation can be objectively dangerous. Accidents happen. A fact I'm keenly aware of as I rest-step up the Angel of Shavano. By the time we reach 13,000 feet, I'm out of gas. Dave finally pauses long enough for me to catch up just as Marcus abandons his ill-fated bootpack and makes his way across the snowfield to join us.

We convene and agree to eat our lunch and turn back, even though we're 1,200 feet below the summit. Marcus looks relieved; he's nearly as wiped as I am. Dave, who spends more time at elevation, skiing nearby Monarch Mountain, is a bit disappointed but understanding. After we switch into ski mode, I pull out my camera and head across the slope to capture the guys' descent.

When I finally make my own way down, it's glorious. The soft corn snow is perfect, and I carve graceful, arching turns across the slope. After ten or fifteen turns, I'm able to catch my breath more easily and relax into the descent. When I meet up with Dave and Marcus at the bottom of the snowfield, we're all smiles and stoke. Of course, I'm bummed we didn't make the summit, but I feel like the day was a success. Fortunately, Dave and Marcus agree.

Unfortunately, we still have a formidable slog to return to the car. As we move from the open snowfield into the woods, the snow deteriorates into a mushy mess. We have to abandon skiing and find ourselves post-holing through the rotten spring snow, skis strapped awkwardly to our packs. I get caught up in a tree and fall over, much to the amusement of Dave and Marcus. Finally, almost eight hours after we first departed the trailhead, we stumble out of the woods. Marcus unlocks the car and opens a bottle of whisky, which we pass around, while sitting contentedly on the hard gravel ground.

Later that night, Marcus and I meet Ben Lara, the Recreation Program Manager on the Salida Ranger District of the Pike San-Isabel National Forest for burritos and beers at a local joint just off Salida's main drag. Ben had planned to join our ski adventure, but a back injury kept him home for the day. It's probably for the best since I wouldn't have had much capacity to interview him while gasping for air on the slopes.

Ben has spent nine years in Salida. His prior post was in California's Inyo National Forest where he oversaw recreation on Mount Whitney, the tallest peak in the Lower 48 and a wildly popular climb. Expecting him to talk about inexperienced hikers getting into trouble or requiring a rescue, I ask Ben about impacts he's seeing from the increasing numbers of people on Colorado's highest peaks. His answer surprises me.

"Poop," he says, unequivocally.

"When one person poops off a trail, either below treeline or high in the alpine, they see it as having one small impact," he explains. "But when there are 20,000 people climbing a fourteener every year and a percentage of them have to poop, you end up with a lot of shit in fragile alpine areas. It's gross in and of itself, but it causes additional problems for wildlife and water quality and through the creation of social trails as people wander around to find an appropriate place to do their thing."

The Colorado Fourteeners Initiative (CFI), a nonprofit dedicated to improving trails, restoring sensitive alpine habitat, and educating people about Colorado's fourteeners, started tracking use in 2016 using infrared trail counters, and they've expanded the program in the years since. In 2018, CFI used twenty-two counters across Colorado's fourteeners to estimate 353,000 hikers accessed the areas. For perspective, that's 19,000 more hikers than they counted in 2017. If just 1 percent of those hikers needed to pop a squat on a hike, that's 3,530 piles of human feces.

So why not just require people to carry wag-bags, lightweight kits made specifically for collecting human poop in sensitive areas?

"Right now, we don't have those rules in place," Ben tells me. "And in truth, we don't have the enforcement capacity to ensure folks would follow them anyway. Also, many people don't really know they're on a national forest when they hike a fourteener. They just follow online directions to a trailhead and start hiking. They know they're hiking Quandary Peak, but they don't know it's on the White River National Forest. If they don't know they're on a national forest, they won't think to check national forest regulations before they go out."

Ben also mentions the suffer concept. What he means is that after hiking for hours up steep terrain, many people feel entitled to defecate where they damn well please. The physical and mental difficulties (of a hike they've chosen to do, on purpose, for fun) have earned them the right to take the path of least resistance when it comes to doing their business. The irony isn't lost on any of us.

Ben believes there are ways to work with the public, but they will require bottom-up approaches led by user groups and outfitters rather than a top-down set of rules imposed by the cash-strapped Forest Service. "It would be better and more effective for the user groups to come up with rules, and then socially enforce them," he concludes.

Colorado's national forests, and its fourteeners in particular, exemplify recreational challenges that are happening on national forests across the country. Communities close to public lands, like Denver, Colorado Springs, and Fort Collins, are growing faster than many other areas of the country. The swelling populations are paralleled by a growing set of online resources that provide directions, route descriptions, photos, and GPS'd tracks that cover an ever-expanding network of trails and peaks. Many of these Instagram photos, GoPro videos, and adventure blogs highlight the summit triumph while downplaying the danger and struggle inherent in outdoor recreation. Desk-bound adventurers consume this content and, photo by photo, video by video, what was once the realm of highly experienced mountaineers starts to seem attainable by anyone with the right brand of hiking boots and trekking poles. And on top of all this, a growing body of science tells us we need to spend more time in nature. It's a potent mix.

THESE 4,000 FEET ARE HARDER THAN YOU THINK

Two-thousand and fifty miles from Denver, a very different mountain range, on New Hampshire's White Mountain National Forest, beckons weekend warriors from Boston and New York City. The Whites, as they're known, sit roughly 8,000–10,000 feet lower than Colorado's fourteeners—but they're no less formidable. While they top out between 4,000 and 6,300 feet above sea level, these rolling, rocky peaks are known for their steep, rugged trails and for the extreme weather that buffets them year-round. Mount Washington, the highest peak in the range (and the most popular) is home to the "world's worst weather," including some of the fastest wind speeds ever recorded. Flora and fauna also belie the low(ish) elevation—the same fragile alpine tundra that tops Colorado's fourteeners is found here too.

Other similarities exist as well. A cog railway ferries tourists to a visitor center and weather station at the top of Mount Washington, just as a cog railway brings people to the top of Pikes Peak. Growing online and print resources highlight the Forest's 1,200 miles of trails and its six Wilderness Areas. In 2016, *Trail Runner Magazine* published a feature story about the White Mountains' ultra-running scene and how the area boasts some of the country's hardest routes and produces some of the country's best runners. It's an inspiring read, even for folks (like me) who would never seriously consider attempting most of the routes, but who are

drawn to the descriptions of steep, remote trails in pristine landscapes. Also, like Colorado's fourteeners, many, if not most, of the visitors from Boston or New York who flock to the Whites for summer recreation and fall foliage season likely don't know they're on a national forest.

For Coloradans, climbing all of the fourteeners is a rarified achievement that speaks to a person's outdoor skills and commitment. The Colorado Mountain Club maintains a list of the people who have officially climbed all of them (1,890 as of 2019). Back east, there's a similar club that, somewhat ironically, began as a way to introduce local hikers to less-visited peaks in the region. The venerable Appalachian Mountain Club, which has been promoting recreation in the White Mountains since 1876, maintains the Four Thousand Footer Club.

First launched in 1957, the 4K Club continues to inspire hikers to rise to the challenge. Membership to the club requires summiting all forty-eight peaks above 4,000 feet in the White Mountain National Forest. As of April 2019, 14,413 people are members. They have a winter version as well, for those folks willing to brave

View of Franconia Ridge from Mount Garfield on the White Mountain National Forest.

Like Pikes Peak, Mount Washington on the White Mountain National Forest also has a railway that ferries visitors to the summit.

New Hampshire's notoriously dark, cold winters and make their way above treeline between Winter Solstice and Spring Equinox. That list is much shorter, but still has more than 800 people on it.

These lists are inspiring to many hikers who get satisfaction from a goal-oriented approach. But they can also obscure the dangers inherent in climbing these peaks. Since 1849, when record-keeping began, more than 200 people have died in New Hampshire's White Mountains. Historic statistics for the fourteeners are harder to find, but from 2010 to 2017, fifty-seven people died on fourteeners across Colorado. In the same period, about twenty people died in the White Mountain's Presidential Range, an iconic sub-range that draws a disproportionate number of hikers.

Despite the proliferation of successful summit videos and glowing magazine stories, the dangers aren't completely unreported. In 2017, Julie Boardman penned *Death in the White Mountains: Hiker Fatalities and How to Avoid Being One*, a chronicle and cautionary tale of the ill-fated hikers who have perished in the region. *Backpacker* magazine published a story called "Why Mount Washington is One of America's Most Dangerous Hikes" in 2008, and *Outside*'s website published a similarly titled piece in 2016 called "Why Mount Washington Kills."

Hikers pick their way along the exposed length of Franconia Ridge in winter on the White Mountain National Forest.

In October 2019, New Hampshire Public Radio interviewed Colonel Kevin Jordan, the Chief Law Enforcement Officer for the New Hampshire Fish and Game Department, which is responsible for coordinating and conducting search and rescue operations throughout New Hampshire, including in the Whites. The interview begins with a brief introduction that explains, "Search and rescue missions in the White Mountains are rising. Over the past decade, the New Hampshire Department of Fish and Game has tracked a steady increase in rescue calls, which now average over 200 each year." That's more than one rescue call every other day.

Jordan points to a number of reasons the tallies are rising, including the basic fact that as cell service improves in remote areas like the White Mountains, more people can use their phones to call for a rescue than ever before. The irony is startling—the same technology that allows more people to record their trips on cell phones, track and share GPS routes, post geo-tagged Instagram photos from summit peaks, and access trailhead and route information also allows them to simply call for a rescue if they get in over their heads.

But inexperience and lack of preparation are truly driving the trend. As Jordan notes, "The vast majority of our incidents that are non-injury related . . . come from inexperience or lack of knowledge." He points to the area's notoriously extreme weather and the fact that at a trailhead below treeline, the temperatures might be in the 40s or 50s as hikers prepare to tackle a summit. Above treeline, the conditions are often markedly different—blustering winds, snow and ice, and 20-degree air can quickly overwhelm unprepared or underprepared hikers. "Very quickly, they realize they're in trouble and they make that call."

Echoing Ben Lara, Jordan points to education as a key strategy in improving how the public recreates. "We need to do a better job at education. We have volunteers now at the trailheads that stop people as they approach . . . we kind of give them a little heads-up about how difficult the trail is. And I just think that public awareness is our best friend to get that message out."

Also like Ben, Jordan isn't interested in keeping people out of the mountains. "I think it's great that people go. I want them outside, but I want them out and safe. We want them dressed appropriately. We want them to have just a few of those emergency pieces of equipment even if they never need it."

Colorado's fourteeners and New Hampshire's Whites provide compelling examples of the challenges facing the Forest Service as it continues to transition from an organization focused mostly on managing timber stands, water, and wildlife. The recreation infrastructure on our national forests is truly impressive. With more than 5,000 campgrounds, nearly 160,000 miles of trails, thousands of miles of rivers

and thousands of lakes, and more than 120 ski resorts that operate on national forests, the list of outdoor options is practically endless. Unlike national parks, national forest boundaries are porous, there are no entrance gates, and most areas don't require a permit. That's great for folks who want to experience nature and our public lands without the crowds and red tape that national parks create, but it adds to the challenge for the Forest Service.

Simply maintaining this infrastructure is a herculean task. A 2015 agency report titled "The Rising Cost of Wildfire Operations: Effects On the Forest Service's Non-Fire Work" presented some sobering facts, including a deferred maintenance backlog of $5.1 billion, which includes administrative buildings, dams, wastewater treatment facilities, research facilities, roads, and, of course, recreational facilities.

Bike-touring along Rock Creek in Montana's Lolo National Forest.

OPPOSITE Roads like this one on the Sawtooth National Forest in Idaho beckon recreationists of all kinds to national forests across the country.

As fighting wildfires has consumed more and more of the Forest Service's annual budget, maintenance isn't the only thing suffering—funding for recreation management has dropped dramatically. From 2001 to 2015, the agency's recreation, heritage, and wilderness programs have seen a 15 percent reduction in funding, or a loss of nearly $80 million. Funding stabilized briefly in 2016 and 2017, but then dropped by several million in 2018.

Meanwhile, across the National Forest System, recreation is a growing and increasingly important use of these public lands. The recreation economy is a real thing, and the agency estimates that national forest recreation provides $10 billion to the Gross Domestic Product annually and contributes 143,000 full- or part-time jobs. The Forest Service isn't especially good at tracking visitation numbers, in part due to the fact that there are no entrance gates through which visitors must pass, but it does have a National Visitor Use Monitoring program, which collects onsite data from interviews and visitor counts over a four-year cycle. The most recent report covers the 2014–2018 fiscal years.

Since 2005, when records were established as a baseline for measuring trends, recreational use has followed an upward trajectory. In the 2005–2009 period, the agency reported just over 142 million visits. In the 2014–2018 period, that number rose to 150 million visits. Eight million additional visits may not seem like a lot, but for an agency that has experienced budget and staffing reductions, managing millions more hikers, paddlers, anglers, picnickers, skiers, ATVers, and campers is difficult at best and impossible in practice.

For decades, the Forest Service has maintained a generally light-handed approach to recreation management. For example, the agency didn't formally prohibit cross-country off-road-vehicle use (driving ATVs or dirt bikes across the

CLOCKWISE FROM TOP LEFT Passing whiskey in the parking lot after our failed bid to summit Mount Shavano.

The Angel of Mount Shavano, viewed at a distance.

The Forest Service has always had a hands-off approach to national forest recreation, as this circa 1916 photo of early visitors to the Okanogan-Wenatchee National Forest highlights.

landscape where there aren't trails or roads) until the year 2000. That same ethos is still prevalent today, and, for the most part, that's a good thing. Yes, some locations require a parking pass and most developed campgrounds require payment (though some still don't). Yes, there are a handful of heavily regulated locations on our national forests—climbing Mount Whitney, floating the Middle Fork of the Salmon River, or paddling the Boundary Waters Canoe Area Wilderness all require permits—but generally, our forests are accessible and open to anyone who can get to a trailhead.

How the agency will respond to growing recreational use is an open question. What isn't debatable is that more and more people are getting inspired to get out and play on their national forests.

As I board a bus to head back to Denver and catch my flight home the day after our Shavano attempt, I recall Ben Lara's comment about how he thinks user groups need to socially enforce rules and educate people about how to recreate responsibly. At first, I thought he was passing the buck, but as I wrestle with feelings about my failed summit bid, I realize he's right. Despite my experience in the mountains, I didn't fully grasp the very real and very difficult challenge of skiing Colorado's high-elevation mountains under my own power. I simply rolled into town, rented the high-tech gear I needed, downloaded directions to the trailhead and a route description, and headed off filled with thoughts of summit glory. Fortunately, my friends were willing to turn around despite clear weather and good snow. We didn't need a rescue, and no one pooped on the trail or anywhere near it. But had we kept going, things might have been different.

The bus shifts into gear and grinds out of the parking lot. I pull out my phone to thumb through photos of the ski, mulling over the perfect Instagram caption.

CAPITAL W WILDERNESS

---

*The Origins and
Future of Wilderness
on National Forests*

IT'S MID-SEPTEMBER AND THE CRISP blue sky hosts a few wisps of clouds high above us. Western larch and Douglas fir trees rise up along the old roadbed, limbs swaying in the gentle breeze. Tim, my trip partner, is ahead of me on his mountain bike, legs pumping. We've been biking for a couple hours, slowly climbing through the thick forest.

Tim slows down, and I catch up to him as we both roll to a stop and dismount.

"Well, that's about as far as we're biking," Tim says, pointing to a small wooden sign ahead that bears the inscription Rattlesnake Wilderness Area. We've ridden

about fifteen miles, and I'm not terribly disappointed to be off the bike. Our goal is McLeod Peak, a rocky pinnacle deep in the Rattlesnake Wilderness on the Lolo National Forest. Tim's tried to get to McLeod three other times and was turned back each trip, but he's confident this itinerary will deliver us to its summit, 8,600 feet above sea-level and about 5,000 feet above Missoula, Montana, where we started our ride.

I unclip my sleeping bag from the seat of my bike and strap it to my small daypack as Tim searches for a tree where we can lock up our bikes. Bikes aren't allowed in Wilderness Areas, so we'll have to hoof it on foot.

We make our way past the sign and onto a single-track trail that winds through dark forest. Bolete mushrooms pop up from the duff and late-season huckleberries dangle seductively on the edges of the trail. Our goal for the night is a lake a few miles up the trail, and we walk silently, listening to a raucous choir of birds calling from the forest.

If you're a fan of what public land aficionados call capital W Wilderness, the mountain town of Missoula, Montana, might be one of the best places you could

Backpackers make their way through the Scapegoat Wilderness, part of Montana's Bob Marshall Wilderness Complex.

OPPOSITE A sign specifies what uses are prohibited in Wilderness Areas, some of the most protected landscapes in the country.

PREVIOUS The Enchantments Area of the Alpine Lakes Wilderness on the Okanogan-Wenatchee National Forest in Washington is so popular that overnight permits are distributed via lottery.

live. Nestled in the northern Rocky Mountains, Missoula sits at the heart of some of the largest swaths of Wilderness in the country. Just south of town, off Highway 93, the massive 1.3-million-acre Selway-Bitterroot Wilderness Area straddles the Idaho-Montana border, encompassing some of the most rugged and remote terrain in the country. Just to the north, sit the Mission Mountain Tribal Wilderness (the only tribally managed wilderness area in the country) and the adjoining Mission Mountains Wilderness Area. The Scapegoat Wilderness, the Great Bear Wilderness, and the famous Bob Marshall Wilderness, known collectively as the Bob Marshall Wilderness Complex, stretch across the continental divide a couple hours' drive from town. Thirty miles or so to the east, along scenic, trout-filled Rock Creek, the Welcome Creek Wilderness covers about 30,000 acres of the rolling Sapphire Mountain range.

Missoulians can literally take a bus from the University of Montana campus in the heart of town to a stop that is just a couple miles from the Rattlesnake Wilderness, where they can camp next to alpine lakes and walk in the footsteps of bears, mountain goats, mountain lions, and moose. Farther afield, the Absaroka-Beartooth, Anaconda-Pintler, Lee Metcalf, Cabinet Mountains, and Gates of the Mountains Wilderness Areas cover a combined total of more than 1.4 million acres of the Big Sky state. Certainly, other communities sit near Wilderness Areas, but few rival Missoula's geographical proximity to so many.

I've been fortunate to live in Missoula since 2007, and over the years, I've visited almost all Montana's vast Wilderness Areas. I've packrafted through the Bob Marshall Wilderness Area on the South Fork of the Flathead River. I've peak-bagged the sky-scraping peaks of the Bitterroot Mountains, still covered in snow in July. I've backcountry skied in the Absaroka-Beartooth Wilderness, traversing an alpine plateau punctuated by 12,000-foot peaks. I've camped under a silent sky so filled with stars it seemed fake. I've drunk directly from creeks so pure they required no filter.

And I've barely scratched the surface.

For folks like me, who love quiet, solitude, and adventure, Wilderness Areas serve up the best of the best—landscapes that, as articulated in 1964's Wilderness Act, which created the National Wilderness Preservation System, have "outstanding opportunities for solitude or a primitive and unconfined type of recreation."

Capital W Wilderness is a specific designation given to landscapes that are managed to preserve the qualities that make them wild, and it is bestowed only by an act of Congress. To be sure, there are thousands, if not millions, of acres of wild country contained within America's public lands, many of which may be as wild and rugged as those areas that bear the capital W, but Congress hasn't designated them as Wilderness, an act that affords them the most protective land-designation status our country offers.

Today, more than 111 million acres of Wilderness are part of the National Wilderness Preservation System. Spread across 803 different areas in forty-four states and Puerto Rico, they are managed by the Forest Service, the National Park Service, the Bureau of Land Management (BLM), the Fish and Wildlife Service, Native American tribes, and states. Generally speaking, all designated Wilderness Areas, regardless of which entity oversees them, share common management practices and have common rules and regulations. And each one was created by Congress.

The National Park Service manages the largest amount of acreage (40 percent of the total), largely due to the Alaska National Interest Lands Conservation Act of 1980, which set aside fifty-six million acres of Alaska as Wilderness. The BLM manages the least with just 9 percent of the total, and the Fish and Wildlife Service manages about 20 percent. The remaining 33 percent of Wilderness acreage is

The Maroon Bells on the White River National Forest's Maroon Bells-Snowmass Wilderness Area outside Aspen, Colorado, are often considered the most photographed mountains in the country.

managed by the Forest Service, with more individual Wilderness Areas than any other agency (447 of the 803 total Wilderness Areas in the country). Just 5 percent of the land area in the United States is managed as Wilderness—only 2.7 percent in the contiguous United States, an area roughly the size of Minnesota.

Most of the Wilderness Areas within a few hours' drive of Missoula are located on national forests. Many of the country's most famous Wilderness Areas are too: Idaho's Frank Church River of No Return through which the Middle Fork of the Salmon River runs, Minnesota's Boundary Waters Canoe Area, Colorado's Indian Peaks and Maroon Bells-Snowmass (containing what are often considered the most photographed mountains in the country), California's Trinity Alps, Washington's Enchantments, Tennessee's Joyce Kilmer-Slickrock, and New Hampshire's Pemigewasset.

It's fitting that many of the most popular and iconic Wilderness Areas in the United States are located on national forests. The origins of wilderness, both as a land-management concept and as a land-management practice rest squarely with the Forest Service, and more specifically, with three Forest Service employees and their conviction that some areas of America's public lands should remain wild and undeveloped forever: Aldo Leopold, Bob Marshall, and Arthur Carhart.

GIANTS OF THE MOVEMENT

Aldo Leopold is a lion of conservation—his name is uttered reverentially by wilderness advocates and conservationists. For nearly a century, his ecocentric approach to land management and his code of environmental ethics has had a lasting and important legacy on American conservation.

Born in 1887 in Burlington, Iowa, Leopold spent his youth ranging through the woods and creeks near his home, cataloging birds and plants, hunting, and fishing. An attentive student, he graduated from the Yale School of Forestry in 1908. In his early career, he was forest assistant for the Apache National Forest in what was then the Arizona Territory, worked to develop the first management plan for the Grand Canyon while at Carson National Forest in northern New Mexico (also still a territory at the time of his appointment), served as associate director of the Forest Products Laboratory in Madison, Wisconsin, and eventually became a professor at the University of Wisconsin. In 1935, he purchased eighty acres of cutover, burned-over, grazed-over land in Baraboo, Wisconsin, and commenced a restoration effort. It was here that he wrote his most well-known and beloved book,

A Sand County Almanac, which was published posthumously in 1949, a year after he died of a heart attack while fighting a grass fire on his neighbor's ranch.

A gifted writer, Leopold championed a new approach to land management that rejected utilitarianism and human interference. The following excerpt sheds light on his transformation from a young Forest Service ranger fresh from Yale to a thoughtful advocate for a natural world that exists outside human influence:

> We were eating lunch on a high rimrock, at the foot of which a turbulent river elbowed its way. We saw what we thought was a doe fording the torrent, her breast awash in white water. When she climbed the bank toward us and shook out her tail, we realized our error: it was a wolf. A half-dozen others, evidently grown pups, sprang from the willows and all joined in a welcoming melee of wagging tails and playful maulings. What was literally a pile of wolves writhed and tumbled in the center of an open flat at the foot of our rimrock. . . .
>
> In those days we had never heard of passing up a chance to kill a wolf. In a second we were pumping lead into the pack, but with more excitement than accuracy . . .
>
> We reached the old wolf in time to watch a fierce green fire dying in her eyes. I realized then, and have known ever since, that there was something new to me in those eyes—something known only to her and to the mountain. I was young then, and full of trigger-itch; I thought that because fewer wolves meant more deer, that no wolves would mean hunters' paradise. But after seeing the green fire die, I sensed that neither the wolf nor the mountain agreed with such a view.
>
> Since then I have lived to see state after state extirpate its wolves. I have watched the face of many a newly wolfless mountain, and seen the south-facing slopes wrinkle with a maze of new deer trails. I have seen every edible bush and seedling browsed, first to anemic desuetude, and then to death. I have seen every edible tree defoliated to the height of a saddlehorn. Such a mountain looks as if someone had given God new pruning shears, and forbidden Him all other exercise. In the end the starved bones of the hoped-for deer herd, dead of its own too-much, bleach with the bones of the dead sage, or molder under the high-lined junipers.

Leopold was so committed to the idea that land could and should be managed by not being managed that he tirelessly worked to convince his superiors in Washington, DC, to set aside a large swath of the Carson National Forest that surrounded the Gila River as a *wilderness*. The term was Leopold's own, and his request was simple: the land should remain wild and undeveloped—no roads, no campgrounds, no timber harvests, no mining, no grazing—just wild land, set aside for wild animals, for trees, for rivers, rocks, mountains. Humans could certainly visit, but their presence would be passing and ephemeral. In 1924, the Forest Service acquiesced, establishing the roughly 750,000-acre Gila Wilderness Area, the first-ever experiment in managing a wild landscape as just that—a wild landscape. It was a bold, if atypical, move for an agency convinced of its technical prowess at managing landscapes.

Four decades passed between the Forest Service administratively designating the Gila Wilderness and President Lyndon Johnson signing the Wilderness Act in 1964. You don't need to be a historian to know that America changed dramatically during those four decades, but some facts help put the changes into context. In 1924, there were roughly 114 million people living in the United States; by 1964, that number

Aldo Leopold overlooking New Mexico, where many of his wilderness and land ethic ideas were first conceived

had swelled 68 percent to 192 million. In 1924, Arizona and New Mexico had been states for a scant twelve years. The western United States, where much of the public lands that could be considered "wild" lay, experienced the fastest population growth rates in the country during the twentieth century. In 1920, the West had just 8.4 percent of the US population; by 1960, that percentage had nearly doubled. According to the US Census Bureau, from 1900 to 1950, states in the West accounted for nine of the ten states with the highest percentage growth in population.

This growth, coupled with an expanding transportation system, massive industrialization, development of both public and private lands, and increasing concern about the environmental impacts of unfettered growth, fostered a community of advocates dedicated to preserving wild landscapes, of which Leopold was a critical, but single, member. John Muir, Stewart Brandborg, Harvey Broome, Arthur Carhart, Frank Church, Marjory Stoneman Douglas, Benton McKaye, George Perkins Marsh, Olaus and Mary Murie, Wallace Stegner, Gaylord Nelson, and countless others championed both the ideals of wilderness and the concept of it as a specific land management statute that would forever preserve the wild nature of certain landscapes.

The list above includes some of the most influential conservationists and environmentalists of the nineteenth and twentieth centuries, and their cumulative and individual contributions to the environmental movement are well documented by historians and authors. But along with Aldo Leopold, Arthur Carhart and Bob Marshall played an outsized role in advocating for the concept of wilderness within the Forest Service.

Marshall, the energetic outdoorsman, was a prolific author, scholar, and an ardent champion of the wild, natural world and indigenous cultures. It was Marshall's 1930-essay "The Problem with Wilderness" that laid the foundation for the group he would help start in 1935—the Wilderness Society—dedicated to preserving large swaths of the American landscape in their natural state.

Marshall worked as the director of forestry for the Bureau of Indian Affairs from 1933 to 1937 and as the head of recreation management for the Forest Service from 1937 to 1939. While in the Forest Service, Marshall directed staff to preserve large areas of road-free western national forests through a variety of rules and regulations, again, bucking general Forest Service dogma that human intervention and management was necessary to the health and value of the nation's public forests. His friendships with Leopold, Harvey Broome (who played a key role in establishing the Great Smoky Mountains National Park), Benton McKaye (father of the Appalachian Trail), and others proved instrumental in founding the

Wilderness Society. His inherited wealth also played a key role in the early days of the fledging organization, as he personally funded it in its first few years. During this period, he wrote numerous articles, essays, and letters extolling the virtues of wild landscapes. Many of Marshall's writings showcase his thinking, but few as succinctly as this one:

> There is just one hope of repulsing the tyrannical ambition of civilization to conquer every niche on the whole earth. That hope is the organization of spirited people who will fight for the freedom of the wilderness. In a civilization which requires most lives to be passed amid inordinate dissonance, pressure and intrusion, the chance of retiring now and then to the quietude and privacy of sylvan haunts becomes for some people a psychic necessity. The preservation of a few samples of undeveloped territory is one of the most clamant issues before us today. Just a few more years of hesitation and the only trace of that wilderness which has exerted such a fundamental influence in molding American character will lie in the musty pages of pioneer books . . . To avoid this catastrophe demands immediate action.

Tragically, Marshall died in 1939 at age thirty-eight from presumed heart failure, nearly two decades before the Wilderness Act was passed.

Arthur Carhart, like Leopold, was from Iowa and was also born at the turn of the nineteenth century. He was the Forest Service's first full-time landscape architect, a role he took on in 1919. Prior to his appointment, the Forest Service was generally disinterested in promoting recreation, leaving that to the Park Service. However, his immediate supervisor, C. J. Stahl, recognized the need and opportunity for promoting recreation on national forests and encouraged Carhart to plan for recreation facilities like roads, cabins, and other infrastructure on national forests in Colorado, where he was based.

One of his first assignments in Colorado was planning summer cabins along the shores of Trapper's Lake in the White River National Forest. According to legend, while lounging by the campfire after a long day of surveying, the outfitter who ran the camp, Paul J. Rainey, pressed Carhart on his intentions for the area. Eventually he asked why Carhart (and the Forest Service bureaucracy) couldn't simply leave at least one mountain lake "as God made it?" That is, free from roads, cabins, and other such "improvements." Moved by, and in agreement with Rainey's plea, Carhart returned to his office with the recommendation that Trapper's Lake remain undeveloped. Stahl agreed, and the lake remains wild and road-free today.

LEFT
Bob Marshall's legacy is still felt today despite his relatively short tenure with the Forest Service and his early death.

RIGHT Arthur Carhart ready for some backpacking in Colorado.

Carhart took a similar approach on the Superior National Forest, eventually recommending that the agency reprogram its road-building budget for the area and let the region remain accessible by canoe only. Today, we know this area as the Boundary Waters Canoe Area Wilderness, the most popular Wilderness Area in the entire National Forest System.

When Carhart joined the Forest Service in 1919, it was still focused mostly on preventing fires and harvesting trees. Recreation planning on national forests wasn't universally embraced by either his colleagues at the agency or by the public at large, and Carhart grew frustrated with what he saw as a lack of action on his planning efforts. His tenure with the Forest Service was short—he resigned after only four years, at first pursuing a career in architecture and eventually becoming an author who devoted much of his writing to bringing hunters and anglers into the broader conservation movement.

The Forest Service came to not only embrace but celebrate Carhart as one of its foremost wilderness advocates. Two of his most visible legacies are Denver Public Library's Conservation Library, which he helped establish in 1960, and the Arthur Carhart National Wilderness Training Center, established in 1933 and housed at the University of Montana.

The Conservation Library contains some of the most important conservation writings of the modern era: essays, memos, and letters from the likes of Aldo Leopold, Olaus Murie, and Howard Zanhiser. It's the official repository of records for organizations such as The Wilderness Society, the Isaac Walton League of America, American Rivers, and the American Bison Society. It reflects Carhart's fervent belief that without a repository of writing, philosophy, and technical literature supporting wilderness preservation, such preservation will ultimately fail.

The Wilderness Training Center, which is still operated out of the University of Montana, works to educate and train wilderness stewards from a variety of public land management agencies and to educate the general public about wilderness. It is staffed by representatives from the Forest Service, the Park Service, the Fish and Wildlife Service, and the Bureau of Land Management and remains a vital and active driver of modern-day wilderness management, policy, and philosophy.

Writing laws is often compared to making sausage. The analogy works on a couple levels: the process itself is messy and the end product is often packed with ingredients most folks may not want to know about. The passage of the Wilderness Act was no different. While the law provides the most protection the US affords to wild landscapes, it still allows certain uses that may be unpalatable to some.

The act itself was written by Howard Zanhiser, first in 1956, then revised more than sixty times in the next eight years. Legend has it that he worked with a tailor in the late 1950s to make a bespoke coat with four supersized inside pockets where he kept books, pamphlets, Wilderness Society information, and other materials. As he lobbied for passage of the act, he availed himself of these materials.

Zanhiser's backstory is similar to Leopold's, Marshall's, and Carhart's. He was born in 1906 just west of what is now the Allegheny National Forest in Pennsylvania. He developed an early love for natural spaces, and he worked for the federal government, including at the Department of Agriculture, which oversees the Forest Service. He penned essays, articles, and papers about the conservation and environmental movement and argued eloquently for the concept of wilderness. In 1945, he became the executive secretary of the Wilderness Society, basing himself in Washington, DC, where he could access politicians and build the support needed to pass a monumental bill like the Wilderness Act.

Although Leopold, Marshall, and Carhart had been successful at working within the Forest Service to preserve wild landscapes, these administrative decisions lacked permanence and were ad-hoc at best. Zanhiser and others in the Wilderness Society felt Congressional action that permanently designated certain landscapes as wilderness and prescribed what was allowed and what was prohibited in those areas was critical to the establishment of a robust and permanent system of wilderness lands in the United States, what they came to call the National Wilderness Preservation System.

A skilled lobbyist and astute judge of public opinion, Zanhiser even employed his children in his lobbying efforts, taking them to Capitol Hill on Saturdays to help distribute his coat-stored materials. In addition to working the halls of Congress, he published articles and scheduled public-speaking events to build public support for his bill. As the decade slipped by, his efforts started bearing fruit, and the first draft of the bill was introduced by John P. Saylor, a Republican from Pennsylvania in 1956.

At first, neither the Forest Service nor the Park Service supported congressionally designated wilderness. Both agencies felt that such legislation would threaten their administrative control over the lands they managed. The Multiple-Use Sustained-Yield Act (MUSY) that provided the Forest Service with its management directives was passed in 1960 and many officials within the agency (and some politicians outside the agency) felt a wilderness bill was unnecessary since wilderness was one of the uses codified in MUSY. Timber, mining, and agricultural interests (also state water agencies) were also opposed to a wilderness bill, and they had the ear of countless congressmen and senators. Eventually though, after its sixty-something rewrites, the bill passed and was signed by President Johnson in September 1964.

Howard Zanhiser, the author of the Wilderness Act, never actually worked for the Forest Service.

When the Wilderness Act was signed into law, it not only laid out the criteria for which public lands could be considered for Wilderness designation and how Wilderness Areas would be managed, it also designated thirty-four Wilderness Areas, covering 9.1 million acres of national forest land. Many of our most beloved wild spaces—including the Ansel Adams Wilderness Area in California's Sierra and Inyo National Forests, the Bob Marshall Wilderness Area in Montana, Minnesota's Boundary Waters Canoe Area Wilderness, California's John Muir Wilderness Area, North Carolina's Linville Gorge Wilderness Area, Oregon's Mount Hood Wilderness Area, and Wyoming's Teton Wilderness Area—were created when the act was passed. Many of these first Wilderness Areas were wild and undeveloped in 1964 because of the direct efforts of Leopold, Marshall, and Carhart, but it was Zanhiser who brought the bill home. Tragically he died a few months before the signing—only Carhart lived to see the Wilderness Act become law.

HOW TO MAKE MORE WILDERNESS

Since 1964, Congress has added more than 100 million acres to the National Wilderness Preservation System (NWPS). Fifty national parks—including the Everglades, Death Valley, Joshua Tree, Shenandoah, and Olympic National Parks—contain designated Wilderness. The Park Service notes that it manages 80 percent of all national parks as if they were congressionally designated wilderness areas, even though the actual percentage of designated wilderness across the national park system is much smaller.

The rules and regulations governing how Wilderness Areas are managed are more complex than you might initially imagine. Compromise is the foundation of most public laws and the Wilderness Act is no different. While the campaign to enact the NWPS was successful, the law contained some ingredients that Zanhiser

The Jedediah Smith Wilderness in Wyoming's Caribou-Targhee National Forest became part of the Wilderness Preservation System in 1984.

and other wilderness advocates likely abhorred. Remember that, when the Wilderness Act was first written, national forests were the primary land type that the law was intended to protect. Because national forests supported logging, mining, grazing, dam building, and other water-development projects, some of these were allowed in the act. Specifically, it allowed for grazing in designated Wilderness Areas. It also allowed, until 1984, hard rock mining on National Forest Wilderness Areas.

The act doesn't give miners and grazers unfettered access to Wilderness Areas generally, but it did allow for grazing and mining that existed on national forests prior to their designation to continue. That grandfathered use was not insignificant. According to the wilderness advocacy group Wilderness Watch, "of the fifty-two million acres of protected wilderness in the lower forty-eight states, livestock are authorized to graze thirteen million acres, over a quarter of the total acreage."

Mining has a complicated history on America's public lands, and mining in Wilderness is even more complicated. Generally speaking, mining in the United States is still governed by the General Mining Act of 1872 (yes, that date is correct, the law is that old), and it states that some tracts of public lands are open to mineral exploration and that all of these lands with valuable minerals are available for occupancy.

In short, American citizens (or foreign companies with American-based subsidiaries) can freely access certain types of public land, make a mining claim, develop that mining claim, and live there as they work the mine. If they maintain the claim and file the right paperwork, they can even come to own it outright. There are specific rules that govern how the process works, and it applies to hard rock mining, that is mining for metals like gold, silver, or copper, and not to coal, oil, or gas. When the Wilderness Act was passed, not only were existing mining claims on national forests permitted but new mining claims in designated Wilderness Areas could be filed and worked up until 31 December 1983.

One other special provision in the Wilderness Act allowed the president to authorize water-development projects in Wilderness Areas, including the building of reservoirs (and the dams that make them), transmission lines, roads, and other infrastructure "upon his determination that such use or uses in the specific area will better serve the interests of the United States and the people thereof than will [the water project's] denial."

While these special provisions prescribe certain uses, in general, most Americans know more about what uses are prohibited in Wilderness Areas than which ones are allowed. These prohibitions are articulated in section 4, subsection C of the Wilderness Act and read as follows:

Except as specifically provided for in this act, and subject to existing private rights, there shall be no commercial enterprise and no permanent road within any wilderness area designated by this act and, except as necessary to meet minimum requirements for the administration of the area for the purpose of this act (including measures required in emergencies involving the health and safety of persons within the area), there shall be no temporary road, no use of motor vehicles, motorized equipment or motorboats, no landing of aircraft, no other form of mechanical transport, and no structure or installation within any such area.

This short paragraph affords Wilderness Areas their protection from natural-resource development, commercial-resort development, and, for many Wilderness fans, the most important prohibition, from motorized use. Without roads, commercial logging is basically impossible. Without commercial resorts and other recreational infrastructure, the wild, undeveloped nature of these landscapes is forever preserved. Without motors, the noise, smell, and crowds that accompany the internal combustion engine wherever it goes, are effectively banished.

Some Americans claim these rules "lock them out" of these public lands. I find that claim hollow at best. The rules bar only machines. This means no cars or trucks obviously, but also no chainsaws, no helicopters, no generators, no motorized boats, no snowmobiles, and no off-road-vehicles are allowed in Wilderness Areas, even by the agencies responsible for managing them. Their staff take horses and mules, or they walk. There are a few exceptions; some areas where motorboats were allowed prior to designation have maintained that allowance, for example. In Alaska where Wilderness Areas are so vast, some uses that occurred prior to their designation in 1980 (like snowmobile use) are still allowed for subsistence hunting and other circumstances.

And that's exactly what the early wilderness advocates sought. They felt that human nature requires wild spaces where the ever-growing, ever-expanding suite of modern technologies was kept at bay. Motors, resorts catering to well-heeled tourists, even modest cabins built along a picturesque lake were antithetical to their vision. On the one hand, they were striving to maintain a connection to the past, a past where one could simply walk for days, fully and completely divorced from civilization, a past that included the American frontier and still-blank areas on a map. On the other hand, they were striving to build a future where the opportunity for such escape might still exist. They feared that in absence of formal constraints, roads and motors and resorts and airplanes would eventually reach every corner of America, making it impossible to ever recapture the wild spaces that once defined the nation.

I for one am grateful for their foresight.

Importantly, Zanhiser and his cohorts at the Wilderness Society fully intended for Congress to add to the National Wilderness Preservation System (NWPS) long after the law was passed. Some of the act's longest paragraphs instruct the secretaries of Agriculture and Interior to review the lands within their jurisdictions (national forests and national parks, respectively) for possible inclusion in the NWPS. The act directed the Secretary of Agriculture to review all lands classified as *primitive* and the Secretary of the Interior to review all roadless lands more than 5,000 acres and to share those reviews and recommendations for inclusion or not with the president. The president in turn, could recommend these areas be added to the NWPS, but only Congress could actually add them.

In pre–Wilderness Act days, the Forest Service had used a variety of administrative designations to protect what it called at first Primitive Areas and later, depending on size, Wilderness Areas or Wild Areas. These designations prohibited many of the same uses as the eventual Wilderness Act, including road building, motorized transportation, commercial timber harvests, and lodges, hotels, or resorts—but, crucially, they were not permanent, inviolable designations. New leadership, a freshly inaugurated pro-development administration, or other political influence could reverse the classifications just as easily as they were first made.

When the Wilderness Act was passed, 9.2 million acres of national forests were designated as Wilderness, but the Forest Service still managed millions of acres of unroaded, unfragmented lands that could qualify as wilderness should Congress decide to designate them. The act forced the agency to analyze these lands and submit that analysis to the president. Over the next several years, they did just that, submitting reports recommending millions of acres as suitable for Wilderness designation. Anti-wilderness groups sued every time, largely voiding the findings.

Following these legal defeats, the fate of our national forests' wildest areas essentially fell, once again, to the Forest Service. Only Congress can designate Wilderness Areas, but the Forest Service can at least implement practices on undesignated land that mirror how official Wilderness is managed. One such administrative tool is labeling a certain tract of land as a Wilderness Study Area or Recommended Wilderness. In effect, these labels allow the Forest Service (or the BLM) to manage the landscape so as not to impair the very characteristics that make it suitable for possible Wilderness designation should Congress decide to act.

One other way the Forest Service can preserve wild areas in its portfolio from development is to simply stop building roads in them. Today, our National Forest System is fragmented by more than 350,000 miles of roads, more than eleven times the number of miles in the interstate highway system. This sprawling network was largely built by timber companies, and they have amassed a maintenance backlog in the billions of dollars.

In 1998, Forest Service Chief Michael Dombeck, instructed the Forest Service to conduct yet another inventory of its roadless areas, which it completed in 2000. This analysis was coupled with a new suite of regulations that became known as the Roadless Area Conservation Rule, the Roadless Rule for short. The Roadless Rule did not directly protect these areas from development or from the various multiple uses for which the national forests are managed. Rather, it placed a moratorium on road building in these areas. Of course, this rule was challenged in the courts as well, by both timber companies and some states like Idaho and Wyoming. This time, the lawsuits were largely dismissed, allowing the Forest Service to maintain its new road-building ban.

While administrative actions and labels provide some guidance, the actual management of roadless areas, Wilderness Study Areas, and Recommended Wilderness is largely up to local Forest Service officials. In some areas, certain non-conforming uses are allowed, provided they don't degrade the area's wilderness qualities. One of them is mountain biking.

THE GREAT BICYCLE DEBATE

When the Wilderness Act was passed in 1964, mountain bikes didn't really exist. The act included "mechanized transport" in its list of prohibited uses. But it wasn't until 1984 that the Forest Service specifically banned mountain bikes from Wilderness Areas, citing the mechanized-transport clause as justification. Bikes are mechanical, it reasoned, and therefore prohibited from Wilderness Areas.

At the time, the prohibition didn't really rankle the mountain biking community. The sport was young, and so few people mountain biked that there was no shortage of trails or places to ride outside of Wilderness Areas. Fast forward a few decades, and things have changed dramatically.

The push to allow mountain bikes in Wilderness Areas has fractured the human-powered-sports community and has pitted user groups that generally have a lot of common ground against each other. Some mountain bikers have long felt

OPPOSITE
Wildflowers hug the steep rock walls on the Selway-Bitterroot Wilderness Area in Montana's Bitterroot National Forest.

the prohibition was unjust, unscientific, and arbitrary. But recent rule changes, specifically in Wilderness Study Areas and Recommended Wilderness, have provided a rallying cry for more in the community to push back against the ban, even in designated Wilderness.

Wilderness Study Areas and Recommended Wilderness may have the same characteristics as designated capital W Wilderness, but they are not officially Wilderness Areas. Often found in remote locations across the West, many have allowed mountain biking for decades. Mountain bike groups have helped maintain trails in these landscapes and have basically biked under the radar for years. As long as the biking didn't jeopardize the areas' wilderness qualities, local officials let the riders ride—after all, there wasn't a specific statute that prohibited their use.

However, as mountain bike technology improved and as new generations of bikers started riding farther and farther into the backcountry, some user groups and Forest Service officials began to feel that such use did, in fact, impact the wilderness qualities that set the areas apart. Some national forests began to strip mountain bikers of the right to ride through these areas. As they lost miles of beloved trails, mountain bikers grew more and more frustrated. Their frustration has manifested in opposition to new Wilderness designations, since the designation would immediately and forever preclude mountain biking, and since the land in question often includes the very Wilderness Study Areas and Recommended Wilderness Areas where cyclists had been riding for years.

Congress hasn't designated a lot of Wilderness in the last twenty years, but there have been some. One of the more recent was the Boulder-White Cloud Wilderness in central Idaho, which was designated in 2015. Renowned for its rocky peaks and remote location, the area also contained several of the country's most iconic backcountry mountain bike routes, including the Castle Divide route. Central Idaho is also home to the Frank Church River of No Return Wilderness, the largest single Wilderness Area in the Lower 48, and many other large Wilderness Areas, so it's not exactly lacking designated Wilderness. Given that they would lose a nationally recognized riding opportunity, mountain bikers fought the Boulder-White Clouds Wilderness designation.

Ironically, Wilderness designation for the region wasn't necessarily preferred by either the conservation community or the Obama Administration, which initially sought to protect the area as a national monument through the Antiquities Act. A national monument designation would have allowed for more permissive recreation uses, including mountain biking, while still protecting the area from natural resource extraction and other industrial uses.

But national monument designations are, arguably, even more controversial than Wilderness designations. Created unilaterally by the president, national monuments are often criticized by conservative politicians and industry groups as an overreach of executive authority. To be sure, these groups aren't fans of Wilderness designations either, but since the power of Wilderness designation rests solely with Congress, they have some influence in the process. National monument designations provide no such opportunity.

So, it was unsurprising that Idaho's conservative representatives vehemently opposed a national monument designation. What was, perhaps, surprising was that they worked with conservation groups and the Obama Administration to craft a compromise that would set aside much of the landscape as Wilderness instead. For

Hikers make their way across Lake Creek in Wallowa-Whitman National Forest's Eagle Cap Wilderness Area.

better or worse, mountain bikers were essentially cut out of those conversations, and the boundaries of Boulder-White Clouds were drawn in such a way that beloved biking routes became off limits to two wheels.

The campaign to repeal the Wilderness Act ban on bikes is led by the Sustainable Trails Coalition, which has worked with two conservative legislators (Representative Tom McClintock of California and Senator Mike Lee of Utah) to introduce legislation that would rewrite the Wilderness Act to allow for mountain biking.

The Sustainable Trails Coalition doesn't advocate for bikes to be allowed in all Wilderness Areas all the time. Rather, it seeks to reverse the blanket ban that prohibits all bikes in all Wildernesses, letting local managers determine if, when,

A mountain biker in the Boulder-White Clouds before the area became a designated wilderness.

and where bikes might be appropriate. The groups also includes strollers and wheel-barrows in their argument against a blanket ban of wheeled devices, and they point to studies that show bikes don't cause any more impact to trails or wildlife than horses, which are allowed in all Wilderness Areas.

Their website leads with the following statement: "The Wilderness Act of 1964 was a beautiful thing. It protected our most precious lands and celebrated the rec-reational opportunities they would provide for generations to come. The act made it clear that things with engines were bad, and living power sources like humans and horses were good. The act didn't ban bikes; that happened twenty years later."

For many mountain biking enthusiasts, especially those in Montana, Idaho, New Mexico, and other states where Forest Service managers have rolled back bike access, it's a reasonable position. Others argue that it's a slippery slope—rewriting the Wilderness Act to allow mountain biking makes it easier to rewrite the Wil-derness Act to allow e-bikes, and then dirt bikes, and then snowmobiles and other off-road vehicles. Soon enough, they fear, Wilderness won't be wild at all.

Some concerns are more immediate, chiefly the simple fact that mountain bikes move much faster than either hikers or equestrians, setting up user conflicts. Many argue the philosophical—Wilderness Areas were created to protect certain land-scapes from creeping modernity, and mountain bikes are an example of this. Sure, they may be human powered, but they are high-tech gadgets that employ a suite of mechanical innovations. Proponents of biking counter that backcountry skis and whitewater rafts (both allowed in Wilderness Areas) are also "mechanized trans-port" and therefore, the same as mountain bikes.

Even for people versed in the nuances of Wilderness law, the arguments are as muddy as a mountain biking trail after a rainstorm.

The largest mountain bike advocacy group in the country, the International Mountain Biking Association (IMBA), does not support the Sustainable Trails Coalition's effort to overturn the ban on bikes in Wilderness. Instead, IMBA sup-ports a pro-active, collaborative approach to public lands conservation and recre-ation. Its model is to work with different groups and agencies to include mountain biking in their plans. While mountain bikers may lose access in some places, like the Boulder-White Clouds, IMBA believes that they can create more mountain biking opportunities in other places, work to shape proposed Wilderness boundaries to preserve existing trail networks, and ultimately build public lands conservation bills that maintain mountain biking while adding new Wilderness to the NWPS.

The debate over mountain bikes in Wilderness is as much about human desires and expectations as it is about science or a strict reading of public law. For advocates of mountain biking, a human-powered sport that inspires love and appreciation for natural places and wild spaces, the ban is unjust and a misinterpretation of what the architects of the Wilderness Act intended. For those who support the Wilderness Act as it is currently written and implemented, bikes are an unnecessary and unwelcome intrusion into the last remaining places where the speed of travel is governed by feet and hooves. Ever lurking in the shadows is the specter of some as-yet-uninvented technology that may also ask to be allowed, be it grounded, winged, or aquatic.

WHAT'S WILD?

Debate surrounding the relatively privileged and niche sport of mountain biking isn't the only philosophical critique of our modern understanding of wilderness. In recent years, the concept of wilderness "as an area where the earth and its community of life are untrammeled by man, where man himself is a visitor who does not remain," has been justly challenged. Many of the early wilderness philosophers and advocates saw wilderness as a place where humankind hadn't yet set foot, where only the "forces of nature" were evidenced.

Of course, humans had long lived in these places and, more importantly, had shaped them. Their impact was everywhere; the most obvious examples being vast stands of stately trees interspersed with large meadows that were the result of their sophisticated use of fire. Even the very nature of the Great Plains was due, in no small part, to the fires indigenous peoples started.

All corners of North America were inhabited, either in passing or more permanently, by Native Americans. No doubt, these people very much intended to "remain" in these areas. That is, until they were consumed by a colonizing force too powerful to rebuff. The irony is fierce—one set of human beings had lived on these lands for millennia; they revered the land and considered it sacred; they kept it "pristine." Another set of human beings had transformed vast amounts of the landscape into an industrial nation, save a few remaining spaces that were too far from civilization, too high and rocky and snow-capped, too impenetrable for exploitation.

The wilderness movement preserved those last remaining pockets of wildness, now emptied of the people who had lived there for generations upon generations. But such preservation ignored the fact that Native Americans had been so displaced and so marginalized that their very presence on the landscape was erased.

Certainly, the wilderness advocates were influenced by the time in which they lived, and labeling them as racist isn't my point, nor is it entirely fair (Marshall, for example, was an advocate for tribes in his role at the Bureau of Indian Affairs and his many writings reflect his respect for and appreciation of Native Americans). Furthermore, we're only just beginning to understand the profound way indigenous cultures shaped and still shape landscapes. That doesn't excuse bigotry, but it helps contextualize it. The Sierra Club has recently wrestled with the conflicted legacy of its founder, John Muir. That the organization is examining its past publicly is heartening. While such soul-searching is important, if perhaps overdue, the fact remains that all of America's lands were inhabited by diverse peoples who left their "footprint," even if this hasn't been acknowledged until recently.

Tentless on a late summer night, Tim and I blow up our sleeping pads and unroll our sleeping bags on a flat spot near the lake as daylight fades to dusk. After we munch on the simple food we brought along, we hang what's left on a limb a couple hundred yards from camp.

The next day, we make our way over game trails to the ridge that leads up to McLeod's lofty summit. Here in the Wilderness, trail signs don't guide your way. Hiking trails themselves are scarce, for that matter, so we navigate the thin game trails with bear spray at the ready, a map in our daypack, and a general sense of where to go (north and up!).

When we finally reach the peak, we raise our arms in triumph and take in the view. To the south, the Rattlesnake Mountains rise and fall in a series of rocky ridges. Missoula is down there somewhere, but it feels a world away. We turn and peer north into the Jocko Valley, part of the Flathead Indian Reservation. The slopes that fall from the summit down to the Jocko are sacred to the Salish, a tribe that lives in the reservation, and the southern part of the Jocko is off-limits to non-tribal members. We're not tempted to trespass; the terrain is nearly vertical and seems impossible to navigate, plus we're headed south.

As we mill about, we spot something Tim had hoped to find—rocks piled about three feet tall, forming an oval platform that looks like it could fit a prone human. Tim has spent the last couple years researching the Rattlesnake Wilderness Area for his graduate thesis, and he tells me that the Salish used to send their young men up McLeod on vision quests. Could this pile of stones be where the teenagers spent a night or two as they fasted and communed with the mountain?

When we finally reunite with our bikes and careen down the double-track, headlamps casting a small cone of light on the rocky, rutted road, I'm still thinking about the pile of stones and what they represented.

This Wilderness didn't even exist, at least not according to the United States of America, until 1980, when Congress created it with pen and paper. It's two years

younger than I am. Tim has told me stories of how the Rattlesnake was the local dirt-biking destination in the 1950s. The lake we camped beside is dammed, as are most of the lakes in the upper basin, all well inside the Wilderness. There are old foundations from early homesteaders just on the fringe of the Wilderness boundary. An old school and a post office used to sit a mile or two from where human-drawn lines have carved this small piece of wild out of a landscape that had been lived in and well used for millennia.

I realize that, to me at least, capital W Wilderness isn't about the past. What makes Wilderness so special isn't whether or not the landscape "appears to have been affected primarily by the forces of nature, with the imprint of man's work substantially unnoticeable" as Zanhiser wrote in the Wilderness Act. Wilderness is about the future and how we, as a country, choose to safeguard those places where we limit our modern presence, even as our collective past haunts the landscape.

OPPOSITE Wilderness isn't just a western phenomenon; the Dolly Sods Wilderness Area on West Virginia's Monongahela National Forest is every bit as stunning as iconic western Wilderness Areas.

THE WOLVERINE
WATCHERS

*How Citizen Science
Helps Wildlife*

THE ROOM IS PACKED. Colorful puffy jackets hang haphazardly from the backs of chairs. The air is warm despite the late-fall weather outside. Dozens of people mill about the high-ceilinged room, chatting softly in small groups.

PREVIOUS
A herd of mule deer bucks on Colorado's Pike-San Isabel National Forest. Like their white-tailed cousins, mule deer are common across our national forests, especially in the West.

At the front of the room, Kylie Paul and Russ Talmo watch the crowd and review the speeches in their hands. Kylie and Russ work with Defenders of Wildlife, a nonprofit organization focused on imperiled wildlife species. It's the first meeting of a new project they've been planning for months and they scan their notes and the crowd nervously.

Eventually, Russ' voice booms out over the din and folks settle into their seats. The crowd is a classic mix of mountain town residents—retirees and college students, bearded outdoor types, and bookish wildlife lovers. Russ and Kylie introduce themselves. People listen closely.

The project is called the Wolverine Watchers, and it leverages the willingness of locals to help the Bitterroot National Forest learn more about the mesocarnivores that live in the forest. Mesocarnivores are mammals whose diet consists of 50–70 percent meat. In the mountains of western Montana, the lineup includes pine martens, fishers, lynx, fox, and, of course, wolverines. Kylie and Russ are hoping to enlist the crowd's help in setting up and monitoring motion-triggered wildlife cameras deep in the forest during the long Montana winter.

Citizen science is a relatively new manner of collecting scientific data. As its name implies, and as the volunteers at that 2014 meeting in Missoula, Montana, exemplified, it utilizes nonprofessional scientists to collect scientific data in a formal and scientifically sound process that professional scientists, wildlife biologists, and land managers can then use to inform their decision making. Importantly, *citizen* is a catchall word used to imply anyone who's not a scientist; one needn't be a citizen in the strict sense to participate.

Volunteers who participate in these efforts increase the scale of research projects, allowing scientists to collect more data from more places than they would be able to reach without help. In the Bitterroot National Forest, which covers more than 1.5 million acres of steep, rugged mountains along the Montana-Idaho border, that additional capacity is especially helpful. The Wolverine Watchers are able to leverage the skills and willingness of cross-country and backcountry skiers, snowshoers, and other interested (and physically fit) members of the community.

Despite its advantages, citizen science—also known as community science, crowd science, crowd-source science, and civic science—took some years to become an accepted part of scientific study. Professional scientists, justifiably, had concerns about data collection and tracking, safety of volunteers, and whether conclusions drawn from science projects conducted by lay people would be fairly treated by the scientific community and the public. The term entered the Oxford English Dictionary in 2014, but the concept is a few decades old.

Eventually, much of the early anxiety faded and this type of science has been embraced by the scientific community and governments, so much so that the US government has a citizen science website expressly set up to help "federal agencies accelerate innovation through public participation." The site provides resources for scientists, citizens, non-governmental organizations (NGOs) and others to participate in projects, initiate their own projects, or read about successful projects and how they've helped advance scientific knowledge and solve real-world problems.

Adventure Scientists is an NGO that has established itself as a key player in the community science movement, in part through smart marketing and good timing, and in part because it capitalized on a group of Americans who spend a lot of time in wild, public spaces—outdoor athletes and adventurers.

The organization was founded by Gregg Treinish in 2011 and now employs thirteen people. While the group works internationally, many of its projects, especially its wildlife-focused projects, have taken place on public lands in the United States, including our national forests. In 2013 and 2014, the group worked with the Olympic National Forest in Washington to set up a monitoring program for elusive Pacific martens, small mesocarnivores in the weasel family. The partnership didn't produce marten sightings while Adventure Scientists was involved, but the field work helped inform the Forest Service's continued monitoring efforts. In the 2018–2019 season, the agency positively detected martens on the forest for the first time since 2008.

Betsy Howell, the Olympic's biologist, was quick to credit the group's work as "crucial" to the project's eventual success, saying, "The surveys [Adventure Scientists] did in 2013 and 2014 helped support our theory that we still needed to get higher in elevation if we were going to find martens. With funds obtained after these two winters, we were able to hire crews that then focused at higher elevations in the national park and forest. These then resulted in a number of detections during the 2018–2019 survey season."

One of the Adventure Scientists' largest projects to date is focused on Wild and Scenic Rivers throughout the United States. These special waterways have Congressional protection from dam building and other types of development, and many originate in national forests. In fact, the Forest Service manages more than 5,000 miles of the 12,700 miles of Wild and Scenic Rivers in the country. In addition to working with the Forest Service, the group is partnering with the National Park Service and the Bureau of Land Management to recruit rafters, canoers, kayakers, hikers, and others to collect data on over 11,000 miles of Wild and Scenic Rivers. Despite the protected nature of these rivers, there is a massive gap in water quality data, which the project aims to fill. Given the fact that these rivers provide 10 percent of the drinking water across the United States, this data is extremely helpful to federal land managers, state and local water providers, and to biologists, hydrologists, and other scientists at the Forest Service, Park Service, and BLM.

Martens are one of the more elusive, and adorable, denizens of our national forests.

Wildlife management is a complex endeavor. With the exception of species named on the Endangered Species List and other specific laws like the Migratory Bird Protection Act, wildlife *populations* are managed by states, regardless of where the wildlife live. That leaves the management of wildlife *habitat*—the forests, rivers, grasslands, and wetlands where wildlife live, eat, breed, rear their young, and migrate—to the agency tasked with managing that particular tract of land or to private land owners. National parks, wildlife refuges, national forests, and other public lands play an outsized role in providing habitat for wildlife, but they are all managed in different ways and for different purposes.

For example, national forests are not managed like national parks. As the first chief of the Forest Service, Gifford Pinchot famously held a utilitarian, or conservationist, view. As such, national forests were always intended to provide a mix of uses, including timber production, water production, grazing opportunities, and mineral and other sub-surface resource development, along with providing healthy wildlife habitat and recreation opportunities. National parks, meanwhile, have always had a preservationist focus, with recreation and wildlife as their twin management priorities.

TIMBER TAKES A STEP BACK

The Organic Act of 1897 didn't explicitly include wildlife habitat in its list of intended uses for the land that would become national forests. For the first four decades of the twentieth century, the Forest Service focused on a three-part mission of protecting forests from illegal logging and destructive wildfires; providing timber to the country by contracting with lumber companies who would harvest the trees, pay the agency for them, and then sell them to mills; and managing national forest water resources for communities, agriculture, and industry. There was plenty of timber for the country's housing needs, the agency made great strides in fighting wildfire, and water flowed from our forests to the communities and downstream users that needed it. For the most part, the agency operated under the public's radar.

Things changed in the post–World War II building boom of the 1940s and 1950s. The agency had honed its industrial silvicultural techniques largely out of public view and, with the help of ever-willing timber companies, had increased the scale of national forest logging significantly. In 1940, America's national forests provided roughly one billion board feet of lumber. By 1960, that amount had sextupled to about six billion board feet. To meet the growing demand for timber, the Forest Service and the logging companies with which it contracted, turned to full-scale industrial logging techniques—primarily clear-cutting.

Ironically, the same demographic demands that drove the logging boom on our national forests also drove a growing recreational interest in these public lands. As soldiers returned from Europe, they needed homes and the timber to build those homes, but they also started recreating in new ways. Surplus military equipment like tents, rafts, backpacks, outerwear, skis and snowshoes, and improvements in automobiles, allowed returning GIs to get out into public lands in new ways and in greater numbers than ever before. Many of the outdoor activities that are common-place today, like downhill skiing, rafting, camping, and hiking were first practiced by returning soldiers and their families. In fact, some of the United States' most iconic ski areas like Vail, Aspen, Sugarbush, and Whiteface were started by soldiers from the army's 10th Mountain Division, a special unit trained in wintertime mountain warfare techniques that included skiing, snowshoeing, and mountain survival. Interestingly, the area where these soldiers trained, called Camp Hale, is located on the White River National Forest, just a few air miles from where Vail Resort would eventually be located.

This growing interest in recreation and other values like wildlife brought more and more everyday Americans out onto their national forests. Many of them were distraught to discover massive clear-cuts, an ever-growing network of forest roads, and an agency unwilling or unable to change the way it managed these vast public lands. By the 1950s, Americans had exerted enough pressure on Congress to enact new laws that forced the agency's hand.

Today, the Organic Act is no longer the main law governing how the Forest Service manages our national forests. In 1960, Congress passed MUSY (the Multiple-Use Sustained-Yield Act) and followed it up in 1970 with the National Environmental Policy Act (NEPA), and in 1976 with the National Forest Management Act (NFMA), which has since been amended several times. Together, these acts stipulate how the agency should manage the 193 million acres under its purview.

Through MUSY, the agency was given statutory authority to manage not only for the protection of the forests, for timber, and for water, but for outdoor recreation and wildlife and fish as well—the act valued outdoor recreation, range, timber, watershed, and wildlife and fish purposes equally. Importantly, when MUSY was passed, the Forest Service was staffed largely by professional foresters trained in silviculture, so that's where it focused its efforts. Certainly, there were some employees

focused on recreation and wildlife, but the agency didn't have a deep bench of expertise and training to handle the expanded duties. Wildlife and recreation were suddenly equal players in the matrix of national forest uses. And a few years later, the door to public input regarding how the Forest Service dealt with resources was not just swung open—it was torn from its hinges.

For better or worse, Congress left it to the agency to figure out how it was supposed to manage each use equally, though it was generous enough to at least define both multiple use and sustained yield. According to MUSY, multiple use means "the management of all the various renewable surface resources of the national forests so that they are utilized in the combination that will best meet the needs of the American people . . . with consideration being given to the relative values of the various resources, and not necessarily the combination of uses that will give the greatest dollar return or the greatest unit output." Sustained yield was defined as "the achievement and maintenance in perpetuity of a high-level annual or regular periodic output of the various renewable resources of the national forests without impairment of the productivity of the land."

If there's a cutest bird award, this baby flammulated owl would be the odds-on favorite; Uinta-Wasatch-Cache National Forest, Utah.

OPPOSITE Once seriously imperiled, the bald eagle is now a regular sight on many of America's national forests, including the Tongass National Forest in Alaska where this eagle is enjoying a fresh salmon dinner.

MUSY was a step toward less intensive and more balanced management of national forests, and it ostensibly put wildlife and recreation on the same footing as other, more profitable uses of the national forests. Bureaucracies are slow to turn, however, and the agency remained more focused on timber harvests than many Americans, and eventually their federal representatives, desired. In fact, despite MUSY, the annual harvests on national forests continued their upward trajectory through the 1960s and into the mid-70s, finally peaking at twelve billion board feet, twice the amount harvested in 1960 and twelve times the amount harvested in 1940.

In 1976, Congress passed the National Forest Management Act (NFMA), which forced the agency to create a management plan for each forest that would guide how different sections of the forest would be managed for the next ten or so years. While it didn't require detailed specifics, it did require the agency to delineate areas where timber, grazing, and mineral extraction could occur and areas where outdoor recreation or the preservation of wildlife habitat would be better uses for that particular part of a forest. The act has been amended several times, as different methods for forest planning have been implemented, but it remains a

foundational, and critically important, tool for forest managers and the public to better understand and plan for national forest management.

By the time NFMA passed things had already changed dramatically thanks to the National Environmental Policy Act (NEPA) of 1970, which created sweeping changes to how the federal government managed and developed projects on the federal estate by forcing federal agencies to consider the environmental impacts of a proposed project and share those impacts with the public in a formal process that includes the public's right to litigate projects if they are deemed illegal or unconstitutional. Though the act wasn't written exclusively for the Forest Service, it was one of the federal agencies required to operate under NEPA, and this provided the public a formal, codified opportunity to push back on both specific projects and broader plans.

New timber harvests, proposed recreation facilities, new mining operations, and water control projects all fall under the purview of NEPA. Even the forest plans the agency was required to develop following the passage of NFMA in 1976 were subjected to NEPA. For the first time in its seventy-year history, the agency

Wild turkey is a popular and plentiful game species that live on national forests from coast to coast.

OPPOSITE While eagles and bears get a lot of the press, less charismatic wildlife that live on our national forests, like this red eft salamander on the Chattanooga National Forest, are no less important.

was forced to navigate the uncharted waters of public participation. It also had to hire an entire suite of new employees to study potential environmental impacts, and Forest Service ranks swelled with biologists, sociologists, hydrologists, and recreation planners.

The public also got organized. Wildlife advocacy organizations, recreation organizations, and other groups built up their memberships and started to engage the agency in a big way. Industry trade organizations dedicated to timber and mining also made their voices heard in the new public-process paradigm.

HABITAT HABITAT HABITAT

The Wolverine Watchers project has come a long way since that first meeting in 2014 when Kylie and Russ first presented the idea to a group of western Montana outdoors people and wildlife fans. Over the next five seasons, roughly 150 people volunteered each winter, lugging the materials needed to set up stations miles deep in the forest.

Once a month, they returned to each location, skis or snowshoes strapped to their feet, bulky winter gear sharing pack space with fresh roadkill, lure (a potent, musk-smelling liquid that attracts carnivores to bait stations and camera traps), gun brushes, and replacement batteries and memory cards for the cameras. Montana's short winter days don't provide much daylight, so volunteers often met in dark mornings and worked late into the waning light to reach the sites and perform their tasks: replacing batteries and memory cards, stringing roadkill to a bait tree, dousing it with lure, and collecting the hair-laden gun brushes. These small wire brushes are placed just below the bait so as critters climb up the tree, some hair gets snagged on the sharp wire bristles. Latex gloves ensure no human DNA is transferred to the sample as volunteers retrieve it and stow it away in labeled Ziploc bags. After analysis at a nearby lab, hair samples help the researchers identify how many individuals of each species visited a particular site. This is a critical part of the data since individual wolverines, fishers, and martens are very difficult to distinguish from others of their species using photos alone. Finally, the volunteers pack up and head back to ice-cold cars and trucks.

With twenty-five sites spread across the forest, and with each site requiring monthly maintenance, organizing the Wolverine Watchers was no small task. But the scale achieved, and the data collected, proved well worth the effort. The Bitterroot National Forest had set up a mesocarnivore monitoring project for the

southern half of the sprawling forest two years prior to the launch of the Wolverine Watchers project. While that effort produced some useful results, it was small in scale and limited in geography. By partnering with hundreds of willing volunteers, Bitterroot was able to conduct a half-decade of valuable monitoring data across the entire northern and eastern stretch of the forest, adding significantly to baseline knowledge about mesocarnivores in the area.

Wolverines are a fascinating species of weasel. Elusive and ferocious, they have earned the respect of scientists, adventurers, and, yes, comic book authors. They live in relatively high-elevation, alpine environments with territories that can range from 100 to 500 square miles. Perhaps unsurprisingly, their population strongholds include Alaska, Scandinavia, Canada, and parts of northern Asia. In the Lower 48, scientists estimate there are fewer than 300 individuals scattered among isolated remnant populations in Idaho, Montana, and some parts of Wyoming, Oregon, and Washington. Recently individuals have been documented in Colorado, California, Utah, North Dakota, and even Michigan, all places where they used to live in higher numbers, but where breeding populations have long been absent. Seeing a wolverine in the wild is extremely rare, which makes it difficult to know how many wolverines live in a particular area, if there are breeding pairs, and how far they roam any given forest—all of which are good things to know if you're a Forest Service biologist tasked with managing wildlife habitat on your forest.

When Congress passed the NFMA in 1976, it instructed the Forest Service to craft comprehensive plans for each forest and to be ready to start implementing those plans in 1982. But it left the process and the intricacies of what those plans needed to include up to the agency. So in 1982, the Forest Service published what is known as 36 CFR 219.

Though cryptic, this seemingly random collection of numbers and letters provide some insight as to its purpose. CFR stands for the Code of Federal Regulations, which is basically a list of the rules and regulations that different agencies and departments of the federal government create based on the laws Congress writes. These rules are considered legally binding, just like case law and legislatively issued statutes. The rules are divided across fifty different subjects, and subject thirty-six is categorized as Parks, Forests, and Public Property. Therefore, any rule or regulation that a federal agency like the Forest Service, the Park Service, or the BLM issues is published in section 36 of the CFR. The CFR is further divided by the regulatory entity issuing the rule and the Forest Service's rules fall between 200 and 299. So, 36 CFR 219 is code for the Forest Service's rule that spells out how it conducts forest planning.

Why this deep dive into the Code of Federal Regulations? Because 36 CFR 219, and specifically subsection 19, is where you can finally find the Forest Service's legally binding approach to how it planned to manage wildlife habitat from 1982 onward (recall, wildlife themselves are managed by the states, unless they are listed by the Endangered Species Act). Here, the agency itself, not Congress, not the courts, not the president, committed to maintaining habitats that support "viable populations of existing native and desired non-native vertebrate species."

The rule has been modified once, in 2012. You might think that updating rules around forest planning would be relatively straightforward, but the process took more than a decade, having first launched under the George W. Bush administration in 2000. The Forest Service has acknowledged that the specific language regarding wildlife and plant habitat management was one of, if not the most, controversial elements of the revised forest planning rules. No doubt, the proliferation of advocacy groups played a meaningful role in the debate. Twelve years, a handful of lawsuits, and significant public input later, a new rule was adopted.

A fluffy mountain goat kid poses among golden larch trees in the Alpine Lakes Wilderness on Washington's Okanogan-Wenatchee National Forest.

In the updated 36 CFR 219, published on the Federal Register in 2012, the agency specifically noted a "disagreement between those who believe that without strong, specific requirements in the rule for maintaining species diversity and viability, the persistence of many species will be at increased risk, and those who believe that putting specific requirements in the rule will result in endless litigation that will keep the agency from moving forward with planning and with projects and activities."

To bridge this divide, the Forest Service adopted a more flexible two-step approach that doesn't bind it to maintaining specific population levels of certain wildlife species but also doesn't abandon its wildlife habitat management duties. The first step of the updated approach focuses on a holistic ecosystem management concept. If, the thinking goes, the entire forest is managed with an ecosystem-wide approach, then "over time, management will create ecological conditions which support the abundance, distribution, and long-term persistence of most native species within a plan area, as well as provide for diversity of plant and animal communities."

As a backstop to this ecosystem focus, the second step details how the agency will manage sensitive and endangered species. Habitats utilized by species listed on the ESA will be managed "to contribute to the recovery of listed species and conserve proposed and candidate species." (Proposed and candidate species are those that the US Fish and Wildlife Service, which maintains the ESA, is considering for listing, but for which no decision has been made.)

This flexible approach parallels a shift in national forest management generally, which has slowly worked itself into the agency's ethos. Rather than focus on particular resources like timber, water, or wildlife habitat, the Forest Service has moved toward a broader, ecosystem approach that takes into account how all the different elements work together to create healthy, functional, though highly managed, landscapes.

An additional backstop includes habitat management for those species considered by regional foresters to be of special conservation concern. The agency requires regional foresters to compile this list and include species that may not be on the ESA but are locally or regionally threatened. Forests must include provisions to improve or maintain habitat for these species to the degree that the particular forest can impact population trends. Of course, those species have to first exist on the forest in question, something that staff- and cash-strapped biologists may struggle to prove on a forest, like the Bitterroot, that covers millions of acres.

SAGA OF THE WOLVERINE

The way the Forest Service manages habitat has a big impact on wildlife populations. Our national forests host more than 3,000 species of vertebrates and innumerable invertebrates. Many animals are well-known and well-studied like white-tailed deer, Rocky Mountain elk, black bears, and mountain lions, while others are elusive and poorly understood, like Pacific martens or wolverines.

The last few hundred years of humanity have not been kind to wildlife populations. Scientists have suggested that we are in the middle of a sixth great extinction. Unlike the previous five mass extinction events in Earth's history, this one hasn't been caused by a massive climatic event or other natural phenomenon; it's being caused by humans.

The Forest Service's Threatened, Endangered, and Sensitive Species program (TES) notes that the number of species listed on the ESA rose from 281 to 1,381 in the thirty-two years between 1980 and 2012. The TES acknowledges the critical role the National Forest System plays for imperiled species. Of the 1,381 species listed in 2012, 32 percent "were known to either use national forest/grassland

Mountain lions, like this one from the Black Hills National Forest in South Dakota, can be difficult to spot, but they live in national forests across the country.

199

habitats, or potentially be affected by Forest Service management activities. Some 251 other species are candidates for listing (i.e., meet listing criteria, but have not yet been formally proposed), and over 50 of those occur on national forest or grasslands."

Today, wolverines are not protected by the ESA. The convoluted history of the wolverine decision illustrates both the controversial and complicated process of adding a species to the ESA and the complex role our national forests play in providing habitat for threatened species.

Typically, the US Fish and Wildlife Service does not decide to propose listing a species on its own, although the Secretary of the Interior, who oversees the USFWS, can decide to consider listing a species. More often, wildlife advocacy groups, like Defenders of Wildlife, the Center for Biological Diversity, or the Endangered Species Coalition (itself a network of groups), petition the agency to list a particular species (individual citizens can petition as well). For example, in 2015, a coalition of twenty-one advocacy groups, including national groups like the Center for Biological Diversity and the Humane Society, and regional groups like the Midwest Environmental Advocates and Friends of the Wisconsin Wolf, petitioned to reclassify gray wolves as threatened under the ESA.

The Superior National Forest in Minnesota hosts a robust population of timber wolves.

If the USFWS finds a petition and evidence compelling, it opens a public comment period, and pending how that process unfolds, adds the species to the list and develops a plan to help the species recover. These plans typically include critical habitat designations, limit certain types of land use, and may even include a process for establishing experimental populations in areas where the species used to live but has been extirpated. They can include both public and private lands.

The first such petition for wolverines occurred in 1994. The USFWS rejected the petition outright, noting that the petitioners failed to provide "substantial information indicating that listing . . . was warranted." Conservation groups tried again in 2000, and again, the USFWS rejected the petition for lack of substantial evidence. A decade of legal wrangling ensued, in which the USFWS decided the listing was not warranted, faced multiple lawsuits and orders to gather more data, rejected the petition again, and finally decided in 2010 that wolverine populations in the Lower 48 did deserve listing on the ESA, but that listing was precluded by higher priority species. This decision effectively kicked the can down the road, buying time for the USFWS to develop conservation plans for other species on the ESA that, it argued, faced more urgent threats of extinction. (To be fair, the USFWS is also cash- and staff-strapped and without the resources necessary to effectively draft recovery plans for all the species on the ESA, it has to make some hard decisions.)

As you might guess, the USFWS once again found itself the subject of lawsuits, this time for failing to consider how climate change presented an urgent threat to wolverines in the Lower 48. And so, in February of 2013, the USFWS announced that it was, yet again, considering listing the wolverine, but any listing would be limited in scope. Human activities like snowmobiling, backcountry skiing, timber harvesting, and infrastructure development that occurred in wolverine habitat would not be prohibited if the species were listed because, according to the USFWS, they did not threaten wolverines. Intentional killing through trapping or hunting, or incidental killing through trapping for other species, would be prohibited. The determination took nearly nineteen months before it ultimately decided, once again, against protection. After another two years of litigation, the US District Court for the District of Montana overturned the withdrawal of the wolverine from the ESA and remanded the case back to the USFWS for further consideration. In October 2020, the USFWS issued the following statement about wolverines and the ESA: "The best available science show that the factors affecting wolverine populations are not as significant as believed in 2013 when the US Fish and Wildlife Service proposed to list the wolverine found in the contiguous United States as threatened . . . The species, therefore, does not meet the definition of threatened or endangered under the Endangered Species Act. Accordingly, the Service has withdrawn its listing proposal."

If you happen to be a biologist working on one of the national forests where an endangered, or potentially endangered species lives, obtaining accurate and detailed information on that species is a critical component of successfully managing habitat in a way that contributes to the species' recovery. But, like so many of the Forest Service's programs, the resources and staff needed to gather this data just aren't available.

Fortunately, community science efforts are expanding. The organization Conservation Northwest has robust community science programs that track wolverines, grizzly bears, wolves, fishers, and Canada lynx across the North Cascades, including in Gifford Pinchot National Forest. Many programs, like those of Conservation Northwest, the Wolverine Watchers, and an effort in southern California where volunteers search for the San Bernardino flying squirrel, are locally or regionally focused. Others, like the Audubon Society's Christmas Bird Count, billed as the "nation's longest-running community science bird project" are national in scope.

In June 2015, months after skis and snowshoes were hung in garages or stored in basements, long after winter snows gave way to summer vegetation, and well after female wolverines emerged from their dens, kits in tow, Kylie emailed the volunteers who participated in the first season of the Wolverine Watchers with a summary of how the season went. The group monitored twenty-two different sites and tallied more than 100 visits to change batteries, refresh bait stations, and collect hair samples. That winter, the project documented more than seventeen different species, including wolverines, which appeared at four different stations, and martens, which appeared at twenty stations. While fishers and lynx were not among the species found that first season, bobcat, gray wolf, red fox, long-tailed weasel, mountain lion, moose, northern flying squirrel, and red squirrels were documented.

In the ensuing years, Kylie and Russ expanded the program, culminating in twenty-eight stations during the 2019 season. Over that time, the project documented twenty-four individual wolverines through genetic analysis. Kylie gave them evocative names like Left-Hook, Back-Spot, Chin-Strap, Big Chunk, Thin-Stripe, and Swoosh. In the 2017, 2018, and 2019 seasons, the project documented fishers at several sites. While wolverines aren't included in the regional forester's species of conservation concern list, fishers are, and the data produced by the Wolverine Watchers will contribute to management for that species.

Finding fisher and wolverine individuals was exciting to be sure. But discerning that the Bitterroot's wolverine population was successfully breeding was the real prize. If seeing a wolverine in the wild is exceedingly rare, seeing kits is like watching a unicorn walk through your backyard. Photographic evidence of young wolverines meant that the Bitterroot's population was growing—good news for the wolverines and a feather in the Watchers' collective caps. When she analyzed the data from 2017, Kylie discovered that a male named Powder Paws and a female named Lefty-White-Toes had, in fact, mated and successfully produced kits. In 2018, one of them appeared on camera. White fur covered his front right paw while the rest of his body was dark brown and black. True to form, Kylie named him Righty.

AFTER THE BURN

The Eagle Creek Fire

CHARRED TREES PARTITION THE VIEW as we hike along the rock-strewn trail, solid black lines rising vertically into the opaque sky. Hundreds of them rise in every direction, some clearly dead, others showing signs of spring growth despite their blackened trunks. Beneath these charcoaled reminders, the ground is awash in green. Ferns rise from the duff, their saw-toothed fronds spreading in emerald spirals. Tiny liverworts drip from the steep rock walls, catching drops of rain and mist. The soft, spring leaves of early-season wildflowers, dark green Oregon grape, and new shoots of ocean spray rise from the damp earth wherever ferns leave space. A thick pillow of moss covers nearly every rock in sight.

April has arrived in Oregon, and alongside a few hundred other visitors, Patrick Shannon, my friend and former colleague at the National Forest Foundation, and I are making our way through the Columbia River Gorge National Scenic Area (CRGNSA). We started our morning at the historic Multnomah Falls Lodge, just off Interstate 84, the epicenter for recreation in "the Gorge" as this area is known locally. The falls for which the lodge is named crash down just behind the stately building, adding a sheen of mist and fog to the already damp scene.

The largest waterfall in Oregon, Multnomah is a sight to behold. Split into two drops, the cascade first crashes 542 feet down a sheer basalt cliff face before pooling briefly then dropping another 69 feet into a second pool. A historic and photogenic bridge spans the upper pool and a riot of ferns, mosses, lichens, and just-budding shrubs cover almost every piece of rock and ground nearby.

Inside the lodge's gift shop, there's ample evidence of artists who have captured Multnomah's sublime majesty—gorgeous photos, posters, postcards, and artwork line the walls. I'm not optimistic that I'll be one of them, as I fiddle with my camera and try to get the entire upper fall in one shot. People mill about in winter hats and rain jackets, setting up tripods or pulling out phones to snag an obligatory selfie as the water plunges behind them. Even on this cold, wet, early spring day, traffic is heavy. Multnomah Falls is considered the most visited natural recreation site in the Pacific Northwest, logging more than two million annual visits. A quick glance

PREVIOUS Firefighters work to protect Multnomah Falls Lodge on the Columbia River Gorge National Scenic Area during the Eagle Creek Fire, September 2017.

Green vegetation bursts from the ground among charred tree trunks following the Eagle Creek Fire.

Multnomah Falls
is an iconic tourist
attraction in the
Columbia River
Gorge National
Scenic Area.

back to the parking lot, where we just barely snagged a spot when we arrived at 9:00 a.m., hints at these numbers. It's already packed with cars.

As Patrick and I head up one of the trails that departs from the falls, evidence of what transpired the year before, here in one of the Pacific Northwest's most beloved and iconic outdoor playgrounds, begins to materialize in earnest. We step past shiny new retaining fences that keep the steep hillsides from sliding onto the downslope trails, roads, and parking areas. Just eighteen months ago a massive wildfire had engulfed the Gorge, closing it to recreation for months.

The Eagle Creek Fire began at about 4:30 p.m. on Saturday 2 September 2017, courtesy of some teenagers playing with fireworks. By Sunday morning, it had grown to 3,000 acres. On Monday, Labor Day, the unofficial last day of summer, thick gray smoke filled the Gorge and blew west into Portland where residents reported ash falling from the sky. Those same winds pushed the fire from Eagle Creek toward Multnomah Lodge, and by Tuesday, the fire had grown to more than 10,000 acres, making a thirteen-mile western run along the Gorge from where it started and even crossing the Columbia River to the north side of the Gorge where it started spot fires in Washington State.

Officials closed I-84, restricted boat traffic on the Columbia River, and closed access to the entire Gorge. As the flames spread, more than 400 homes in the small town of Cascade Locks, just two-and-a-half miles from Eagle Creek, were evacuated. For the next two months, the fire worked its way across more than 48,000 acres.

As the fire spread, so did stories about its devastating effects and about the heroic efforts of those battling it. *Oregon Live*, an online property of the *Oregonian* newspaper, published a riveting account of how firefighters spent a sleepless night protecting Multnomah Lodge from the flames with a hastily built, but successful, system of sprinklers and hoses that kept the building wet while the fire surrounded it on three sides. Local news reported on the 153 stranded hikers forced to spend an uncomfortable and unplanned night in the woods before hiking nearly fourteen miles to safety via a long, alternative route. Footage and imagery of the Gorge engulfed in orange flames spread across the country, becoming national news. *USA Today* covered it, and a larger *New York Times* story about forest fires in Oregon and Washington focused its imagery on the Eagle Creek Fire.

As coverage grew, the public responded. Area residents took to social media to air their grief and find community (so great was the outrage, that the identity of the teenager responsible for starting the fire was kept from the public due to concerns over his safety). A Portland-area musician wrote a song about the fire called the "Eagle Creek Elegy." *Portland Monthly*, a glossy lifestyle magazine ran a story just

a few days after the blaze started that featured writing from a half-dozen locals who all expressed their heartbreak over the fire.

Within weeks, the National Forest Foundation had raised more than a hundred thousand dollars to help the Gorge recover. Helped by good publicity and by the Forest Service, who directed would-be donors and concerned citizens to the NFF's effort, it was the largest post-fire fundraising success the organization had experienced to date, eclipsing all previous recovery efforts, despite most having followed far larger and more devastating fires.

This response was heartening to be sure, and it was understandable. But it was also disproportionate to the fire's size and impact. All told, the Eagle Creek fire affected roughly 48,000 acres and destroyed one house and three other buildings. For perspective, the Chetco Bar Fire, which burned in Oregon's Rogue River-

A helicopter readies to drop water on the Eagle Creek Fire, September 2017.

OPPOSITE The Eagle Creek Fire burned in a mosaic pattern across the Columbia River Gorge National Scenic Area.

Siskiyou National Forest from mid-July to early November the same year the Eagle Creek fire raged, burned more than 190,000 acres. The Miller Complex, also on the Rogue River-Siskiyou burned 39,700 acres. In fact, more than 350,000 acres of Oregon's national forests burned in 2017 (not including Eagle Creek), and an additional 52,000 acres of Bureau of Land Management land also burned. Yet no one penned a song or devoted pages of a monthly magazine to the Chetco Bar or the Miller Complex fires.

Explanation for the outsized response to the Eagle Creek Fire can be found in the Gorge's beloved natural resources, its proximity to Portland, and to the unique management scheme that first created the Columbia River Gorge National Scenic Area nearly forty years ago.

FROM CELILO TO SILENCE

The Columbia River Gorge winds for about eighty-five miles through the Cascade Range. While these mountains may be less well known than the Rockies or the Appalachians, two of the range's most prominent peaks, Mount Rainier and Mount Saint Helens, are familiar to most Americans. The steep, rugged, and biologically diverse Cascades extend from Lassen Peak in northern California through Oregon and Washington and into Canada. In northern Washington, North Cascades National Park (bordered to the south and west by the Mount Baker-Snoqualmie National Forest and to the south and east by the Okanogan-Wenatchee National Forest) is often called the American Alps because it rivals the scenic grandeur of Europe's most famous range.

The Columbia River cuts through the heart of the Cascades, connecting the Columbia Plateau with the Pacific Ocean and creating a natural boundary between Oregon and Washington. It's one of three rivers in the United States that cross the range and it's by far the largest. Without the river and the mountains, there would be no Gorge. Beginning in the Miocene, roughly 15 million years ago, as the Cascades themselves were rising, the Columbia began relentlessly cutting its course to the Pacific. More recently, at the end of the last ice age roughly 15,000–13,000 years ago, a series of cataclysmic floods known as the Missoula Floods ripped across the Pacific Northwest and through the Columbia River basin. The repeated violent flooding scoured the volcanic rock lining the river and helped create the steep cliffs and buttresses that draw millions of visitors to the Gorge today.

Size and location have made the Gorge a critical transportation corridor—I-84 and US Route 30 run along the river on the Oregon side, Washington State Route 14 runs along the Washington side, and major railroad lines run along both banks. Barges ply the river itself, and, through dredging, locks, and other manipulations, are able to travel inland all the way to Lewiston, Idaho. Major dams, including two in the Gorge, provide hydroelectric power throughout the Pacific Northwest and control the river flows, effectively making it a series of slack-water pools.

Visitors driving east from Portland through the Gorge's eighty-five miles witness a stunning transformation as the ecology changes from a verdant, fern- and tree-choked temperate rainforest to a semi-arid sagebrush steppe. The western portion of the Gorge receives between 75 and 100 inches of precipitation a year, while the eastern side sees a fraction of that—between 10 and 15 inches annually. This dramatic difference makes the Gorge one of the most captivating and biologically diverse landscapes in the United States.

Significant elevation changes add to the diversity as well. Just east of Portland, where the boundaries of the National Scenic Area reach their western terminus, the Columbia River sits only twenty or so feet above the Pacific Ocean. Roughly thirty-five air miles to the east, Mount Defiance, the highest point in the Gorge, reaches 4,960 feet into the sky. (Lest confusion reign, another Mount Defiance rises in Washington's Mount Baker-Snoqualmie National Forest, which is outside Seattle and several hours north.) Microclimates abound in all of this transition, fostering an astounding diversity of plant communities, including 800 species of wildflowers, thirteen of which are found only in the Gorge.

The Gorge possesses rich cultural and historical significance as well. Archeologists have found evidence of humans inhabiting the area that stretches back more than 10,000 years. Massive salmon runs and natural transportation routes combined to make the Gorge a center for Native American life in the Pacific Northwest.

Arguably, no site was more important to Pacific Northwest Native cultures than the fishing grounds around Celilo Falls, which was located about twelve miles

Basalt cliffs, carved by the Missoula Floods, help make the Columbia River Gorge an absolutely stunning landscape.

east of the modern-day town of The Dalles. Considered the longest continuously inhabited location in North America, Celilo Falls, called Wy-am by local tribes, served as a supermarket, trading center, and transportation and cultural crossroads for tribes stretching from Alaska to the American Southwest and the Great Plains.

Before the Army Corps of Engineers turned the mighty Columbia River into a series of reservoirs, it thundered over rapids and waterfalls on its route from British Columbia to Astoria, Oregon, where it meets the Pacific Ocean. In the Gorge, Celilo Falls marked the start of a stretch of dangerous water that ran 12–15 miles downstream. Here, the Columbia, elsewhere more than a mile wide, was squeezed into a basalt canyon about 140 feet across. The constriction provided access to the incredible salmon runs that made their way from the Pacific Ocean to spawning grounds as far upstream as Idaho and Canada. An estimated fifteen to twenty million salmon made the annual migration, and the miles-long constriction was the perfect spot for fishing. Indian fishermen used nets attached to long poles, called dip nets, to catch fish after massive fish.

In 1805, Lewis and Clark paddled down the Columbia and witnessed between 7,000 and 10,000 people (one of the highest densities of people they encountered in their entire trip) living and trading along the fishing grounds. They called it, "a great emporium . . . where all the neighboring nations assembled." According to the Columbia River Inter-Tribal Fish Commission, "for thousands of years, Wy-am was one of history's great marketplaces. A half-dozen tribes had permanent villages between the falls and where the city of The Dalles now stands. As many as 5,000 people would gather to trade, feast, and participate in games and religious ceremonies." In addition to the thousands who traveled to gather, permanent residents included the Wasco people who traditionally lived on the south side of the river and the Wisham people who lived on the north side.

The tribes' long-standing uses of Celilo Falls and the Columbia in general were effectively brushed aside in the twentieth century. The Columbia's potential for hydropower had long been recognized, and the effort to construct the massive dams that now slow its once tumultuous run to the sea began following the passage of the Federal Water Power Act of 1920. This law gave authority for building hydropower dams to the federal government, removing it from the states where it had previously rested. Shortly after it passed, Congress instructed the Army Corps of Engineers and the Federal Power Commission (itself a creation of the Federal Water Power Act) to survey the nation's waterways for their suitability to water control structures that would improve navigability, control flooding, provide irrigation, and generate hydropower. Their report was presented in 1926 and in it, the authors named the Columbia River as "the greatest system for water power to be found anywhere in the United States."

All told, the report called for ten large dams on the main Columbia, and in the ensuring years, funding and effort was devoted to surveying dam sites. In 1929, the Great Depression began to ravage the country and when Franklin Roosevelt won the Presidency in 1932, the appetite for massive public works projects was immense. Bonneville and Grand Coulee dams were started in 1933 and finished in 1938 and 1941 respectively. Three thousand laborers, comprised largely of men from welfare and relief rolls, built the Bonneville Dam, working in continuous eight-hour shifts for fifty cents an hour.

Today, according to the Northwest Power and Conservation Council, there are 274 hydroelectric dams in the Columbia River watershed, including fourteen on the main stem of the Columbia from the Mica Dam, near Revelstoke in British Columbia, to the Bonneville Dam, just forty miles from Portland.

In 1957, the gates of The Dalles Dam closed, inundating Wy-am and closing a millennia-long chapter in North American history. The tribal villages that once dotted the area are now under water. Today, the largely Native American Celilo Village

Celilo Falls in the early 1900s, before it was inundated.

sits on a bluff above the still water that obscures Wy-am (in 2008, the Army Corps used sonar technology to determine the falls do still exist beneath the artificial lake). While the US government compensated tribes for the loss of their ancient fishing grounds, no financial remuneration can offset the cultural losses.

DESIGNATION SCENIC

Euro-American settlement of the Columbia River Gorge happened quickly. In 1850, forty-five years after Lewis and Clark passed through and a decade before the Civil War started, Portland claimed roughly 800 residents. Fifty-five years later, in 1905, it boasted 90,000 people and hosted a world's fair centennial celebration of the Lewis and Clark Expedition. Three million people came for the festivities. Evidently, Portland threw quite a party; by 1910, its population more than doubled. By 1980, the Portland Metro Area, which includes suburbs in both Oregon and Washington, hosted over 1 million residents.

As the region grew, many who cherished the Gorge's incredible natural beauty believed unmitigated development posed enough of a threat to demand action. The Gorge's scenic splendor and proximity to Portland had long made it attractive for developers, both industrial and recreational. The website for Friends of the Columbia Gorge details some of them. Some early concepts included a golf course and polo grounds at present-day Angel's Rest, the highest elevator in the world at Mist Falls, and a power plant at Wahkeena Falls. Later, Bonneville Dam's cheap power had businessmen envisioning (and championing) a Pittsburgh of the West with steel mills lining the river, gorging on hydropower. Alarmed locals pushed back on these early efforts, and fortunately they weren't the only ones concerned. In 1979, the National Park Service initiated a study to determine if the Gorge would be appropriate as a National Park.

The Park Service's report recognized the Gorge's "national scenic value" and recommended a National Scenic Area designation, to be managed by the Forest Service, even though the concept was new and ill-defined (no such actual designation existed at the time). Existing towns, railroads, and dams made a National Park designation impractical, but the Park Service reasoned that the Gorge's scenic values possessed national importance and a Scenic Area designation would provide organized, regulatory oversight to development in the Gorge, something that had been absent to date.

In 1980, shortly after the Park Service issued its report, local conservationists started the Friends of the Columbia Gorge to advocate for federal protection. Led by Nancy Russell, the group marshaled an impressive roster of supporters that, by 1981, included many influential backers, including two former Oregon governors, a former Washington governor, and several city and county commissioners from Oregon and Washington. A thirty-one-member steering committee helped plan and execute a campaign to protect the Gorge.

In 1982 and 1983, completion of Interstate 205 and a bridge (now called the Glenn Jackson Bridge) that spanned the Columbia, connecting Portland to Vancouver, Washington, literally and metaphorically paved the way for potentially unchecked suburban sprawl to mar iconic Gorge vistas. Subdivisions proposed near Multnomah Falls and Beacon Rock proved especially controversial. Through smart lobbying, access to key people, and growing public support, Friends of the Columbia River Gorge blocked these developments and eventually achieved its vision of federal protection for the Gorge in 1986. Oregon's Senator, Mark O. Hatfield carried the legislation and lobbied hard for its passage. Developers, private property advocates, and some residents of the many communities that border the Gorge opposed federal protection. But President Reagan signed the bill at the last moment, literally hours before it would have been pocket vetoed through inaction.

The front page of the *Oregonian* on 17 November declared, "It has been an uphill battle, won only by consensus, compromise and commitment. The obvious winners are the thousands of residents of the gorge—who will no longer be subject to political turmoil and indecision—and the tens of thousands of Americans and people the world over who will forever be able to view this beautiful area."

National Scenic Area is a somewhat rare federal designation that Congress has used to protect a handful of especially scenic spots in the country. It was first applied to the Mono Basin in 1984. The Columbia River Gorge National Scenic Area was the second, just two years later. The designation was intended to do two things: one, protect and enhance the scenic, cultural, recreational, and natural resources of the Gorge; two, protect and support the economy of the Gorge by encouraging sustainable growth in existing urban areas and by allowing future economic development in a manner consistent with the above purpose.

To accomplish this, the legislation assigning the designation also created the Columbia River Gorge Commission and designated three types of land within the Gorge: Urban Areas (10 percent of the total area, where development is generally unrestricted), General Management Areas (50 percent, where development is managed by the commission to allow agriculture, forestry, and some small-scale commercial and residential development—this includes about 31,000 acres of the Columbia River itself), and Special Management Areas (40 percent, mostly managed

by the Forest Service for recreation and other natural services, but allowing some forestry, agriculture, and even residential development). So, while the Forest Service comanages the Columbia River Gorge National Scenic Area with the Columbia River Gorge Commission, it "owns" less than half of the 293,000 acres.

Bridal Veil Creek in autumn on the Columbia River Gorge National Scenic Area.

It's a unique system that has allowed the thirteen communities within the Gorge to grow while also preserving much of the natural splendor that makes the area unique and drives the recreation economy that has taken root here.

Just driving through the Gorge is inspiring and historic. Cliffs, buttes, bluffs, and mountains rise 3,000 feet above the river, growing ever greener and more lush as you snake west. From Troutdale to The Dalles, history buffs can navigate sections of the Historic Columbia River Highway, the first scenic highway built in the United States. Much of the historic route is now replaced by I-84, but some sections of the old highway are still drivable; others are slowly being converted to a trail system for cyclists and pedestrians. Atmospheric differences on the east and west sides of the Gorge create strong winds that whip up the river, and windsurfers, kite surfers, and paddleboarders have turned the riverside town of Hood River into a wind- and water-sports mecca. For more terrestrially minded folks, over 300 miles of trails wind through the Gorge, including the Pacific Crest Trail, one of the country's premier long-distance trails. And when they get thirsty or need a place to crash for the night, there are half a dozen breweries, chic hotels and mom-and-pop motels, and, of course, farm-to-table restaurants sprinkled throughout the Gorge's quaint towns.

I didn't bring a bicycle or a paddleboard on my visit. But I did bring hiking boots, which I make good use of as Patrick and I tromp along one of the more popular trails, winding through forests of Douglas fir, ponderosa, and hemlock trees. While most are fire scarred, many are still alive, and the profusion of green rising from the forest floor certainly shows that the fire had little lasting effect on many of the plants here. In truth, this forest, like virtually all forests in North America is adapted to fire.

Throughout the United States, from the hardwood forests of Appalachia to the high-elevation forests of the Rocky Mountains and from the longleaf pine stands of the Gulf Coast states to the damp forests of the Pacific Northwest, fire has been a driver of forest ecology. Part of this can be attributed to Native Americans whose deft use of fire helped shape the ecology of the entire continent since the glaciers retreated.

While many consider the Organic Act of 1897 to be the Forest Service's foundational legislation, the agency wasn't formally created until President Theodore Roosevelt transferred management of forests from the Department of the Interior to the Department of Agriculture and placed Gifford Pinchot as the head of the newly minted Forest Service through the Transfer Act of 1905. Just five years later, Pinchot's agency would be challenged by one of the most important events in the history of our nation's forests, one that dramatically changed how the agency managed our forests—decisions we are still grappling with more than 100 years later.

THE BIG BURN

An uncharacteristically dry and warm winter in 1909–1910 preceded a dry spring and a hot summer. By mid-August, there were reports that between 1,000 and 3,000 small wildfires were burning in federally managed forests across Montana, Idaho, and Washington. Then, on 20 August, hurricane-force winds whipped across the region, effectively combining the thousands of fires into one major conglomeration. White pine trees, at the time the dominant tree in the region, reacted to the extreme heat in ways no one predicted. The trees' resinous sap, made up of hydrocarbons, essentially boiled out of the trunks, creating a cloud of highly flammable gas that spread across hundreds of square miles. The gasified sap ignited in a series of horrific explosions that sent fireballs thousands of feet into the air and touched off yet more fires. In two terrifying days, the Great Fire (or Big Burn or Big Blowup) torched three million acres of Montana, Idaho, eastern Washington, and southern British Columbia. Eighty-six people (most firefighters) died, towns were incinerated, and the Forest Service was forever changed.

First, the young agency received more funding from Congress, which nearly doubled the Forest Service's budget the year after the fire. This helped address the manpower and equipment shortage that agency leaders blamed for hampering its ability to control the 1910 fires. Second, as its staff and funding grew, and as it sought to prove its worth, the agency became obsessed with fighting any and all fires on lands in its purview.

Severe fire seasons in the 1930s further encouraged the agency to fight all fires on national forests. At the same time, it began helping other public and even private land managers prevent timber-destroying fires on their lands. The agency used the incredible manpower available through the New Deal–era Civilian Conservation Corps to not only battle fires, but to build roads, fire lookout towers, and ranger stations, most of which were built to help spot and thus prevent large, uncontrollable wildfires. In 1935, the Forest Service enacted its 10 a.m. policy, which decreed that all fires should be suppressed by 10 a.m. the morning after they were first detected.

After World War II, surplus military equipment found its way into the agency's firefighting efforts. Planes, trucks, jeeps, and bulldozers became standard firefighting equipment. Smokejumpers leveraged military training and equipment to parachute into remote, inaccessible areas to fight fires as soon as they were spotted. By the 1960s, the Forest Service was arguably the best wildland firefighting organization on the planet. It also effectively set fire policy for all federal land management agencies, which brought Forest Service firefighting practices and its 10 a.m. policy into national parks and BLM lands. For the most part, this decades-long effort successfully prevented massive fires like the Great Burn. It also radically altered the ecology of the West's fire-adapted and fire-dependent forests.

While eliminating fire from the landscape can temporarily save valuable timber stands, it also allows a buildup of the types of fuels that make fires bigger and hotter. Forests that saw fire every ten, fifteen, or twenty-five years, hadn't experienced it in forty or fifty years or more—when they did eventually burn, they burned hotter and more destructively. Climate change, something Gifford Pinchot never had to

consider, also began to impact the planet, drying out and stressing forests. And all the while, more and more people moved closer and closer to national forests, building homes in what's called the wildland urban interface or WUI.

By the 1970s, Forest Service staff had begun to rethink their attitudes about fire. Slowly, they came to understand the critical role it played in forest ecosystems and that more frequent but lower intensity fires were, in fact, beneficial to forests. Small fires recycled nutrients back into the soil instead of sterilizing it. They removed fine fuels—sticks, needles, shrubs, and even small trees—from the ground before they could pile up and become fuel reservoirs for larger fires. Agency biologists learned that many types of wildlife depend on fire, and slowly the policies changed course. The 10 a.m. policy was abandoned, replaced by a let-it-burn policy, which allowed fires to burn themselves out in areas where they didn't threaten people or infrastructure.

Aftermath of the Big Burn of 1910 on the Coeur d'Alene (now part of the Idaho Panhandle) National Forest.

From an ecological standpoint, this new direction was welcomed, but it didn't directly address the imbalance a century of fire suppression had created. Beginning in the late 1990s and continuing through today, the agency began to see its firefighting budget spiral ever upward. Firefighting costs in 1995 represented 16 percent of the agency's annual budget. By 2015, they consumed 52 percent. One might assume that Congress would give the agency more money to offset these rising costs, but that hasn't happened. Instead, the Forest Service has shifted resources from programs like recreation, wildlife, and vegetation management programs, even though the latter is a key tool in reducing the susceptibility of forests to burn and in reducing the severity of fires once they start. Dollars aren't the only resource the agency has shifted, it has also seen a 39 percent reduction in non-fire personnel since 1995.

Fire season (the time of the year when forest fires are most likely to start) has lengthened by seventy-eight days since the 1970s. Nearly twice as many acres burn

Charred trees dot the Anaconda-Pintler Wilderness on Montana's Beaverhead-Deerlodge National Forest.

each season than in seasons thirty years ago. The six worst fire seasons since 1960 have all occurred since 2000, and many western states have recently experienced the largest fires in their history. These mega-fires are very expensive. In 2014, the ten largest fires on national forests cost the agency more than $320 million to battle.

In 2017, Congress finally addressed the firefighting budget. Historically, the agency forecasted its firefighting budget based on a rolling ten-year average. In other words, it took the average of firefighting costs over the last ten years and requested that amount for the year ahead. When the average size of fires and the costs to fight them were stable, this worked out okay. But as the fire season lengthened, as fires grew in size and impact, and as costs rose commensurately, that process left the firefighting budget perpetually underfunded. The latest fix will provide some relief by allowing the agency to tap into other emergency funds the government has on hand (like those used for hurricanes), but firefighting costs continue to consume a disproportionate amount of the money Congress provides to the Forest Service each year.

COMMUNITY FROM CALAMITY

Like most forest fires, the Eagle Creek Fire burned in a mosaic pattern. According to Forest Service reports, 55 percent of the area within the burn perimeter was unburned or burned at low severity, 30 percent of the area burned at moderate intensity, and only 15 percent burned at high intensity. So, from an ecological perspective, the Eagle Creek Fire wasn't particularly damaging. Despite its unnatural inception, it triggered a natural and needed cycle in the forest's ecology.

From a recreational perspective, the damage was more significant. Part of what makes the Gorge so scenic, and waterfalls like Multnomah possible, are its steep cliffs. These walls are beautiful but they're also unstable. As the fire swept through, it burned the moss and lichen that act as cement for the loose rocks that make up much of the Gorge. Without that glue, landslides and rockslides, already common, occurred with more frequency, washing out trails and posing a danger to hikers.

The fire also damaged recreational infrastructure. The day after Patrick and I finished our hike, I returned to Multnomah Lodge to talk with Stan Hinatsu, a recreation staff officer for the Columbia River Gorge National Scenic Area. As we sipped coffee in the lodge's historic, high-ceilinged dining room, we talked about how the fire had impacted the area's most popular activities—hiking and walking. Stan explained that even prior to the fire, the Gorge was experiencing challenges due to ever-increasing use. While Multnomah Falls is the main attraction, the rest of the Gorge is immensely popular as well, with more than two million people enjoying trails each year. "After the fire, the entire Oregon side of the Gorge was closed to recreation," he told me. "And as a result, the Washington side was overrun, as were parts of the Gifford Pinchot National Forest which borders the Scenic Area in Washington."

Prior to the fire, the Forest Service had been working with Travel Oregon and Friends of the Columbia River Gorge on a campaign (called Ready, Set, GOrge!) aimed at distributing people across the entire Gorge to reduce usage at trailheads nearest to Portland. The burn and the closures created another angle for education. "In some places, communities are used to forest fires and what happens after a fire, but Portland is different," Stan told me. "We saw this as an opportunity to educate the public on how large fires are managed. It was a good opportunity and we took good advantage of it."

While Portland's residents may have been unaccustomed to wildfire impacting their backyard, the CRGNSA also required a different response than would have happened on virtually any other unit in the National Forest System. When the CRGNSA was created, its boundaries included thirteen towns that had grown up along the river; today, roughly 70,000 people live in these towns. There are also twenty-one state parks and recreation areas managed by the state of Oregon scattered throughout the Gorge. The Historic Columbia River Highway and I-84, both managed by the Oregon Department of Transportation (ODOT), run through as well. All this meant coordinating with multiple partners to manage the fire and to manage people after the fire was put out.

"Once the fire was controlled, we had two meetings a week with Oregon State Parks and ODOT," Stan continues. These meetings helped coordinate staff, tackle post-fire projects efficiently and appropriately, and ensure that public-facing messaging was consistent. But Stan and his colleagues were able to tap into other groups as well.

"Local trail groups stepped up, as did local volunteers," he told me. "More than 4,000 people signed up to volunteer across the different groups, so we had to figure out what to do with that energy and capacity."

The Gorge's steep, rocky walls, always prone to collapse, are especially unstable following fire, threatening trails and hikers.

OPPOSITE Several organizations are working to restore trails in the Gorge, including replacing infrastructure like this charred post that used to mark an overlook.

That meant yet more meetings to bring all of these groups together and craft a collective strategy. In effect, the fire catalyzed new partnerships and new approaches to dealing with recreation in the Gorge. Just like the local residents who came together to protect the Gorge forty years earlier, a new group of Gorge fans found themselves building alliances and proving that engaged, committed people can make a real difference.

Scattered trail groups, which often competed against each other for members and funding, set aside their provinciality and worked across the entire Gorge. The Washington Trails Association for example, focused on ensuring the trails on the Washington side of the Gorge could handle the increase in recreation stemming from the closure of the Oregon side. They also helped out on projects on the Oregon side as needed. The Forest Service and other groups even helped a new organization called Trailkeepers of Oregon get up and running.

Stan says, "Now, more than a year after the fire, we have a great set of partnerships in place that we didn't have prior to the fire. We're working more strategically and are generally able to get more done more efficiently. It's been a good thing. Already, we've had something like 300 work parties out on the forest."

Because the ecological damage wasn't that severe, and much of the fire burned in designated Wilderness where the Forest Service doesn't replant trees after fire as a general rule, the agency was able to spend much of the funding from Congress, the NFF, and other groups like Oregon's Kitchen Table (which raised nearly $150,000 through a crowd-funding campaign) on rehabilitating the recreational infrastructure that was damaged by the fire. This infrastructure, while seemingly simple, is expensive. Stan estimated that in Eagle Creek, where the fire started, it was going to cost at least $1 million just to replace the three bridges that the fire destroyed.

Trail-focused organizations weren't the only groups that came together. Residents and businesses of the town of Cascade Locks, which was largely evacuated during the fire, also forged new partnerships. One of the businesses that got a lot of press for its community efforts during the fire was Thunder Island Brewing, located in a small warehouse on the banks of the Columbia River, just off the Cascade Locks main drag.

Thunder Island bills itself as the "closest brewery to Multnomah Falls." The Pacific Crest Trail, the Historic Columbia River Highway State Trail, and the Cascade Locks International Mountain Bike Trail all run through town, so the brewery has always had a close connection to the area's natural amenities. They've long offered a free beer to trail crews who come in after a day of swinging pulaskis

A trail crew made up of volunteers from the Pacific Crest Trail Association work with hand tools to clear a massive log on the Mark O'Hatfield Wilderness in the Columbia River Gorge National Scenic Area. Chainsaws, though easier, aren't allowed in designated Wilderness Areas.

OPPOSITE
After the fire, charred tree trunks line trails in the Gorge, but the forest is bursting with fresh green life.

New signs mark one aspect of restoration progress in the Gorge.

and brushing trails. A Trail Magic board allows PCT thru-hikers to pay forward a beer by buying a coaster and pinning it to the wall. Other thru-hikers can redeem the coaster and get a beer. Owner David Lipps estimates they do about 800 coasters a year and the brewery throws in a bunch of free beer at the end of the hiking season as well for any hikers who may have missed the chance to grab one from the wall.

Tall and thin with a big, wild beard and a bald head, Lipps is proud of how the business community came together during the fire. "Everybody left their personal and business rivalries aside then, and much of it is still gone now," he told me as we nursed a Remember the Forest IPA at the brewery bar. "During the fire, Shelly at the Alehouse [another local restaurant] got special permission to come back to town to cook meals for the fire crews that were stationed here. She brought a lot of the local restaurants together in that effort. Dave's Killer Bread donated a bunch of food and Tillamook offered 4,000 pounds of cheese. In the end, I think it was a good thing for the town."

Thunder Island sponsored fundraisers for local residents impacted by the fire— as did other businesses, which Lipps is quick to point out. "Thunder Island got a lot of press, which was maybe a bit unfair since so many others were also helping out. In the end, I don't think the fire hurt us or the town."

Lipps's comments echo what Stan Hinatsu told me the day before. The fire was a dramatic and frightening event, but it wasn't devastating. Just as the fire had ecological benefits, it also had social benefits. Groups and businesses that might have competed for funding or patrons, came together not only during the fire itself, but also in the years after.

Back in Multnomah Falls Lodge, Stan and I are sipping the last of our coffee when Stan's radio crackles to life. A rock fall has cascaded onto a trail near the lodge. It's a direct result of the fire, and a constant challenge the agency has faced since the blaze was extinguished. Stan gulps the last of his coffee, apologizes for cutting our interview short, and heads out to investigate.

Back in my truck on the long drive home to Missoula, I wind along the serpentine blacktop of I-84 and steal glimpses of the forest high above me. In some places, grey trunks stand as skeletal reminders of the fire. But green is the dominant hue. I ponder a counterfactual as I drive. How might the Gorge be different if that sixteen-year-old hadn't carelessly tossed a firework out into dry tinder? Would the forest have burned eventually? Likely it would have; it certainly needed to, as do pretty much all forests. Would the passion of Portland's residents to heal the fire's damage have been as strong if lightning had started the blaze? I doubt it. It certainly seems plausible that this combination of cause and timing converged to leave the Gorge better off than it was and might have been.

Community often rises from calamity. For the Gorge and the millions of people who visit it, live within it, or love it from afar, the trauma of the Eagle Creek Fire is irrefutable. But so too are the partnerships and cooperation that are expanding in its aftermath. Like tender green shoots sprouting from charred remains, a new, energetic community of Gorge supporters is rising. Spring rains and sunshine will nurture the former. Collaboration and optimism will sustain the latter.

9

ALL THE PEOPLE'S LAND

Diversity and Representation in the Forest Service, National Forests, and the Great Outdoors

EARLY IN MY GRADUATE STUDIES, I took a class about national forest policy. It was one of my first and best introductions to this system of public lands, and I wish it were part of every Americans' coursework whether in high school, college, or beyond. In that class, I learned that natural resource conflicts are driven primarily by scarcity.

For those whose livelihoods depend on work in a local timber mill, such as those in northern California and southern Oregon during the spotted owl wars of the late 1990s, the scarcity in question was lumber from national forests. For wildlife advocates embroiled in the same issue, the scarcity was northern spotted owls. For those whose knees and ankles no longer support long hikes and heavy backpacks, that scarcity is motorized access to wild country and the opportunity to ride an ATV or snowmobile as far into the woods as they can. For those who have enough motors and mechanized equipment in their daily lives, the scarcity is quiet places to hike and find escape from the long arm of our mechanized society.

Scarcity drives the debate over mountain biking in capital W Wilderness. It drives the debate over issues as impactful as oil, gas, and hard rock mining, and it drives more mundane debates, like those over whitewater kayaking and wade angling. Talk to someone who feels that managed forests can better prevent massive and destructive wildfires and someone who feels that managed forests are just another term for industrial logging, and scarcity rears its head there too. For proponents of managed forests, the scarcity is funding for science-based management that can allow fires to burn less intensely and less destructively. For proponents of forests absent human intervention, the scarcity is a long-term view that ecosystems can, and should, manage themselves if we would just get the heck out of the way (it's also probably a scarcity of public policy that limits housing developments in the wildland urban interface, codes that require those developments to include fire-safe building practices, and insurance policies that don't externalize firefighting costs to such a huge degree). For every stakeholder who highlights one scarcity, another is ready to highlight its opposite.

It can be hard to wade through the arguments over whose version of scarcity is the most compelling. Are timber jobs worth more than the northern spotted owl? For some, they surely are. For others, the answer is a hard no. I don't profess to have an answer to these competing values and the infinite others that form the beating heart of debates over public lands management. I have my own perspective and my own experiences, but they are mine and shouldn't be peddled as *the solution*. At the least, the concept of scarcity as a driver of natural resource conflict is a valuable lens through which to view our national forests.

Scarcity also drove the editorial choices I made when conceiving of and writing this book—which topics I covered and which I didn't, which threads I followed and which I abandoned. In the end, for every story I included, I left out a hundred, a thousand, ten thousand others. There are only so many pages to a book after all. Our national forests are so diverse, so broad, and so enmeshed in our history as a nation that telling all the stories they contain is an impossible task. This chapter aims to speak, however briefly, to two of these stories in particular: the stories of Americans of color and of women.

A viewing platform provides a great view of a waterfall on the Chattahoochee-Oconee National Forest in Georgia.

IMAGES MATTER

Let me be 100 percent clear here. I am white. I am male. I grew up in a comfortably upper-middle-class family in Maine, and my first experience on a national forest was a family ski vacation in Utah. I've lived in Alaska and now in Missoula, Montana. None of these places are particularly diverse. Quite the opposite. I am not personally familiar with the prejudice that Americans of color have faced. I have no experience with the economic realities of living tantalizingly close to the wide-open spaces of a national forest yet having no way of accessing them. I'm also unable to fully comprehend the stifling hand of sexism and how it's impacted so many women.

Let me be clear about another matter. I don't know that I'm the best person to tell these stories, and I've wrestled with that lack of confidence. But I can use the bully pulpit that is this book to share some history and some context about these two topics and, though it may be filtered through my own perspective, some optimism for the future.

When I worked at the National Forest Foundation, we collaborated with the Forest Service on a public awareness campaign about national forests. As we unveiled the creative content supporting the campaign to Forest Service employees outside of the small cadre with whom we'd been working, we encountered a consistent critique: all of the images we had sourced included only white people.

It wasn't a choice we'd made intentionally, but we had struggled to find quality photos featuring members of BIPOC (Black, Indigenous, and People of Color) communities in an authentic way. Those photos we had found (and could legally obtain within the limited budget and time constraints under which we were working) looked like ads for designer clothes or other consumer products—so inauthentic, they didn't fit the context in which we were using them. Acknowledging our failure, we redoubled our efforts, reached out to partners, found additional funds to hire photographers, and made some progress. This was in 2015, so not that long ago.

There is no doubt that many Black Americans today don't feel welcome in the outdoors. Much of that feeling stems from the issue we faced at the NFF—few Black or brown faces are depicted in outdoor settings, whether in the ranks of public lands management agencies, in the pages of an REI or Cabela's catalogue, or in photos on websites for conservation organizations. (For decades, conservation groups have been majority white and male, both in terms of their members and their leadership. Many groups have worked diligently over the last decade to change this, but there is still much work to do.)

We are a visual society, and we take our cues from the images we see. If those images only show white people outdoors, it appears as if the outdoors is the exclusive province of white people. Of course, there are socio-economic, physical, and historic factors as well, but the lack of diversity in outdoors media plays a big role in the perception that only fit, affluent white people hike, rock climb, fish, bird watch, or camp.

In 2009, the comedy website *Funny or Die* produced a video that's garnered half-a-million views to date. It's called "Black Hiker." In it, a Black man played by Blair Underwood goes for a hike. (Judging from the scenery, he's outside Los Angeles, perhaps on the Angeles National Forest, though I don't know exactly.) Throughout his hike, white hikers on the trail regard him as an object of fascination, almost like an endangered species. First a white couple asks if he's lost. Then a young white man puts on an Obama t-shirt after noticing him. At the summit, where he's stopped to take in the view, two rangers pop breathless from the bushes. They ask if he's signed the guest book at the start of the trail—they want proof that a Black man was there. A moment and an indignant exchange later, the other white hikers he's seen also emerge from the bushes, awed and captivated by his presence. They all insist on a photograph, and he asks them if they've ever seen a Black hiker before. None of them have, and they, too, want proof.

Like many of the best parodies, this one is rooted in truth. Black hikers, Black rock climbers, Black paddlers, Black mountaineers, they're all rare in America's outdoor spaces. Much recent scholarship has focused on the myriad benefits that being outside in natural settings has on mental and physical health and statistics suggest that BIPOC communities are prevented from realizing those benefits. This dynamic has profound implications for the future of public lands management, and for the ecosystem services, wildlife, and other nonhuman values these lands provide. Scholars have noted that by 2044, America will be a majority-minority country. In short, there will be more BIPOC than whites. If the majority of Americans have little experience in outdoor spaces like national forests and national parks, they're less likely to agitate for funding of those spaces and engage in their management. For public lands management agencies already starved of funding, and for those conservation groups whose primary members are aging white males, this is a serious and potentially devastating problem.

In 2006, the Forest Service published a short, six-page document called "A Brief History of African Americans and Forests." It's available online and worth reading in full. Its authors cruise through the history of African Americans and forests generally and African Americans and the Forest Service more specifically.

According to the document, in the early colonial period, many enslaved Africans found safety in the forests of the south, even if it was hard won and difficult. Escaped slaves found refuge among Native American tribes that were able to maintain autonomy from white settlers (at least until those Indians were attacked or forcibly moved). Some formed their own all-Black communities in the thick, virtually impenetrable forests and swamps of the deep south.

Over time, however, forests became places where Black people were exploited, first through the forestry trade where they labored in brutal conditions making

turpentine and other products, and later, in the Jim Crow period when forests were places where Black people were murdered and lynched. Many Black people living today still associate forests with lynching, rape, and murder.

Yet, despite these oppressive histories, there are some examples of Black men working in national forests during the mid-twentieth century. During the Great Depression, all-Black CCC camps provided economic opportunity to roughly 200,000 Black men, but they were limited and segregated opportunities. An all-Black battalion of paratroopers in World War II, known as the 555th Parachute

CLOCKWISE FROM OPPOSITE TOP
Most CCC camps, like this one on the Chippewa National Forest, were segregated.

Women sorting seedlings on the Ashe Nursery, DeSoto National Forest, Mississippi, circa 1951.

The Triple Nickles, or 555th Parachute Infantry Battalion was an all-Black firefighting unit during WWII.

Infantry Battalion or the Triple Nickles pioneered wildland firefighting practices, serving as smokejumpers tasked with putting out blazes on national forests and other timberlands caused by fire bomb balloons the Japanese launched during the last months of the war.

Charles "Chip" Cartwright, joined the Forest Service in 1970 (after being discouraged from the forestry trade by his professors at Virginia Tech). He became the first Black district ranger in 1979, the first Black forest supervisor in 1988, and the first Black regional forester in 1994. The first Black female forest supervisor, Eleanor "Ellie" Towns, received her appointment as recently as 1998.

Today, Black people make up only 4 percent of Forest Service staff. It's hard to envision how urban Black youth might be inspired to pursue a career in public lands conservation when they have limited or no experience in outdoor spaces. Certainly, many professional conservationists attribute their chosen careers to formative experiences outdoors. That's the route I followed, as did many of my colleagues at both the NFF and other conservation organizations where I've worked.

While 4 percent is low, statistics show that there are more Black people working in the Forest Service than visiting the national forests. According to a paper in the May 2018 *Journal of Forestry*, "national forest visitors who identify as white

BELOW LEFT
Chip Cartwright was the Forest Service's first Black district ranger, first Black forest supervisor, and first Black regional forester.

BELOW RIGHT
Ellie Towns was the first Black female forest supervisor in the Forest Service.

comprise 94.6 percent of all visitors between 2010 and 2014, while visitors who identify as Hispanic or Latino comprise only 5.7 percent of visitors during this same time frame; visitors identifying as Black make up a mere 1.2 percent of total visitors to national forests across the continental United States."

The first Black person to climb Denali, North America's highest peak, was Charles Crenchaw. That was in 1964, the year the Civil Rights Act was passed, four years before Martin Luther King, Jr. was assassinated, and fifty-one years after the first all-white team of men reached the summit. It would be another forty-nine years before an all-Black team would climb the peak. That 2013 expedition was organized by the venerable National Outdoor Leadership School, better known by its acronym, NOLS, and by journalist and outdoor adventurer, James Edward Mills, who chronicled it in his book *The Adventure Gap: Changing the Face of the Outdoors*. An excellent documentary of the expedition called *An American Ascent* followed in 2016.

In the ensuing years, Mills has continued his advocacy for and exploration of Black Americans in outdoor spaces. I was fortunate to meet him through my work at the National Forest Foundation and to interview him in 2016. In that interview, we discussed Expedition Denali and the motivation behind it. He told me, "Our

This photo from 1972 shows early efforts at the Forest Service to diversify its workforce.

hope was to encourage an elevated discussion of who spends time in the outdoors and who doesn't. We wanted to create a modern adventure story that depicted people of color as central characters and hopefully inspire minority youth to seek out an exciting outdoor experience of their own."

And how did Mills feel the outdoor community reacted to the book, the film, and the expedition in general?

I think the outdoor community as a whole embraced Expedition Denali. Several organizations have been very helpful and supportive in our efforts to bring the message of diversity to a broad audience. But to be honest, I was disappointed by some of the comments I received in a few of the articles that I and others have posted about the project. People who identify themselves as outdoor enthusiasts have objected to proactively introducing people of color to nature. They claim that we're bringing controversy into an environment where none exists—as if outdoor recreation is above the complicated issues of racial bias, privilege, or discrimination. Our documentary of the climb, *An American Ascent*, was rejected by two of the most prominent outdoor-facing film festivals despite having won several awards at other events and being screened at the White House. So, despite our best efforts to connect with the outdoor community, we still seem to have fallen a bit short.

In 2013, National Geographic magazine published an article by Mills highlighting the then-upcoming Expedition Denali. The post quotes one of the female members of the team, Erica Wynn, who says, "When you think about the story that mountaineering has been, it's been predominantly white male. If a little Black girl were to look into mountaineering and hear that single story, she would probably say 'I don't have much of a place there, or the odds are against me.' I hope that Expedition Denali and being a part of this helps to change that story."

In that same article, Mills writes, "It's not a question of whether or not African Americans can climb high mountains. What matters is as a group we tend not to . . . Without any deliberate effort to prevent Blacks and other minorities from becoming involved in the sport, the number of non-white participants is conspicuously low. The organizers of Expedition Denali merely hope to change that by introducing a new narrative into the mix and perhaps redefine what it means to be a climber."

In the last decade, a number of organizations have emerged to redress the lack of BIPOC participation and representation in the outdoors. Diversify Outdoors is one of them. It's a coalition of social media influencers, bloggers, athletes, activists, and entrepreneurs who "share the goal of promoting diversity in outdoor spaces where BIPOC, LGBTQ+, and other diverse identities have historically been marginalized and silenced." Their roster of influencers includes Ambreen Tariq, founder of @BrownPeopleCamping; Tyhree Moore, one of the Expedition Denali team members; Michael A. Estrada, founder of Brown Environmentalist; Len Necefer, founder of Natives Outdoors; Pinar Ateş Sinopoulos-Lloyd, cofounder of Queer Nature; Summer Michaud-Skog, founder of Fat Girls Hiking; and more than a half-dozen other talented leaders focused on specific groups of people who have been historically absent in outdoor media.

That this particular coalition operates largely in the digital sphere is telling (some member groups do organize outdoor meetups and host events targeted at their specific demographic, but the coalition itself is primarily digital). It's also purposeful, as the language on its website demonstrates by not only stating so explicitly but also setting this goal in bold face.

> **We created the Diversify Outdoors coalition to better connect those leading the movement through social media** and, by providing a united front platform, we aim to grow our community and provide resources to others seeking information, allyship, and collaboration opportunities. . . .
>
> **The one thing we all have in common: we are leaders in social media advocacy of promoting diversity and equity in the outdoors.** Collectively, we reach over **154K** followers through Instagram alone.

The mission of Diversify Outdoors is similar to that of Expedition Denali: better representation of minorities in outdoor media. The hope is that improved representation leads to more participation, which leads to even better representation and even more participation. But their mission isn't just about getting more BIPOC in outdoor magazines or catalogues and by extension on trails or climbing routes; it's also focused on building a broader constituency of Americans who care about public lands and are engaged in their management. Diversify Outdoors isn't just for BIPOC or LGTBQ+ communities, it's for anyone who cares about these landscapes and about building an engaged constituency of Americans regardless of skin color, body shape, socio-economic status, or sexual orientation.

These groups and others like them aren't necessarily focused on getting their constituents onto national forests specifically—Denali, is of course, in Denali National Park—but given that seven in ten Americans live within a two-hour drive of a national forest, that forests are often less expensive than national or state parks, and that they tend to offer a wider variety of recreational experiences, they certainly play a big role in providing outdoor opportunities to minority communities.

To that end, nonprofits like Big City Mountaineers raise funds to take youth from disinvested communities onto national forests (and national parks and state lands) for everything from day hikes to week-long backpacking trips. The group, based in Golden, Colorado, operates across the country and provides free gear, transportation, food, and professional guides for its participants. Big City Mountaineers was founded in 1990 and has evolved over the decades. In 2020, the organization initiated an internal effort to update its mission statement and, more broadly, the language it uses on its website and in its promotional material. Gone are terms like *at-risk* and *inner-city* and the implications they carry. While some may dismiss this as politically correct wokeness run amuck, language, like imagery, plays an important role in how people see themselves.

Groups like Big City Mountaineers or the National Forest Foundation, which has several successful efforts that bring minority youth onto national forests for paid summer-internship and youth-corps programs, work directly with the Forest Service to implement and manage these initiatives. But the agency has programs of its own as well.

Smokey Bear greets young kids on Alabama's Tuskegee National Forest; outreach events like this Festival of the Forest help the Forest Service bring diverse users onto national forests.

The Freedom Trails Initiative focuses on how the Wayne, the Hoosier, and Shawnee National Forests in Ohio, Indiana, and Illinois played important roles in the Underground Railroad long before they became national forests. Forest Service archeologists are cataloguing and preserving historic sites and sharing their discoveries with the public. Part of this innovative program included a small grant to Tennessee State University for Black students to spend their summer on the forests, conducting research through a paid-internship program. (That grant is part of a larger USDA initiative called the 1890 National Scholars Program that awards scholarships to students so they can attend one of the nineteen Historically Black Land-Grant Universities, of which Tennessee State is a member.) This opportunity was highlighted in a press release when the program won a USDA Honor Award in 2001. "There are currently only about twenty African American archaeologists [in the Forest Service]. We saw this research as an opportunity to get college students excited about their heritage and perhaps interested in a career in archaeology."

National efforts like Every Kid Outdoors provide free entrance to all federally managed public lands whether national forests, national parks, or wildlife refuges for every fourth-grader in the country (the free entrance extends to all children under sixteen who are part of a fourth-grader's group and to three accompanying adults, effectively an entire family). Of course, Every Kid Outdoors doesn't magically erase other, very real barriers like transportation, lack of gear, and the legitimate fear many have of outdoor spaces, but it's a step in the right direction.

A MAN'S WORLD

Black and brown Americans aren't the only groups underrepresented in the Forest Service. Today, the agency is led by Vicki Christiansen, the second woman to act as chief. The first was Abigail Kimbell who was appointed under George W. Bush's administration and led the agency from February 2007 until July 2009. The National Park Service hasn't fared any better (Bush's appointee Fran P. Mainella was the first woman to serve as director in 2001), as of 2016, only 37 percent of the NPS workforce was female.

The hard truth is that both agencies have a long history of misogyny and sexual discrimination.

Chief Christiansen's appointment followed allegations of sexual misconduct involving her predecessor, Tony Tooke. In 2018, shortly after his appointment as chief, a *PBS NewsHour* investigation surfaced the allegations against Tooke, along with additional allegations of broader sexual misconduct, harassment, assault, and retaliation leveled against the agency by thirty-four current and former Forest Service employees. Tooke himself was accused of inappropriate touching and affairs with subordinates and elected to resign days after the allegations came to light. The investigation revealed that the Forest Service had received more than 1,000 reports of harassment between 2016 and 2018, of which it investigated 632 cases and found misconduct in 150. This is the context in which Christiansen had to step into her leadership role. The agency has updated its anti-harassment policy, but it remains to be seen how effective their strategy will be against the long-standing challenges women have faced in the Forest Service.

Chief Vicki Christiansen is the second female chief in the agency.

Women have long been part of the Forest Service, but as in many other companies and industries through the first half of the twentieth century, their roles were largely administrative and secretarial. As with all things, there were exceptions. For example, Eloise Gerry worked in the Forest Products Laboratory as a research scientist in the 1910s. Hallie M. Daggett became the agency's first female fire lookout in 1913, when she went to work on the Klamath National Forest in California. World War II provided women an opportunity to do the work traditionally done by men, but those opportunities evaporated after the war ended and the men returned home. For the most part, during the first half of the twentieth century, women worked in the office. Field work like rangering, firefighting, riding the range, delineating logging units, and building recreational infrastructure was reserved for men.

The Civil Rights Act of 1964, the National Environmental Policy Act of 1970, and the National Forest Management Act of 1976 forced the agency to change, though the change was slow. The Civil Rights Act required employers to provide equal employment opportunities regardless of race or sex. The other two acts required rigorous environmental review of management activities that might have "a substantial impact" on the environment and imposed broad science-based management on the forests in general. To implement those requirements the Forest Service had to

hire a large set of *ologists*—biologists, ecologists, hydrologists, geologists, archeologists, sociologists, etc. Many women gained employment through these twin pieces of legislation, but the agency remained largely a men's club because men held the leadership positions.

James G. Lewis shined a light on the Forest Service's history of sexism and sexual harassment in his article "New Faces, Same Old Values: A History of Discrimination in the Forest Service," published in *Forest History Today*. He notes that "as late as 1976, women held 84 percent of clerical jobs in the agency and 15 percent of administrative and technical jobs, but fewer than 2 percent of full-time professional jobs."

In 1973, Gene Bernardi, a sociologist at the agency's experiment station in Berkley, California, applied for a new position, but, as Lewis explains, the hiring supervisor decided to wait for a male applicant. "Bernardi sued on the basis of sexual discrimination under Title VII of the Civil Rights Act of 1964, as amended by the Equal Employment Opportunity Act of 1972, and won compensation but not the job. She and several other women then filed a class-action lawsuit over the hiring and promotion of women and minorities in Region 5, which covers all of California."

LEFT Hallie M. Daggett was the first female fire lookout in the Forest Service when she began on the Klamath National Forest in 1913.

RIGHT Ms. Daggett's pioneering work notwithstanding, staffing fire lookout towers was a job that WWII made more available to women—until the men returned from war.

During the first several decades of the Forest Service, women performed mostly clerical roles in the agency.

Six years later, in 1979, the lawsuit resulted in a consent decree (approved another two years later by the district court) which, according to Lewis, instructed the Forest Service to "bring its California workforce into line with that of the state's civilian labor force by having women in more than 43 percent of the jobs in each job series and grade. The Forest Service agreed to monitor progress and enforce the rulings." But even that didn't go quite as planned.

For one, the Reagan Administration balked, arguing that the decree was, in essence, a hiring quota system. That delayed Forest Service implementation, and so the decree was extended through 1991. Additionally, once the improved hiring practices were implemented, unintended consequences followed. As Lewis puts it:

> The rapid promotions of women, however, proved a powerfully divisive issue among employees. Many felt that the consent decree put "accelerated" women in an unfair position, forcing them to succeed or be judged as failures. Some did succeed, to the benefit of the Forest Service, but others did not, and both they and the agency lost. The shift away from the concept of meritocracy in hiring and promotion practices generated resentment within a few years and created a difficult work atmosphere in Region 5.

One of my favorite tasks at the National Forest Foundation was publishing the organization's semiannual magazine, *Your National Forests*. For the Summer/Fall 2017 issue, we focused on fire on our national forests. We explored the topic in several ways, but the issue's main feature was a story that Dayle Wallien wrote about female firefighters. Dayle is the conservation partnerships director and raises much-needed funds for the NFF, but her past employment included a five-year stint working for the Forest Service as a wildland firefighter. During this time, she wasn't just on a ground-based hotshot crew (an impressive enough entry for a resume, as hotshot crews work very hard in dangerous conditions)—she rappelled into wildfires from a helicopter.

Rappellers and their smokejumper counterparts are elite firefighters who rappel or parachute into fires from helicopters and airplanes respectively. They must pass rigorous physical standards to ensure they can withstand the demands of the job.

Dayle's article balanced the basics of wildland firefighting (what the different types of firefighters do, the unique terminology used by firefighters, the equipment they use) with personal stories from four female firefighters in the Forest Service.

The story (which is available online if you would like to read it in its entirety) was fun to produce. But the reaction of our readers was the best part. In my time working on the magazine, we rarely received reader feedback (most often, we were alerted to small mistakes or typos), but that issue struck a chord. One reader emailed how proud she was when she showed the cover, which featured a female firefighter, face blackened from charcoal, to her young daughter. That cover photo (and other photos in the story, all of which featured women) provided visual proof that women could do anything—including fight wildland fires. She thanked us for helping to show her daughter that her world was open. It was, perhaps, a small thing—the NFF's magazine has a limited reach and it was one reader—but to me and my colleagues, it was gratifying and humbling.

Of all the jobs in the Forest Service, firefighting, and smokejumping particularly, was historically seen as men's work. It's crazy dangerous and requires peak physical conditioning. The McCall Smokejumper Base in Idaho details training requirements on their website—candidates have to be able to do seven pull-ups, forty-five sit-ups, twenty-five push-ups, and then run 1.5 miles in less than eleven minutes (a 7:20 mile), and they have do to all those things with only five minutes break between exercises. And if that's not hard enough, they also have to hump a pack that weighs 110 pounds for 3 miles in ninety minutes or less. I'm not sure if you've ever hoisted a 110-pound pack, but it's a serious amount of weight.

These requirements aren't meant to discriminate, they're meant to mirror the rigors of the job. After the smokejumper launches him or herself from the airplane, a pack of gear that weighs at least 100 pounds follows. Once smokejumpers have done their work, they have to haul that gear to the nearest road, trail, or helispot. The terrain (unlike the test, which is done on flat ground) is often rugged, steep and thick with vegetation. It is also, potentially, on fire. And the pickup location is often a lot more than three miles from where the smokejumper landed.

The agency also imposes height and weight standards—smokejumpers have to be at least sixty inches tall (without shoes) but not more than seventy-seven inches, and they must weigh at least 120 pounds but not more than 210 pounds (without clothes). Hearing and vision standards are also imposed. In short, becoming a smokejumper ain't easy. But it isn't for men only.

In 1979, Deanne Shulman, who had been a seasonal firefighter since 1974 and who had worked on a hotshot crew and a helitack unit (positions that require more training and more physical capabilities than other, basic firefighting duties), applied for and was accepted into the McCall smokejumpers program. When she arrived, the diminutive, but tough, Shulman was told she didn't meet the weight requirement. She packed her bags and readied to leave.

But others in the program told her the agency had waived those requirements for certain men. According to Lewis: "Allen 'Mouse' Owens, a four-foot-eleven, 120-pound Vietnam War vet who had received congressional waivers on the height and weight requirements and had been with the smokejumpers for ten years, contacted her and encouraged her to fight for her rights."

Shulman eventually filed an Equal Employment Opportunity complaint, not because she felt the standards were unfair themselves, but because if others had received height or weight waivers, she felt that she should too. Faced with media scrutiny, the agency relented and offered her another chance, provided she met the weight requirement, which she did when she next reported to the McCall training station. In 1981, Shulman became the first female smokejumper in the United States.

In 1979, as Shulman was battling the entrenched male smokejumper culture, the Forest Service appointed its first female district ranger, Wendy Milner Herrett. A landscape architect by training (she worked as a landscape architect at the Region 6 headquarters in Portland, Oregon), Herrett wasn't just female, she also wasn't an engineer or a trained forester, bucking agency precedent on two fronts.

As women were struggling to climb the Forest Service's leadership ladders, the agency was undergoing a shift in how it approached forest management. Driven in part by the National Environmental Policy Act and the National Forest Management

Act, but also by the broader environmental movement and by on-the-ground realities, the agency was shifting from focusing on timber management as its primary function to a more holistic management ethos that focused on whole ecosystems. It was also engaging with the public far more frequently than ever before, largely because NEPA and NFMA required it to. As Lewis explains, the combination created an opportunity for more women in leadership roles.

Wendy Milner Herrett was the first female district ranger in the Forest Service.

> Professional women entering the Forest Service brought with them a different perspective on the relationship between humans and the environment. A survey conducted in 1990 found that "women in the Forest Service exhibit greater general environmental concern than men" and in particular were more in favor of reducing timber-harvest levels on national forests and designating additional wilderness areas. Another survey found that nontraditional professionals (regardless of gender) held beliefs similar to those of the women in the first survey. Subsequent studies have shown little or no difference in attitudes concerning general environmental issues between men and women, but women exhibited "significantly more concern than men about local or community-based environmental problems." Taken together, the studies suggest that the increase in the number of nontraditional employees had a measurable impact on the attitudes of other employees and was changing the agency's management focus. Forest Service employees' values are now more closely aligned with those of the general public they serve.

To be fair, not all efforts by the Forest Service to diversify its workforce (either in terms of gender or race) were forced through lawsuits. And many men throughout the agency supported their female colleagues' efforts for more equal treatment. No organization is a monolith. And while it still struggles with sexual harassment complaints and other less-intense but still-unfortunate examples of misogyny, the Forest Service is certainly a different organization than it was twenty or thirty years ago.

SMALL ACTION, BIG CHANGE

In May 2015, the Deputy Chief of National Forest System, Leslie Weldon (a Black woman serving in one of the most senior leadership positions in the agency), gave a speech to the Federal Asian Pacific American Council at its 30th Annual National Leadership Training Program meeting. In the speech, Weldon focused on the Forest Service's pursuit of gender and racial equity in its workforce. While she acknowledged the agency's history, she also highlighted the progress it's made.

Members of the Forest Service Girl's Club pose below a sign near a tree plantation they helped establish on the Chequamegon-Nicolet National Forest in Wisconsin circa 1939.

At one time in our history, especially in our leadership, the Forest Service was mainly an elite cadre of white men, almost all of them professional foresters. Since they came from identical backgrounds, they all thought in the same way, so their decisions mirrored each other. It made for a very cohesive organization, and it worked very well for many decades.

But in the long run it made for a weak organization, because when conditions changed, we were too stuck in our ways, and we refused to change ourselves. And that's because we were missing out on the ideas and perspectives of the vast majority of our fellow citizens—citizens whose backgrounds were different—citizens such as women, such as minorities, such as folks whose training was in something other than forestry.

Today, I am happy to say that we are a very different kind of organization. If you just look at our leadership alone—our Senior Executive Service—you can see a tremendous difference. More than thirty-five percent of our top leadership is made up of racial minorities. Almost sixty percent of our top leadership reflects either gender or racial diversity. And we have folks from all kinds of professional backgrounds throughout our organization now. We have engineers, wildlife biologists, social scientists, public affairs specialists, you name it.

In the last thirty to forty years, we have made great strides in building diversity into our workforce as a whole. . . . But we do fall short in some professions for both women and minorities. We are working hard to make up the shortfall.

Chip Cartwright, Ellie Townes, Deane Shulman, Wendy Milner Herrett, and Abigail Kimbell are remembered as firsts. But that remembrance is built on foundations laid by others. The contributions of the women and Black Americans who preceded the big firsts can't be ignored, even if traditional history often leaves them out. Also important are the allies who challenged the white-male-dominated norms that pervaded America during the twentieth century and the first decades of the twenty-first. Unfortunately, as the Black Lives Matter and Me Too movements have shown, America still has a lot of work to do in its move toward a more equitable society.

When James Edward Mills first started promoting Expedition Denali, he encountered pushback from some members of the outdoor community. They argued that the project's focus on an all-Black team was divisive and unnecessary. The outdoors isn't racist, they claimed. Why introduce race into it? Certainly, many, if not most, of those commentators probably don't consider themselves to be racist, but it's also likely many are white males with plenty of means and examples to follow in enjoying public lands. Their comments reveal the challenges that journalists like Mills and groups like Diversify Outdoors face. In addition to fighting active racism, which does rear its ugly head in the outdoors (recall the 2020 example of a white woman playing victim and trying to incite police violence toward a Black man birding in New York's

Central Park, after he had the gall to ask that she follow the rules and leash her dog), they also have to battle the claim that the outdoors welcomes everyone even as 95 percent of the people who actually use the outdoors are white.

Images on social media or a film about an all-Black climbing team may seem like small things to those of us accustomed to seeing people who look like us in the outdoors. To minorities and especially minority women, the growing presence of Black and brown faces in outdoor media represents something important, allowing them to picture themselves in spaces white men have dominated for generations. This intentionality is manifesting in other ways as well. There's a growing movement, spearheaded by conservation nonprofits and environmental justice organizations, to recognize the indigenous cultures that once lived on our public lands by naming them in blog posts, photo captions, event speeches, and literature. These relatively simple acts are powerful, as they force us to acknowledge, even briefly, that the lands we enjoy are part of a history that extends far beyond the National Forest System.

Rarely does one single action cause irreparable harm to the environment. More often, a series of actions whittles away at the integrity and resilience of our natural world—death by a thousand cuts. The converse is also true. No single action—a lawsuit, a social media movement, an all-Black adventure film, or a magazine cover—can heal our degraded landscapes or our fractured society. Just as one errant plastic bag does not make the Great Pacific Garbage Patch, one image of a soot-covered woman on the cover of a small nonprofit's magazine does not erase decades of sexism and misogyny. Yet, one less bag floating in the ocean might save a young sea turtle, and one magazine cover might give a girl the confidence to follow whichever path she desires. So we must do many things, even if each feels small and insignificant, because we cannot know the difference that one thing might make. As a diverse group of Americans build physical and emotional connections to the outdoors, they grow the ranks of those who care about our forests and parks—and more people who give a damn is precisely what our outdoor spaces need.

Our national forests don't care if we live in a city, a suburb, or a rural town of 2,000 people. They most certainly don't care what color skin we have or what gender we are. Wind and rain buffet us equally and bright sunshine warms us all regardless of whom we love or what size pants we wear. In the end, it will take all of us who care about these places—white, Black, brown, male and female, queer and straight, fat and thin, young and old—to see past our small differences and focus on the big commonality we share: our love of the outdoors.

There is no doubt in my mind that the forces who would like to privatize our public lands, profit from them, and externalize the costs of that profit back onto

society would like to see us fractured, divided, and focused elsewhere so they can hatch their dark conspiracies while we dither. Their goals will be much more easily realized if we're arguing about who belongs and who doesn't instead of fighting tooth and nail to ensure a sustainable future for our public lands. If we fail to unify because we feel threatened by "others," we've already lost. If we fail to grow our ranks because we don't think it's important for a young Black girl to see someone who looks like her in an Instagram post, or, because we dismiss or minimize the fear many people have of outdoor spaces, we've already lost. If we don't participate in the stewardship of these lands and don't engage in their management because it's something only white people do, we've already lost.

Apathy is the true enemy of our public lands. When we hobble our capacity to fight by failing to show all Americans that they have a rightful place in that fight, we diminish our collective power. If we are united, apathy will lose.

Our national forests need as many champions as they can get.

AFTERWORD

THE PONDEROSA PINE, THAT CLASSIC western tree with its rust-tinged bark and its sweet, vanilla scent, can live for 500 years or more. Their eastern cousins, the longleaf pine that once grew throughout the Southeast, live for 300 years. Giant sequoias are still youngsters when longleafs and ponderosas finally fall to the ground from old age—they can live for 3,000 years. And yet even sequoias are eclipsed by the gnarled, twisted trunks of the bristlecone pine, the oldest of which has lived on the Inyo National Forest for almost 5,000 years (though the Forest Service won't share exactly which bristlecone it is because they've learned that some humans can't be trusted with such magnificent secrets). Even relatively short-lived deciduous trees, like oaks and maples, whose gorgeously intricate leaves burst with color every fall before dropping to the ground ahead of long, white winters, will grow for 150 years or more when conditions allow.

The Forest Service, and by direct extension, the National Forest System, was 115 years old when I wrote this book.

I find this fascinating. An agency whose existence is just a blip in a sequoia's lifespan has been tasked with managing the sequoia's fate. And the ponderosa, the longleaf, the maple, the oak, and thousands of other species. That's no small task.

Humans have difficulty understanding time. The average American life (in 2020 anyway) lasts 78.93 years, roughly the same as a black willow, one of the shortest-lived trees around. Those of us who've only lived a few decades are even less capable of comprehending time than those who've lived into their seventies or eighties. We struggle to process that women have only been able to vote for 100 years. On the one hand, 100 years seems like ancient history, on the other, there are people alive today who were alive when the right was finally realized. The thick woods that cover New Hampshire, North Carolina, and many parts of the West today, aren't much older than women's suffrage, though to most of us walking through them, they feel ancient and eternal. Even those old-growth groves spared the sawyer's sharpened crosscut aren't that old, despite their name. Both the place I grew up, Maine, and the city in which I live, Missoula, were covered by massive sheets of ice just 20,000 years ago, a fraction of a fraction of a pixel in the 4K display that is geological time.

The stories in this book mostly cover the last 200 years of American history, though some drift farther back into our collective past. But it's not a history book, and the stories that did make their way onto these pages are intended to provide context and perspective through which we can better understand current attitudes, events, and adventures.

Of course, I've included stories about the Forest Service (lots of them)—some positive, others negative. But in the story of the NFS, the Forest Service is only one actor, a principal one to be sure, but just one in the sweeping saga that has shaped these landscapes. The government and its departments (of agriculture, of interior) is another. And the citizens of the United States are yet another, both as individuals and as groups coalesced around a specific cause, be it wildlife, the timber industry, or motorized recreation.

ABOVE In autumn, western larch turn golden yellow and light up Montana's Lolo National Forest.

PREVIOUS The fissures in a stately ponderosa pine's bark grow deeper with age.

Our national forests were created from lands our country effectively stole from people who have lived here for millennia. But they have also protected those same lands from the ravages of unfettered private enterprise concerned only with profit. Some have been subjected to poor management at the hands of those tasked with ensuring their long-term viability. But others comprise the most protected landscapes in the world, places that helped generate the very concept of wilderness and were the first examples of that concept put into real-world practice. They contain ski areas where it costs hundreds of dollars a day for the right to ride the lifts, and also areas where families can camp, picnic, hike, or fish for free any day of the year.

These contradictions are at the heart of our national forests and of the agency that manages them, an agency now firmly rooted in managing entire ecosystems, not just specific stands of timber. Tasked with a mandate to manage a finite set of lands

What do we want our national forests to become in the future? Their fate is up to us.

for an infinite set of priorities, the Forest Service has made (and continues to make) mistakes to be sure, but those mistakes should be seen in the context of the task with which it has been charged. I hope this book has provided some of that context.

If, in some small way, this book has helped you understand the complexity of these lands and the pure messiness of managing such an unruly set of landscapes for a conflicting set of objectives, then I consider it a success.

The United States is a fortunate nation. We have national parks and wildlife refuges and have managed to protect the scenic and biotic resources that they contain. We have vast tracts of private land and a robust set of laws that allow that land to be used pretty much however its owners decide. We have places where motors aren't allowed and places where revving engines and the smell of exhaust are the main draws. We have some of the world's most rigorous environmental laws, and we still produce more oil and gas than any other nation. We have almost limitless personal freedom and also families and communities for whom we sacrifice that freedom. We have a fraught, complicated history with which we're still wrestling, and yet we possess an optimism for the future that remains unrivaled. And we have our national forests, where these contradictions, triumphs, tragedies, and histories play out.

Our national forests are a mirror of our society. And just like a mirror, they reflect our best and our worst as they challenge our perceptions and the very way we see ourselves. They are the lands where we both celebrate and wrestle with the past, and through which we debate how we should realize our future. Just as we peer at our reflection and see our younger selves, ripe with potential and promise, we also see the years gone by, rendered in scars and blemishes that life has inflicted. Yet despite those imperfections, we carry on, drawing on our past to help us manage our finite lives for an infinite set of priorities.

If we fail to act as agents of our lives, or of our forests, they will be managed by external forces—to our benefit or our peril. The stories in this book reflect that agency. In the mid-1990s, a group of citizens decided that they could, and should, turn an abandoned military-industrial complex into a tallgrass prairie. Farther west, a motley assortment of skiers and snowshoers self-organized so they could spend their weekends searching for wolverines. Outside Portland, Oregon, groups have come together to heal a landscape they love—their work is a metaphorical phoenix rising from the literal ashes of a massive wildfire. Across the country, people who have historically been absent in the outdoors are showing that they have a place in our forests and in the media that has spent decades shunning them. The very genesis of our eastern forests proves that one person with vision and commitment can affect real progress. Sometimes, such agency takes a long time to bear fruit, as evidenced by the long-running saga of the Badger-Two Medicine. But even here, recent progress highlights how sustained effort and patience can overcome centuries of marginalization.

The future of our forests is yet unwritten. What they will become, and how, is up to us.

ACKNOWLEDGMENTS

I AM DEEPLY GRATEFUL FOR AND HUMBLED BY the help I received on this project. Thanks to the team at Timber Press, especially to Will McKay, who helped shape the book and reviewed early drafts, and to Jacoba Lawson, whose great edits made the book so much better. Thanks to all my former NFF colleagues who helped answer questions, hosted me when I visited their backyard forests, and who are all genuinely great people. I'm likewise grateful to the Forest Service employees with whom I spoke and who helped in countless other ways. Thanks to all the photographers whose images help bring these special places to life; especially to Brian Chaszar, who not only provided many of the best images but also helped me source others that appear throughout the book. Special thanks to my dear friend Andy Mitchell, who took time from his busy life to read the entire manuscript and offer suggestions that greatly improved the final product. Thanks also to the scholars, authors, writers, and historians whose work helped me navigate the captivating history, policy, and modern-day controversies that make our national forests so interesting. And, finally, thanks to everyone else who helped but who I failed to mention; you know who you are!

NOTES

INTRODUCTION

"Where conflicting interests must be reconciled . . ." —Pages 16–17, The Greatest Good: A Forest Service Centennial Film (website), US Forest Service, "Pinchot and Utilitarianism," Accessed January 2021. www.fs.fed.us/greatestgood/press/mediakit/facts/pinchot.shtml

"were known to either use National Forest/Grassland habitats" and "Some 251 other species are candidates for listing . . ." —Page 27, US Forest Service, "TES-Program-Summary," February 2012. www.fs.fed.us/biology/tes/index.html

CHAPTER ONE

"As private lumber interests ravaged Michigan's forests . . ." —Page 39, Joseph J. Jones, "Transforming the Cutover: The Establishment of National Forests in Northern Michigan," Forest History Today, Spring/Fall 2011. https://foresthistory.org/wp-content/uploads/2016/12/2011_National_Forests_Michigan_transforming-cutover.pdf

"practically all of it, whether cut or not . . ." —Page 40, Susan L. Yarnell, General Technical Report SRS-18, "The Southern Appalachians: A History of the Landscape," US Forest Service, May 1998. www.srs.fs.usda.gov/pubs/gtr/gtr_srs018.pdf

"The President of the United States may, from time to time" —Page 43, Gerald W. Williams, The USDA Forest Service—The First Century, USDA Forest Service Office of Communication, Revised 2005. www.fs.usda.gov/sites/default/files/media/2015/06/The_USDA_Forest_Service_TheFirstCentury.pdf

"In the West there was an articulation . . ." —Page 44, Kevin Dennehy, "First Forester: The Enduring Conservation Legacy of Gifford Pinchot," Yale School of the Environment, September 2016. https://environment.yale.edu/news/article/first-forester-the-conservation-legacy-of-gifford-pinchot/

"more than 40 bills to create eastern national forests were introduced between 1901 and 1911." —Page 47, Forest History Society (website), "Passing the Weeks Act," Accessed January 2021. https://foresthistory.org/research-explore/us-forest-service-history/policy-and-law/the-weeks-act/passing-weeks-act/

"deplorable in the extreme." —Page 50, Harold T. Pinkett, "Gifford Pinchot at Biltmore," The North Carolina Historical Review, Vol. 34, No. 3, July 1957.

Page 53, Tom Tidwell, "Forests and America's Water Security," speech at American Water Resources Association. Hartford, CT. 27 June 2013. www.fs.usda.gov/speeches/forests-and-americas-water-security

"The agency estimates that 75 percent . . ." —Page 53, US Forest Service (website), "Water Facts," Accessed January 2021. www.fs.usda.gov/managing-land/national-forests-grasslands/water-facts

"180 million people in 68,000 communities who get their water from forested lands . . ." —Page 58, US Forest Service (website), "Water Facts," Accessed January 2021. www.fs.usda.gov/managing-land/national-forests-grasslands/water-facts

"Forests to Faucets 2.0" —Page 58, US Forest Service (website), "Forests to Faucets," Accessed January 2021. www.fs.fed.us/ecosystemservices/FS_Efforts/forests2faucets.shtml

"In 2018, the Forest Service budget . . ." —Page 59, US Forest Service, "FY 2019 Budget Justification." www.fs.usda.gov/sites/default/files/usfs-fy19-budget-justification.pdf

"In perhaps its most important role, . . ." —Page 61, US Forest Service (website), "Forests to Faucets," Accessed January 2021. www.fs.fed.us/ecosystemservices/FS_Efforts/forests2faucets.shtml

CHAPTER TWO

"The art and science of controlling the establishment . . ." —Page 64, US Forest Service (website), "Silviculture," Accessed January 2021. www.fs.fed.us/forestmanagement/vegetation-management/silviculture/index.shtml

"The Organic Administration Act of 1897 explicitly . . ." —Pages 64–65, US Forest Service (website), "Reforestation Overview," Accessed January 2021. www.fs.fed.us/restoration/reforestation/overview.shtml

Origins of tree planting program in Nebraska, —Pages 66–67, Thomas R. Walsh, "The American Green of Charles Bessey," *Nebraska History*, Vol. 53 (1972): 35–57.

Origins of tree planting program in Nebraska, —Pages <XXX>, John F. Freeman, *High Plains Horticulture: A History*, University of Colorado Press, November 2008.

CHAPTER THREE

"I started with surprise and delight . . ." —Pages 85–87, Eliza R. Steele, *A Summer Journey in the West*, John S. Taylor and Co. (New York), 1841.

"Today, only 2,500 acres of virgin tallgrass . . ." —Page 89, Openlands (website), "Have You Discovered Midewin National Tallgrass Prarie?" Accessed January 2021. www.openlands.org/2016/12/14have-you-discovered-midewin-national-tallgrass-prairie/

Midewin remediation statistics —Page 91, Federal Facilities Restoration and Reuse Office (pdf), "Collaboration Leads to Early Cleanup Completion: Joliet Army Ammunition Plant," April 2008. www.epa.gov/sites/production/files/documents/success_story_joliet_0.pdf

"Midewin (pronounced mi-DAY-win) . . ." —Pages 92–93, US Forest Service (website), Midewin National Tallgrass Prarie, "Where did Midewin's name come from?" Accessed January 2021. www.fs.usda.gov/detail/midewin/learning/history-culture/?cid=stelprdb5155329

"Midewin was crisscrossed by nearly 200 miles of road . . ." —Page 94, US Forest Service (website), "The Joliet Army Ammunition Plant," Accessed January 2019. www.fs.usda.gov/detail/midewin/learning/history-culture/?cid=stelprdb5155180

"First, the federal government planned to purchase..." —Page 98, Hurt, R. Douglas. "The National Grasslands: Origin and Development in the Dust Bowl." *Agricultural History* 59, no. 2 (1985): 246-59.

"Our national grasslands remain beautiful examples . . ." and "provide tremendous benefits including pollination of native and agricultural plants . . ." —Pages 100–101, US Forest Service Press Office, News Release, "US Forest Service Celebrates 75 Years of National Grasslands," 18 June 2012. www.fs.usda.gov/news/releases/us-forest-service-celebrates-75-years-national-grasslands

"According to a grim timeline compiled by the US Fish and Wildlife Service . . ." —Page 102, US Fish and Wildlife Service (website), National Bison range Wildlife Refuge Complex, "Time Line of the American Bison," Accessed January 2021. www.fws.gov/bisonrange/timeline.htm

CHAPTER FOUR

"Most were killed by diseases . . ." and "In their absence . . ." —Page 112, Mark Maslin and Simon Lewis, "Why the Anthropocene Began with European Colonisation, Mass Slavery, and the 'Great Dying' of the 16th Century," *The Conversation* (online edition), 25 June 2020.

Treaty of Fort Pitt text —Page 114, Treaty with the Delawares (1778), Yale Law School, Lillian Goldman Law Library, The Avalon Project, Accessed January 2021. https://avalon.law.yale.edu/18th_century/del1778.asp

"The treaty established the Great Sioux Reservation . . ." —Page 116, Kimbra Cutlip, "In 1868, Two Nations Made a Treaty, the US Broke It and Plains Indian Tribes are Still Seeking Justice," *Smithsonian Magazine* (online), 7 November 2018.

"Even though Moncrief Oil believes . . ." —Page 131, Tristan Scott, "Last Lease on the Line," *Flathead Beacon*, 20 January 2020.

"prohibit future commercial timber harvest, . . ." —Page 131, Rob Chaney, "Badger-Two Medicine Gets Protection Bill," *Missoulian*, 22 July 2020.

"facilitate consistency and effectiveness . . ." and "oversight of Forest Service programs . . ." —Page 131, US Forest Service (website), "About the Office of Tribal Relations," Accessed January 2021. www.fs.fed.us/spf/tribalrelations/aboutOTR.shtml

OpEd by Blackfeet Tribal Members —Page 133, Tim Davis, John Murray, Terry Tatsey, Tyson Running Wolf, and Darrell Hall, "Badger-Two Medicine Needs Permanent Protection," *Flathead Beacon*, 27 June 2020.

CHAPTER FIVE

"According to the Denver Post . . ." —Page 142, Jon Murray, "Denver's Population Has Grown By Nearly 20 Percent Since 2010—and It's Picking up Again," *The Denver Post*, 18 April 2019.

"for sounding the alarm . . ." —Page 142, Nancy Severance, "Author Richard Louv Honored with the 50th Audubon Medal," Audubon Society Press Release, January 24, 2008. https://www.audubon.org/news/author-richard-louv-honored-50th-audubon-medal

New Hampshire Public Radio Interview with Colonel Kevin Jordan —Page 151, Sharon Brody, Hannah Chanatry, "As Hikers Flock to the White Mountains, Search and Rescue Missions are on the Rise," *WBUR News*, New Hampshire Public Radio, 13 October 2019. www.wbur.org/news/2019/10/13/new-hampshire-hiking-colonel-kevin-jordan

The Rising Cost of Wildfire Operations: Effects on the Forest Service's Non-Fire Work —Page 152, US Forest Service, *The Rising Cost of Wildfire Operations: Effects on the Forest Service's Non-Fire Work*, 4 August 2015. www.fs.usda.gov/sites/default/files/2015-Fire-Budget-Report.pdf

US Forest Service, National Visitor Use Monitoring Program —Page 154, US Forest Service (website), "National Visitor Use Monitoring Program," 17 August 2020. www.fs.usda.gov/about-agency/nvum/

CHAPTER SIX

Aldo Leopold quote —Page 163, Aldo Leopold, *A Sand Country Almanac: And Sketches Here and There*, Oxford University Press, 1949. Retrieved from Wilderness Connect, January 2021. https://wilderness.net/learn-about-wilderness/aldo-leopold.php

Bob Marshall quote —Page 166, Robert Marshall, "The Problem of the Wilderness," *The Scientific Monthly*, February 1930. Retrieved from Wilderness Connect, January 2021. https://wilderness.net/learn-about-wilderness/bob-marshall.php

"Of the 52 million acres of protected wilderness . . ." —Page 171, Wilderness Watch, "The Cattle Compromise: Livestock Grazing's Damaging Effect On Wilderness And The Way Toward A Livestock-Free Wilderness System," A Wilderness Watch Policy Paper, January 2019. https://wildernesswatch.org/images/wild-issues/2019/01-2019-WW-Policy-Paper-Grazing.pdf

CHAPTER SEVEN

"The surveys AS did in 2013 and 2014 . . ." —Page 187, Adventure Scientists (website), Welcome to Field Notes, "Martens Located at Last!" 25 October 2019, www.adventurescientists.org/blog/martens-located-at-last

CHAPTER EIGHT

"For thousands of years, . . ." —Page 214, Columbia Inter-Tribal Fish Commission (website), "Celilo Falls," Accessed January 2021. www.critfc.org/salmon-culture/tribal-salmon-culture/celilo-falls/

"the greatest system for water power to be found anywhere in the United States." —Page 215, Northwest Power and Conservation Council (website), "Dams: History and Purpose," Accessed January 2021. www.nwcouncil.org/reports/columbia-river-history/damshistory

"Some early concepts included . . ." —Page 216, Friends of the Columbia River Gorge (website), "Early Threats and Protection Efforts," Accessed January 2021. https://gorgefriends.org/about-the-gorge/early-threats-and-protection-efforts.html

"It has been an uphill battle, . . ." and ""initially advocated for management . . ." —Page 217, Friends of the Columbia River Gorge (website), "Our History," Accessed January 2021. https://gorgefriends.org/who-we-are/history.html

CHAPTER NINE

"A Brief History of African Americans and Forests" —Page 235, James G. Lewis and Robert Hendricks, "A Brief History of African Americans and Forests," US Forest Service, 21 March 2006. https://www.fs.fed.us/people/aasg/PDFs/African_Americans_and_forests_March21%202006.pdf

"national forest visitors who identify as white..." —Page 239, David Flores, Gennaro Falco, Nina S. Roberts, Francisco P. Valenzuela, III, "Recreation Equity: Is the Forest Service Serving Its Diverse Publics?" *Journal of Forestry*, Vol. 116, Issue 3, 21 April 2018.

"Our hope was to encourage an elevated discussion..." and "I think the outdoor community..." —Pages 240, Greg M. Peters, "Outdoors for All: An Interview With James Edward Mills," *Your National Forests Magazine*, Summer/Fall 2016.

"When you think about the story that mountaineering has been..." —Page 240, James Mills, "All African-American Team Takes on Denali—Why It Matters," *National Geographic* (online), 9 May 2013.

"There are currently only about 20 African American archaeologists..." —Page 243, US Forest Service (website), "Freedom Trails Initiative Wins Honor Award," Accessed January 2021. www.fs.usda.gov/Internet/FSE_DOCUMENTS/stelprdb5061449.pdf

Leslie Weldon speech —Pages 250–251, Leslie Weldon, "Diversity and Inclusiveness at the Forest Service," speech at Federal Asian Pacific American Council, 30th Annual National Leadership Training Program. Rockville, MD. 5 May 2015. www.fs.usda.gov/speeches/diversity-and-inclusiveness-forest-service

PHOTO CREDITS

Map on pages 8–9 by Best Maps Ever

Bain News Service, Publisher. J.W. Weeks., ca. 1915, 47
Brian Chazar, 20 middle, 62, 65, 159, 170, 193, 222, 253, 254, 256–257, 258
Burton Historical Collection, Detroit Public Library. *Bison skull pile.* Circa. 1892, 104
Carol R Montoya, Dreamstime, 50
Chicago Tribune Archives/TCA, 91
Courtesy of the Forest History Society, Durham, N.C., 167
Courtesy of IMBA. Photo by Leslie Kehmeir., 178
Courtesy of Kylie Paul/Wolverine Watchers, 195
Courtesy of the Wilderness Institute, 167
Courtesy of The Wilderness Society, 169
Detroit Publishing Co., Publisher. *Logging a Big Load.* United States Michigan, 39
Dust Bowl farm. Coldwater District, north of Dalhart, Texas. Photo by Dorothea Lange, 1938, 98
Forest Service, USDA, 238 left, 246, 249
Forest Service, USDA, Southern Region, 242
Forest Service, USDA. Photo by J. Zapell, 27 bottom
Forest Service, USDA. Photo by Rudo L. Fromme, 2
Greg M. Peters, 13, 30, 57, 71, 73, 74, 77, 78, 79, 80, 81, 137, 138, 144, 153, 154 top left, 154 right, 174, 207, 208, 224, 225, 226, 228
Intermountain Forest Service, USDA Region 4. Photo by Charity Parks, 23 top
Johnston, R. W., Copyright Claimant. Fifth & Liberty Sts. flood of. Pennsylvania Pittsburgh United States, 1907, 48–49
Lee, Russell, photographer. *Lon Allen's son raking brushings from land which will be planted in potatoes.* Near Iron River, Michigan. United States Iron River. Michigan Iron County Iron River, 1937, 40
Michelle Wendling, 84, 88, 94
National Park Service, 92–93
The far west—shooting buffalo on the line of the Kansas-Pacific Railroad/Bghs. Great Plains, 1871, 103
The plow that broke the plains; look at it now. Oklahoma. Photo by Arthur Rothstein, 1936, 99

Tony Bynum, 108, 132
U.S. Fish and Wildlife Service. Photo by Bauer, Erwin and Peggy, 188

iStock

2pluscolors, 41
4nadia, 213
Adventure_Photo, 140
aimintang, 14
BenjaminSullivan, 118–119
BlueHorizonImages, 36
bradleyhebdon, 23 bottom
christiannafzger, 152
DaveAlan, 210
Dee, 218
DenisTangneyJr, 148–149
dennisvdw, 20 top
Douglas Rissing, 192
Eifel Kreutz, 56
EJ-J, 182
Eva2k0, 43
GeorgeBurba, 139
Gerald Corsi, 22
JacobH, 20 bottom
JeffGouldon, 197
JillLang, 60
joesephfotos, 199
JohnPitcher, 200
jumaydesigns, 134
MarkNH, 150
MichaelWarrenPix, 45
MikeCherim, 147
RobertWaltman, 101
RONSAN4D, 28
sarkophoto, 190
Spondylolithesis, 161
sshepard, 158
SWKrulllmaging, 184

tacojim, 27 top

VisualCommunications, 6

Wildnerdpix, 26

Flickr

American Jounal of Botany. Vol 2 (1915), Plate XVIII, 67

Forest Service, USDA, 238 right, 239, 245

Forest Service, USDA, Alaska Region. Photo by Carey Case, 32–33

Forest Service, USDA, Alaska Region. Photo by Harvey Hergett, 28–29

Forest Service, USDA, Eastern Region, 38, 54–55, 95, 97, 105, 106

Forest Service, USDA, Intermountain Region, 230

Forest Service, USDA, Northern Region, 100, 221

Forest Service, USDA, Northern Region. Photo by K.D Swan, 245

Forest Service, USDA, Pacific Northwest Region, 215, 227, 236 bottom

Forest Service, USDA, Pacific Northwest Region. Photo by Eagle Creek Fire Response Team, 204, 211

Forest Service, USDA, Pacific Northwest Region. Photo by Matthew Tharp, 19, 156, 177

Forest Service, USDA, Pacific Southwest Region. Photo courtesy Aldo Leopold Foundation, 161

Forest Service, USDA, Southern Region, 52, 233

Forest Service, USDA. Active stratovolcano, Mount Hood National Forest, Oregon. Photo by Cecilio Ricardo, 24–25

Forest Service, USDA. Photo by C.A. Scott, 68

Forest Service, USDA. Photo by C.M. Archbold, 125 bottom

Forest Service, USDA. Photo by Cowling, 154

Forest Service, USDA. Photo by Daniel O. Todd, 237

Forest Service, USDA. Photo by E.S. Shipp, 53

Forest Service, USDA. Photo by Jay Higgins, 66

Forest Service, USDA. Photo by K.D. Swan, 80, 129

Forest Service, USDA. Photo by Ken Hammond, 244

Forest Service, USDA. Photo by L.J. Prater, 236 top

Forest Service, USDA. Photo by Otto Schallerer, 125 top

Forest Service, USDA. Photo by R.Dale Sanders, 250

Forest Service, USDA. Photo by S.T Dana, 123

Forest Service, USDA. Photo by W.S. Clime, 70

Forest Service, USDA. Photo by Walter Akins, 126

Intermountain Forest Service, USDA Region 4. Photo by Jose Abrego, 191

INDEX